NEW YORK CITY CARTMEN, 1667–1850

for Carl,
who is always a
cooperative,
your student

New York City
Cartmen
1667–1850

REVISED EDITION

❋ Graham Russell Gao Hodges ❋

NEW YORK UNIVERSITY PRESS
New York and London

LIBRARY OF CONGRESS CATALOGING IN PUBLICATION DATA

Hodges, Graham Russell, 1946-

New York City cartmen, 1667-1850.

The American social experience series; 4

Bibliography: p.

Includes index.

Teamsters—New York (N.Y.)—History.

New York (N.Y.)—History—Colonial period, ca.1600-1775.

New York (N.Y.)—History—1775-1865.

I. Title. II. Series

HD8039.T22U54   1986   331.7'6138841324   85-28492

ISBN 978-0-8147-2461-3 pbk.(alk. paper)

ISBN-13: 978-1-4798-0057-5 (e-book)

ISBN-13: 978-1-4798-0045-2 (e-book)

New York University Press books are printed on acid-free paper,

and their binding materials are chosen for strength and durability.

We strive to use environmentally responsible suppliers and materials

to the greatest extent possible in publishing our books.

Manufactured in the United States of America

10 9 8 7 6 5 4 3 2 1

In memory of my parents,
the Reverend Graham Rushing and
Elsie Russell Hodges

"Those who live in a trading street are not disturbed by the passage of carts."
Sir Richard Steele, *The Spectator*, September 9, 1712

CONTENTS

Illustrations

ACKNOWLEDGMENTS TO FIRST EDITION

I was assisted in preparing this book by many people and institutions. I wish to express my thanks to all those who helped me with this work.

Of particular help were the librarians, curators and clerks of the New York Public Library, the New-York Historical Society, the New York City Municipal Archives, Trinity Church Archives, the Library Company of Philadelphia, Columbia University Library, the Edinburgh University Library, the British Library, the Guildhall Library, London, the Boonton Historical Society and the New Jersey Historical Society.

Many individuals helped me on the research for this book and by careful and critical readings and suggestions. My thanks go to Don Gerardi, Iver Bernstein, Phyllis Barr, William Pencak and Conrad Wright. Special thanks goes to Barbara Cohen and her New York Bound Bookstore where I was able to obtain many rare materials related to New York City history. Ms. Cohen also reprinted Isaac Lyons' *Recollections of an Old Cartman*. My father, the Reverend Graham R. Hodges, was especially helpful; he discovered many of the illustrations used in the book. Portions of this book were offered as papers before the Society for Historians of the Early American Republic, the New-York Historical Society, the SUNY-Stony Brook Colloquium, the New School for Social Research, Bard College Conference on Regional History, the New York State Historical Association Conference, the Boonton Historical Society, the New Jersey Historical Society and the Worshipful Company of Carmen in London. I thank the participants and commentators at those events for their valuable advice and criticism. This book began as a doctoral dissertation at New York University. Special thanks go to the committee which included Daniel Walkowitz, Tom Bender and Alfred F. Young of Northern Illinois University. Patricia U. Bonomi offered valuable advice and encouragement. The chairman of the committee, Carl E. Prince, gave unstintingly of his time and support. Mary-Lou Lustig, Emerita Professor of History, West Virginia University, made several full reviews of this manuscript and was immensely helpful in sharpening concepts and clarifying language.

New York City Cartmen is about a class of workers seldom discussed in American histories, but who were of seminal importance in their time and whose examples resonate through the labors and lives of a sizable fraction of today's laborers. New York City's early cartmen were the principal haulers of goods as were their counterparts in other American cities and towns. As our country urbanized, the cartmen's interactions with municipal government, with merchants and other townspeople became significant strains in the daily lives of our cities. Teamsters, cab drivers, delivery workers, and other movers of goods and services will find their ancestry in New York City Cartmen. America's great, historical shift to cities produced a second cartmen legacy. In the early nineteenth century, as New York and American cities desperately tried to clear the mounds of street filth, they organized a class of cartmen as the first sanitation workers. Decades before the creation of police and fire departments, these "dirt carters" became the prototype of the municipal worker, a group with a vast heritage today. Private and public carters, locked in an embrace with municipal government, developed their own culture, as will be displayed in this book. That heritage of government intervention and an often surly job culture makes the history of the cartmen meaningful today.

Revising and republishing this book stimulates memories of the struggle for a scholarly presence in conditions similar to the hardships young scholars face today: finding a meaningful research topic, writing a dissertation, and then facing a very uncertain academic job market. I wrote the first version of this book as a fledgling doctoral candidate in the 1970s while receiving a "transportation fellowship," from my earnings from the Dalk Service Company, which employed me as a taxi driver. My five years driving taxis in New York City prepared me wonderfully for understanding the world of civic regulation that governed the cartmen and for comprehending their unique trade personality and significance to the movement of goods and people in New York. Publishing this book at NYU Press in

1986 helped me secure a job and then tenure at Colgate University, my academic home since then.

Dusting off scholarship from my early career revives hours spent scouring old licenses, laws, and petitions at the first New York Municipal Archives, then located on Park Row, a flight up from a Burger King Restaurant, and at the Chancery Lane Public Record Office in London where I opened documents some undisturbed since the fifteenth century, or scouring old economic texts at the New York Public Library. During those years I did researched for this book at the New-York Historical Society that venerable archive that was in serious financial trouble. Its archivists continually warned me to finish my work quickly because there might not be a tomorrow. Fortunately, the N-YHS survived and is in much better condition today. One archive that was immensely useful but is no longer open is the Trinity Church library. During its brief period of public access, I found in the Trinity Church archives extraordinary and seldom seen maps of downtown Manhattan and gleaned the long-term leases that the carters and other laborers secured for land on the Trinity Church farm, that extended up the lower west side to Greenwich Village. I read widely in English, Dutch, and early American political and legal histories while preparing this book. One scholarly work that remains undiminished in my estimation is Richard B. Morris' *Government and Labor in Early America* (Columbia University Press, 1946), which taught me about the importance or regulation in colonial New York City. Morris' work continues to influence my scholarship as may be seen in the book, *Taxi: A Social History of the New York City Cabdriver* (NYU Press paperback, 2012). Catching the eye on the hood of any yellow cab in New York City today is a medallion that is a direct descendant of the monopoly licenses held by the city's cartmen centuries ago.

Morris's work on economic regulation is significant for interpreting the history of early American workers. In a significant debate, Christopher Tomlins and Robert Steinfeld disagree about the effect of regulation in early America. Steinfeld argues that regulating labor created an "oppressive regime of exploitation," by criminalizing all forms of labor disputes. Tomlins criticizes Steinfeld for excessive valorizing of "free labor." Tomlins also contends that historians must look at local and regional conditions when interpreting the transplanting of European government regulation to the colonies and subsequently to the early United States. In this book, I take pains to show that the cartmen and government's regulatory embrace had at times turbulent qualities and had a mutually satisfactory character of protection and political activism. The cartmen were occasionally oppressed but always desired to continue their regulatory bargain with the city government. Free labor was not for them.[1]

This history of New York City's cartmen has influenced a variety of scholarships, particularly anyone interested in early American labor and urban life. Scholars of the making of race find the story of the white cartmen's control and segregation of their generic skill as evidence of the "wages of whiteness." Debaters about the uneven development of capitalism among urban workers discern variations among carters. Over the years, I have received many communications from the descendants of the cartmen, which has indicated to me their importance of family history. Finally, discussion of the political social benefits of the American Revolution for our nation's workers may focus on the example of the cartmen and their steadfast maintenance of traditions, monopolistic control of their work, and their negotiation with political forces and figures. This improved book thereby reflects upon and uses the sizable scholarship on early American workers and cities published since 1986.

Since publication of the first edition of this book, historical studies of New York City are now far richer with the addition of two monumental works. The first is Edwin G. Burrows and Mike Wallace, *Gotham: A History of New York City to 1898*. Their sweeping, informed book is the best book ever done on New York City. I am grateful that their arguments fully supported the contentions made about the cartmen in the first edition of this book. The second major achievement is *The Encyclopedia of New York City*, now in a second edition. Kenneth Jackson's massive compilation undergirds nearly all scholarship on the city.[2]

I am grateful to New York University Press for giving me the chance to bring this book back to life. More then simply reprinting the book with a small introduction, NYU Press has created a new file that allows introduction of new evidence and updated arguments and to correct errors that have plagued my conscience for years. I am grateful to the patience and hard work of Steve Maikowski, Margie Guerra, Adam Bohannon, Deborah Gershenowitz, Edith Alston, and Despina Papazoglou Gimbel, at the press.

I am also grateful to the Newman Family Old Print Shop on Lexington Avenue for continued use of Nicolino Calyo's watercolors and to Leonard Milberg for use of the cover illustration and other images. My wife, Gao Yunxiang and sons, Graham Zhen Gao-Hodges and Russell Du Gao-Hodges, supported this project as only they can. I repeat the dedication of this book to my parents, the Reverend Graham Rushing and Elsie Russell Hodges, who deaths I mourn each day and whose examples I strive, however inadequately, to emulate.

INTRODUCTION

On May 31, 1799, James Townsend, a New York City merchant, hired Charles Gillerd, a cartman,* to "ride" a load of hardware from his shop on Water Street over to the New Albany Dock. After Gillerd carted the goods to the dock he returned for his cartage fee. He asked for the three shillings set by municipal law for such a load; the merchant demurred and suggested that the work seemed only half a load and not worth over two shillings. "Three shillings or nothing," responded the cartman. The merchant, stung by the obstinacy of the carter, refused to pay more than his offer, believing it to be a reasonable one.

The cartman angrily drove off. A few days later the merchant received a summons to appear before the Mayor's Court to answer a suit placed by Gillerd. Not having the time to spend in court, the merchant settled with the cartman by paying the three shillings. Displeased by the cartman's independence, he wrote a letter of complaint to his alderman asking that Gillerd be suspended from being a licensed carter. Jacob DeLaMontaigne, the alderman, declined to take any action because the cartman was right.[1]

Gillerd challenged the merchant's attempt to bilk him because of his confidence in his status as a cartman of New York City. Born in New York, Gillerd was a Revolutionary War veteran. He returned from battle to become a freeman of New York City which entitled him to take a license to work, in his case as a cartman, and to vote in municipal and assembly elections.[2] For the next 15 years he drove a cart. New York City was his home and he knew every street and lane and most of the people in it. No merchant was going to cheat him of his lawful earnings.

The cartmen, haulers of commodities on one-horse carts, dominated intra-urban transportation for the first two centuries of New York City's

---

*Throughout this study, cartman, carman, carter and karman will be used interchangeably to denote haulers of commodities using a single horse and a two-wheeled cart. Historically, carman was employed initially, but other terms soon entered popular custom.

existence. During a period when other vehicles such as carriages and farm wagons were either rare or banned from the city, their two-wheeled carts were ubiquitous around the docks, markets and narrow streets of the city. The cartmen, dressed in a uniform of a white frock, trousers, boots, farmer's hat and long-stemmed pipe, were all-purpose carriers of the city's merchandise and possessions.

The cartmen's story has never been fully told. They were key laborers in New York's mercantile economy, their numbers ranging into the thousands by the early nineteenth century. They were wise and active participants in politics as well. They established a unique ideology and were courted by politicians using appeals designed for the cartmen's interests. They were not led by the nose, however, but voted and acted with independence and resolution. Historians have noted the need to comprehend the ideology of the common man;[3] the cartmen's hard-nosed political awareness offers an important opportunity.

The cartmen's history reveals a system of government regulation which characterized the political economy of New York between 1650 and 1850. Derived from English and Dutch legal customs, New York's municipal regulations governed the work habits and prices of trades held to be in the public interest. This broad definition included such occupations as cartmen, butchers, bakers, tavernkeepers, porters, chimney sweeps and river pilots, as well as a small army of municipal employees including gaugers, packers and weighmasters. The Common Council and mayor regulated their activities and prices; one of the mayor's principal duties was to license the cartmen and other workers.

The city government's regulation of cartmen extended to all aspects of the trade. Municipal laws defined the size, shape and composition of the cart. The identity of each cartman and his license number were painted on the side of his cart, or in the wintertime, his sleigh. He was not allowed to refuse work or to charge more than carefully set rates which were published in newspapers, chapbooks and broadsides.

Each cartman was required to own only one horse and cart, free and clear of debt. He could not hire employees beyond a daily basis. When working the streets, he was supposed to walk the horse and cart at a leisurely pace; constant abuse of this law caused great consternation among the citizens.

Between 1695 and 1801 every cartman had to become a freeman of the city. This status, derived from ancient English law, granted the right to work in the city and to vote in municipal and assembly elections regardless of wealth. The freemanship bonded together city government and laborers such as the cartmen.

The history of the freemanship, central to the cartman's ideology, offers insights into the meaning of citizenship in early America. As the freemanship provided the right to work and vote in the city, it created citizenship for urbanities in the same way the freehold provided a civic sensibility for rural Americans. A man's occupation became synonymous with citizenship. In the mercantile economy of New York City, occupations were regarded in proportion to their perceived contribution to the economy.[4] As movers of commodities or essential goods such as firewood and hay, the carters achieved a status far above their skills or financial worth.

In time, the freemanship and the stability it provided helped the cartmen develop strong traditions. Exempt from competition and benefiting from the corporate patronage of city government, the cartmen customarily had long careers and passed their license on to sons and grandsons. Corporate paternalism (the municipal government viewed itself as a body and citizens as parts of that body) insured that citizens would have steady employment and would even create work for them in hard times.[5]

The special legal ties between the cartmen and the merchants who ran the government created a unique class relationship This relationship included both tangible and psychic rewards for the carters and acknowledged the interdependence of the two. Since, after all, the prosperity of the merchants depended upon orderly economic activities, safe and essential delivery of goods was essential. During the city's early history, New York City's elite merchants dominated its political economy. Yet, myriad, smaller traders were part of roughly forty percent of New York's population commercial community. The cartmen serviced great and small merchants as well as the rest of the city's population. The lack of a centralized trading community meant that publically employed cartmen constituted a superior work force to hiring or owning private carters.[6] The cartmen gained secure employment and other benefits from the merchants including favorable leases, loans and bonds. Moreover, as city officers, merchants rewarded cartmen with appointments to lower-echelon municipal offices.

An example of the close ties between merchants and cartmen may be found in a story told by John Bernard, an actor visiting New York in 1799. Several merchants invited Bernard to a tavern. Believing that Bernard could not tell a laboring man from a wealthy citizen, the merchants exchanged costumes with cartmen. The merchants dressed in the carter's white frock, trousers, farmer's hat and boots and reclined about the tavern smoking clay pipes. The carters dressed in fine coats, wigs and breeches. Bernard, however, heard about the deception and came to the tavern dressed as a cartman. He watched with amusement as the would-be pranksters grew impatient for his arrival. Finally he revealed himself and all enjoyed a good laugh and many toasts. Dressed in a white frock, any man could be a cartman or in fine clothes any man a gentleman.[7]

We should not make the mistake of merchant James Townsend, however, and think that this special relationship with the merchants made the cartmen "deferential." Historical studies often assert that colonial New York was a deferential society. It has yet to be proven and there is ample evidence to the contrary. The cartmen were anything but obsequious. Indeed, their sense of citizenship and knowledge of their importance to the city's economy gave them a belief in their equality with all men. One difficulty with deferential theory derives from a limited reading by scholars of J. G. A. Pocock's famous essay. After describing this theory Pocock discussed patronage as an alternative ideology to explain social bonds.[8] In New York City, patronage, not deference, cemented the ties between merchants and cartmen.

This is also a story of labor discrimination. New York City was not an easy place in which to find work and exclusion was always part of social custom. Popular attitudes in early New York City dictated the general exclusion of outsiders. Bolstered by the residency requirements of the freemanship, some occupations in New York City, particularly the cartmen, ostracized vagrants or farmers seeking to work in the city who might possibly undercut the prices of local tradesmen. Similar biases shaped the cartmen's attitudes toward black New Yorkers. Enslaved and free blacks were excluded by law from numerous trades not only because of the negrophobia of white workers but also because they believed the blacks would undercut prices and create competition for jobs. A similar attitude toward soldiers was the most frequently cited resentment of New Yorkers in the prerevolutionary era.[9] After the. Revolution, this attitude of resentment toward outsiders created animosity toward the Irish.

Civic support and discrimination helped the cartmen to create a community and culture of their own. This community was characterized by special sets of behavior, loyalties and ideas which were manifest and internalized by the cartmen. Their culture, a complex of rules and values which guided their behavior,[10] was both unique to them and supplemented by ancillary occupations such as wheelwrights, stablekeepers, tavernkeepers, blacksmiths and politicians. The New York City cartmen inherited much of their culture from English patterns, but also developed certain traits peculiar to the New World.

Their culture was a vibrant and visible part of life in early New York. It was evident in neighborhoods known locally as the cartmen's, in favorite taverns, at wheelwrights' and blacksmiths' shops and in the streets of the city which their heavy carts and ponderous horses dominated. The cartmen were present as a group in such social events as parades, political rallies and riots. In short, they were ubiquitous in early New York society.

Their ubiquity created an "everyman" quality about the cartmen. One incident which suggests this universality is the case in 1804 of Thomas Hoag alias Joseph Parker. Hoag or Parker was accused by Susan Faesch of marital desertion and bigamy. Miss Faesch testified that she married Hoag in 1797 in Rockland County and, although he ran away two years later, she still thought him "the finest looking man she ever met."

In 1803 Miss Faesch learned that her husband was working in New York City as a cartman. She hurried to New York to the spot where he kept his cart, saw him reclining on it and heard him speak to his horse. She immediately recognized her husband's shrill, nasal voice and upon closer inspection saw a vivid scar on his forehead which she remembered had been occasioned by a horse's kick. She then reclaimed her husband.

But it was not Thomas Hoag. Rather, as several witnessess testified, the cartman was Joseph Parker who generally worked carrying lime and building materials and labored nights as a watchman. Although Parker thought Faesch very charming, he was already married to Elizabeth Secor. Undeterred, Susan Faesch charged him with bigamy.

After many witnesses testified for each side, the case was decided by inspection of the bottom of the defendant's right foot, where Hoag had a long scar. As Joseph Parker's foot was scarless, he won the case and returned to his life as a cartman. Miss Faesch's suit was the fourth such case of mistaken identity against the cartman.[11]

Although the cartmen were not "everyman," their story is important for understanding the nature and organization of work in early America. Labor historians have neglected semiskilled workers such as the cartmen and have concentrated on skilled artisans. Largely concerned with union organization or, more recently, with the transition from preindustrial labor to industrial capitalism, such labor history is of undeniable value.[12] However, it is not the whole story. Semi- or unskilled workers such as the cartmen constituted large percentages of urban workers in colonial and early nineteenth-century America.[13] Ignoring their history slights the full history of American labor.

While the cartmen were not considered skilled, they were not without talents. They were excellent horsemen, knowledgeable of farriery, and were hardy and deft at driving and loading their carts. Although occupational diseases such as facial paralysis, phlebitis and pneumonia curtailed some cartmen's careers, the carters generally remained on the job for decades. They also knew the streets thoroughly. They were, according to cartman-historian Isaac Lyon, a "combination of encyclopedia and intelligence office," and understood all the affairs and actors on the New York scene. Businessmen, noted Lyon, knew the value of a good cartman and treated him accordingly.[14]

This is also a book about New York City. As street-level observers and participants in a horse-redolent New York, the cartmen offer an unusual opportunity to study the city through the eyes of the common man. Like their descendants, the taxicab drivers of New York, the cartmen's ubiquity, political and social concerns, and traditional behavior all insured that when important events occurred in New York, the cartmen would play a part.

Although the cartmen were quintessential New Yorkers, they were deeply affected by their European roots, particularly Dutch and English. First generation cartmen were Europeans who brought with them ingrained traditions, culture and work habits. These attitudes were transformed to America, even though modified by the American environment. Even so, the strength of the popular ideology in New York insured that conceptions of citizenship, of government intervention in the economy, discrimination and intolerance of luxury and immorality, all derived from European practice, would remain important for understanding New York life for two centuries.

CHAPTER ONE

The London Cartmen

The history of the New York City cartmen begins in medieval London. There, city authorities, merchants and cartmen created a web of legal customs which shaped the organization and conduct of the trade for centuries to come. Among the most important developments were fixed prices and exacting standards of performance. These laws, along with a myriad of lesser regulations, were mediating forces between the cartmen and the general public. At the same time the mercantile nature of the London economy fostered ties between cartmen and merchants. The cartmen's need for protection from competition and their desire to maintain self-control compelled them to act politically. Within this structure of laws, politics and economic interdependence emerged the cartmen's culture of London.

Although formal organization of the cartmen did not occur until 1517, there is evidence that some regulation did exist long before then. The London city government enacted fixed prices for carting as early as 1350. A series of incidents between angry farmers complaining of extortionate rates charged by carters for delivering their produce inside city walls to the markets necessitated the price codes. From this, it appears that the cartmen already possessed some exclusive rights to cart within the city.[1]

Around the same time the London aldermen forbade the carters the practice of "engrossing," the purchase of essential goods for the purpose of monopoly, and "forestalling," the purchase of necessities before they reached the market with an eye toward raising prices.[2] As public carriers, the carters were in a good position to gain control over the exchange of firewood, hay and meat. Since urban citizens considered forestalling and engrossing to be heinous crimes, severe penalties were set for violations of these laws. Subsequent regulations of the cartmen in London always included high fines to discourage these practices.

London citizens wanted the carters under the regulation of law. Their caustic comments about the cartmen's behavior indicate another consistent historical strain; in the eyes of most city dwellers, carters were "rude and surly." Indeed, the occupation became synonymous with boorishness; to behave in a "carterly" manner was to be offensive, ill-mannered, and antisocial.[3] The hostile descriptions of the inhabitants of Lower Thames Street are a good example. The good citizens of this important London thoroughfare derided the carters, stating that "their employment requires stout bodies and naturally renders their minds unthinking and unheeding . . . rough and sturdy, intractable and ungovernable by themselves or one another, or without great complaint by their superiors."[4] The motivation for this complaint were the reckless driving and frequent fistfights between the cartmen and citizens over right-of-way. There was an underlying message as well. To the urban, medieval mind, the cartmen were badly in need of strong governance. It was not considered possible or in the public interest to allow the trade self-control; rather the government should regulate them. Alarmed citizens noted "the number of carres and carters . . . must need be dangerous as dayly experience proveth."[5]

Such complaints would have been futile were it not for the development of a stronger municipal government during this time. Throughout England independent municipalities emerged between the thirteenth and fifteenth centuries. Organized around principles of commerce, many such towns and cities passed laws creating the offices of Mayor and Common Council. The promotion of commerce was chief among the goals and governments passed ordinances and laws designed to enhance it. Such perceptions and actions became known as the corporate method of government.[6]

Essential to the concerns of commerce in early London was the need to regulate trades considered to be in the "public good." These included carpentry, baking, butchery, gravedigging, portering and carting. In this way the ideals of the merchant governors intersected with those of the workers. Carting, however, presented special problems of regulation. Concern over its regulation included not only local grievances, the desire to promote commerce and the need to protect local tradesmen, but also involved disputes with the Crown and local anxieties over social control. Royal prerogatives in London included the right to impress all carts at will. This occurred during festivities and in wartime. When the carters were summoned for royal duty, the city found itself at the mercy of a casual work force composed largely of "sturdy beggars and vagrants." Such a situation was intolerable to London merchants and irritated the cartmen.[7]

Before regulation, London cartmen tended to be "masterless" men who roved from city to city in search of work.[8] This situation, combined with occasional Royal impressment, meant that the city corporation and merchants were faced with a work force in which they had no confidence. Added to this was the intolerable behavior of the transient carters. London, like other English cities, was plagued with wanderers; as a result there were frequently more potential carters than available work. The low, generic level of skill and the overabundance of labor created strong competition for jobs. Fights and brawls in the streets over work were frequent. Gangs fought pitched battles over the right to work in certain lucrative areas of the city.[9]

As can be imagined, this situation caused great alarm among authorities and merchants. Few desired to entrust their goods to such turbulent workers; fewer still were happy with the chaotic and dangerous conditions in the streets. The solution lay in organization and restriction of the "carrying trade." The key was to create regulation acceptable to merchants, the city government and cartmen.[10]

Under terms of the agreement of 1517, the city government controlled entrance to the trade. This was not, as in the skilled trades, under a system of apprenticeship, but rather by appointment from the mayor who received an excise tax for each license. The carters, in turn, received monopolistic privileges within city limits. While the original number of carters was fixed at 26, the mayor reserved the right to appoint others as needed. As a further concession, the carters agreed to "cleanse and purge" the streets once a week. Standard fees were set for all work provided by the carters and were posted throughout the city.

In order to convince wary merchants of the advantages of using city carters instead of cheaper, transient labor, the city required that each carter take the oath of freemanship and provide a bond similar to the porters'. The bond could be a cash pledge, a recommendation from a merchant familiar with the applicant, or a pledge of person and property. Thus the government created a stable, loyal work force tied to the well-being of local affairs and secured against potential damages.[11]

Under freemanship law only residents of the city could practice trades within the city. This allowed the city government to bar farmers, recent migrants and a host of others considered to be aliens from working within the city limits. This, naturally, was supported by the carters. In both London and later New York this provision was to be of the utmost importance.[12]

Although the freemanship eventually declined in England as concepts of free trade eroded its powers, it remained fundamentally important for manual workers, particularly cartmen, who enjoyed its political and licensing powers. Another reason for its importance, even until the 1830s, was the protection the freemanship provided for Londoners from being seized by the press gang.[13]

The importance of the freemanship cannot be overestimated. In London and New York it solved problems of social control which had vexed the cartmen, the civic government, commerce and the ordinary citizen. No longer would a carter face unwanted competition. As an urban citizen he had privileges and protection. No longer would the merchants, city government and citizens be dependent upon floating, transient labor. This is not to say there would not be problems in London or New York between cartmen and the other groups, but now at least there were boundaries to the relationship.

Problems did arise, over the exclusionary nature of the regulations. New standards enacted in 1528 called for the licensing of all carts. Each carter was restricted to ownership of only one cart; "horse-hiring" or subleasing of carts was forbidden. The new standards sought to encompass the activities of wood deliverers and scavengers but infringed upon the influential guild of woodmongers. Its members carted firewood from long distances and would not submit to local delivery by city carters. Moreover, the woodmongers had obtained friends among city alderman. Their anger over the encompassing nature of the new regulations was bolstered by their own ambitions to increase their control over the cartmen and hegemony over urban transportation.[14]

The dispute raged for over a century. At various times the woodmongers gained control of the cartmen's charters and were able to draw the general trade under their guild. At other times, the cartmen were able to gain independence from the woodmongers and achieve authority over all intra-city transportation. A principal area of dispute was over the "car-rooms" or space on the street. These assigned spots on the curbside where carters awaited work held the value of a shop and could be sold or bequeathed. By 1717 some spots were valued at over £150. Control over them was of great financial importance.[15]

It was not until 1667 that the issue of control was finally settled. The Common Council, seeking to dismantle the woodmongers' monopoly over fuel transportation, awarded a charter of fellowship to the carters.[16] While internal organization was decided by the cartmen, external or legal control lay in the hands of the city government. For the cartmen to maintain an effective fellowship, a balance had to be established between the benefits of government regulation and its hindrances.

From this long period of struggle with the woodmongers, the carters learned an important lesson. Maintenance of their fellowship privileges was wholly dependent upon favorable political action. Far more than any other fellowship or guild, the fortunes of the cartmen were inextricably linked to politics and government.

Regulations placed London carters and government in a unique relationship. While other trades experienced a degree of regulation, none, even the porters, were quite as controlled as the cartmen. Yet, of all the trades, none was as essential to the commerce of the city as the cartmen. Local politicians controlled entrance to the trade by protecting the chosen carters against interlopers and by providing civic labor. In return, the cartmen gave their labor to commerce at fixed rates and provided an inexpensive supply of workers for necessary civic chores such as sanitation. The freemanship and its privileges glued the relationship together.

As the London economy boomed in the sixteenth and seventeenth centuries, both sides benefited. The number of carters grew steadily. From the original 26 in 1517, their numbers grew to over 400 by 1580. The Common Council then limited further expansion of licenses and eventually permitted carters to hire others and to take apprentices under the privileges of their licenses.

A monopolistic license with the power to employ others meant that London's carters achieved another tradesman's goal: a competence to be passed along to their heirs. Fathers passed their licenses down to their sons

"The London Cartman and Creeler," 1614, from the Notebook of Michael Van Meer, Edinburgh University Library, Scotland.

and grandsons. As the value of a license soared higher, the trade became more tightly bound to a few families.[17]

The regulatory relationships of the government toward the carters soon became more administrative and generally concerned with public order and safety. As the number of carts grew, the city government passed safety measures. It enacted a speed limit of five miles per hour in 1580. Riding on carts was forbidden; carters were instructed to walk their carts through the streets using a leash on the horse no more than three feet long. To avoid congestion and accidents, carts were to maintain a distance of at least one cart-length.[18] Further problems with traffic jams and resulting brawls caused the council to make most streets one-way. Streetmen akin to present-day police were appointed to direct traffic and to issue summonses for improper driving. These streetmen were often accused of working in conjunction with the carters. A system of informants and inspectors was set up by the city to check on street activities. In this way the function of carting in London, and later in New York, required the establishment of a bureaucracy to govern its activities.[19]

The problems of traffic regulation and resulting public attitudes were well expressed in an appeal for stronger laws and penalties in 1617. The preamble of a petition by local citizens read "the disorder and rude behavior of the cartmen and draymen of this city is of late grown to excesse that manny man, women and children have been indangered and some have lostye their lives by the stoppinge upp of passages and streets of the city by carrs, carts and drays and by the carrlesse leadinge and guarding of horses." The citizens asked for and received new and stronger regulations in which the cartmen were held criminally responsible for reckless driving and injury. Fines were stiffened and greater amounts required for bonding.[20]

To make the carters more responsive to citizens, the council instituted license tags. Each cart was to display a brass plate with a license number. The number was also painted on the front and side of the cart along with the owner's name and address. There were frequent complaints, however, that carters smudged the numbers or turned plates upside down.[21] Public attitudes and concerns invariably resulted in further regulations. Not only was the occupation considered in the commercial interest of the city, but the nature of the work and its close relationship to prices for essential goods such as food, hay and firewood mandated full regulation.

While the cartmen generally obeyed the price rates, crisis brought out the worst in them. A good example was the extortion committed by cartmen during the Fire of London in 1666. Thomas Vincent, a clergyman, condemned the carters when he observed that "any money is given for help, five, ten, twenty, thirty pounds for a cart to bear forth into the fields some choice thing." The eminent diarist, Samuel Pepys, confirmed this by noting in his journal that the "streets were clogged with carts which are not to be had but at the dearest rates." Such profiteering in times of crisis would be repeated at every opportunity.[22]

Some Londoners supported the cartmen. The arrival of private carriages and coachmen on the streets of the city constituted a challenge to the cartmen's monopoly and caused John Taylor, the Water Poet, to rise to their defense. Taylor was a licensed waterman who rowed passengers along the Thames. Taylor and his cohorts were outraged by the presence in the streets of coachmen whom they saw as threatening to the carters and an offense to the concepts of social equity. Taylor wrote a ringing assertion of the virtues of the carter entitled *The World Runnes on Wheeles, or Oddes Betwixt Carts and Coaches.* Taylor's epic poem compared the honest cartman with the image of mankind while the coachman was akin to the Devil and the Harlot. While the carter carried honest and essential goods, the coachman and his coach created evil and avarice. Compared to the humble cart which was "ancient beyond the limits of Records or writings," the coach had "a mouth gaping on each side like a monster."

The drivers were equally the subject of Taylor's moral lecture. For Taylor, the cartman "doth signify a Verse or a Song . . . there is a good correspondence for versing, singing and Whistling which are all three musically and much practiced by the Cartman." The coachman on the other hand was akin to a brothelmaster because a coach has "loose curtains while a whore has loose skirts." While the cartman carried "Stones, timber, Corne, Beer and Whine," which by "necessity must be carried . . . which necessity the honest cart doth supply," the coach was a "running House of Abomination."

Taylor's poem equated the coach with prostitution: "If adultery and fornication bee committed in a Coach, it may be gravely and discreetly punished in a cart, for as by this Means the Coach, is a running Bawdy-House of Abomination, so the Cart . . . is the sober, modest and civil pac'd Instrument of Reformation; so the Coach may be vices infection, the Cart is often vices correction."[23] In Taylor's eyes the cartmen were representatives of the mentality of the common man. The cartmen were agents of the civic morality and symbolic instruments of correction.

By the mid-eighteenth century an extensive series of regulations and prices governed the cartmen's labor. In addition to the requirements and ownership, cartmen worked under additional codes.[24] Much of the downtown was declared off-limits for cruising. Once a delivery was made, cartmen were supposed to leave the main arteries by the next side street and return to their stands. Although heavy fines were levied for reckless driving, surly behavior and rate-gouging, the effectiveness of these codes may be seen in John Jervis' comment that "the commercial streets are always the most dangerous." Jervis warned coachmen automatically to give the right-

Frontispiece of "The World Runnes on Wheeles," by John Taylor, London, 1623. By permission of the British Library.

of-way to cartmen because their fierce driving is necessary "to make up for time wasted in tippling."[25]

Much of the cartmen's work occurred on the wharves. Each morning, beginning at five o'clock, carters lined up by the sides of waiting ships to remove their wares. Employers could not choose cartmen at random but had to adhere to a carefully defined order. Although laws forbade the cartmen from spending the night on the wharves, many arrived as early as four a.m. in order to be first in line.

To insure lawful price performance, the London Common Council publicly displayed price codes on the wharves and made them available in chapbooks and commercial guides. The standard load was any parcel between 19 and 25 cwt. While allowances were made for small and half-loads, no cartman could be forced to carry more than a standard load. For distances close to the London Bridge the rate in 1757 was one shilling and six pence; this was the first increase since 1691, indicating the strong stability in such prices. Fares for distances of up to six miles from the bridge ranged up to five shillings. Disputes over prices were settled by the lord mayor or, more commonly, by local justices of the peace.[26]

Within the framework of these regulations the carters evolved into a particular breed of worker with recognizable traditions. Their uniform was composed of a white frock, farmer's hat, trousers and heavy boots. Their hands held either a thin-stemmed pipe or a long, standard-sized whip.[27] As with many other trades, their voices rang out their presence. Mansie Wauch, a tailor visiting London, described the carters "bawling 'ye yo, ye yo' yellow sand, yellow sand, with mouths as wide as a barndoor and voices that made the drums of your ears dirl and ring."

May 1 was the Carters' Day throughout England. On that day carters and horses paraded through the streets bedecked with flowers. Mansie Wauch was deeply impressed by "the whole regiment of carters ... with great bunches of wallflower, thyme, spearment ... stuck in their buttonholes; and broad belts of stripped silk, of every color of the rainbow, flung across their shoulders.... Their hats were all rowed with ribbons, and puffed about the rim, with long green or white feathers; and cockades were stuck on the off side, to say nothing of long strips behind them like streamers." The horses were "a sight of fleeing ribbons." The parade was accompanied by "a chield ... carrying a new car-saddle over his shoulder with a well-cleaned pitchfork," followed by drummers and pipers. The procession was climaxed by a cart-race between the four swiftest pacers and drivers. The winner of each year's race was made "King of Carts," in a coronation held at the trade guildhall on Carter Street. Other cartmen won awards for longest service. Afterwards the trade would celebrate at taverns.[28]

The cartmen developed a close relationship with their horses, animals that were considered near-human. Indeed, their manure was thought sweet-smelling because of their proximity to mankind. One seventeenth-century author declared that "Horses and mules understand carters' language." Terms such as "Gee" and "Ree" and the like will make horses go and stop, turn right or left, as the driver wishes. Experienced drivers learned to whisper in the animal's ear, doubtless exploiting their sense of smell. Horse names such as Scot and Brock remained popular across the centuries. Despite the horses' high value and perceived proximity to human life, carters were known to mistreat them. Poet John Gay described a London street scene:

The lashing Whip resounds, the Horses Strain,
And Blood in Anguish bursts the swelling Vein.[29]

The nineteenth-century cartmen remained much like his predecessors. Hone described them as "hardy, healthy and long-lived if sufficiently fed and temperate." In an amusing account of a particular type of cartman, the brewer's carter, Hone cited them as "a rough specimen of an unsophisti-cated John Bull Englishman." The carter and his horse, argued Hone, "were adapted to each other's use: the one eats abundantly of grains and prospers in the traces, the other drinks porter by the canful and is hardly able to but-ton his jerken." The cartmen's driving was compared to an army's, "Woe to the patience of the crowd, waiting to cross the roadway, while the long lines of the cartmen are passing in review, like a troop of unyielding soldiers."[30]

Henry Mayhew described the cartmen as a combination of hard-work-ing journeyman and semicriminal tough. He believed that carters seldom came from the skilled trades but rather were ill-trained, loutish youths without a possibility of training. A few fallen tradesmen filled the remain-der of the ranks. The behavior of the carman was restrained only by the dictates of employment and by the expectations of the merchant elite. Mayhew commented that the cartmen were not so much servile to the

merchants as interdependent. Only at hiring time was there a hint of deference. Moreover, carters expected reciprocal recognition of their rights.[31] In
one incident wine merchants attempted to save on cartage fees by rolling
casks through the streets themselves. Angry cartmen blocked their passage
until the merchants agreed to use their services.[32]

Eventually the fellowship of cartmen, like that of the porters, lost its
strength in London. The reasons were threefold. First, by the onset of the
nineteenth century, the port of London had outgrown the old city. Because
the cartmen's privileges and licenses did not apply outside the old city limits the value of the license dropped drastically. Unlicensed carters undercut
the fees of legitimate carters. By the 1840s licenses were virtually worthless.

Second, as the London economy became more diversified, many carters
became full-time employees of particular businesses. A number of tradesmen, notable wharfingers, coalmerchants, butchers and victuallers purchased carrooms. Rather than providing a general skill, cartmen became
more identified with a particular type of business, most notably hay and
corn, dairy, and the largest group, greengrocers. Though such carmen continued to share cultural traits, such as strong drinking and an addiction to
horse-racing, specialization denied the trade the unity of previous eras.[33]

A third reason emerged from the organization of the carters. As they
obtained semiguild status the fellowship of carters was able to shake off
many of the demands of the city for public labor. This meant that other unlicensed laborers performed the necessary tasks of street cleaning and repair,
to cite but two examples. This weakened the bonds between the city and
carters and subsequently the city hired others to do these tasks. When the
shipping work of the London carters declined they could not, as New York
carters were able to do, turn to the city government for employment.[34]

The London experience of the cartmen provided legacies for their
brethren in New York City. Strong regulation by local government, an often hostile relationship with the citizenry, and a dependence on the shipping trade and mercantilism for support were among these. Unlike New
York carters, their London counterparts were able to achieve control of
their occupation at an early date and maintain a large degree of self-control.
They were able to develop a strong culture which could not wane until
expansion of the city diluted the value of their monopoly. Until then the
London carters provided a living example to their New York brethren.

CHAPTER TWO

Creation of the Bond
in New York City, 1667–1700

Local governments in colonial cities along the Atlantic Coast in the seventeenth century based their legal and political systems on European models. The municipal government in New York followed precedents established in Dutch and English law to insure fair and equal distribution of essential goods and labor and to protect local residents from competition from outsiders.[1]

Like their English counterparts, the merchants who dominated local government in New York saw the promotion of commerce as their purpose. Examination of the contents of laws, ordinances and council minutes of New York and other early American cities demonstrates their focus to be overwhelmingly concerned with commercial issues. This was particularly true in revenue expenditures and labor relations. Cities such as New York, Philadelphia, Annapolis and Albany used much of their available revenue to build wharves, piers, cranes, and jetties, while residents "trod dusty streets along open sewers to draw putrid water from city wells."[2]

Coastal cities regulated the activities and prices of trades considered to be in the public interest and in the interests of commerce. Regulated trades in New York included those involved in food production such as baking and butchery and in transportation such as carting, portering, ferrying and piloting. Other regulated trades included those of coopers, tavernkeepers, sailors and printers. In order to insure fair trade the Common Council appointed inspectors and measurers of various commodities and rewarded informants who uncovered violators of public codes.[3]

New York's local government drew on the influence of two fairly compatible legal systems. When the English took control of New Amsterdam in 1664 and renamed it after the Duke of York they encountered a political and social philosophy much like their own. There were ethnic tensions, as we shall see, but the transfer of power was remarkably smooth.[4] Important English government institutions, such as the Common Council, mayor and the freemanship, fit easily into the Dutch counterparts of the court of burghomasters and shepens and the burgher right. There were also similarities in labor control. The English permitted continuation of Dutch regulation of the sale of bread and meat. Markets were established which made New York the center of commerce for the area. The English, as concerned about the quality of essential goods as the Dutch, and equally determined to halt forestalling and engrossing, designated spots along the river fronts for the gauging, weighing and measuring of firewood, hay and meat. By law only cartmen, porters, river pilots and ferrymen enrolled in the freemanship were allowed to use the city docks.[5]

Early in New Amsterdam's history the Dutch sought to retain the loyalty of laborers. In 1648 the council governing the small colony ruled that "tradesmen will not be permitted to carry on any business ... unless they take up fire and light in New Amsterdam for three consecutive years."[6] Designed to protect local tradesmen from incursions by sailors visiting from the Netherlands, the act was part of the overall monopolistic nature of Dutch law in the new colony.

Nine years later the municipal government of New Amsterdam[7] officially established the burgher right. The ostensible reason was to protect the citizens against "pedlars travelling up and down the coast," but the danger of competition from sailors and traders from Holland was mentioned. The burgher right was also a reward to local inhabitants for their service in the "late wars against the English and the Indians" and in anticipation of future service.[8] Thus it was a recognition of the privileges and responsibilities of citizenship.

The Dutch divided the burgher right into great and small according to the wealth of the applicant. Fees were initially set at fifty guilders for the "great burghers" and twenty for the small, but were soon lowered in order to encourage universal participation. All burghers were required to live in New Amsterdam and to take an oath of allegiance. City laws required constant residence. A return to the Netherlands for a lengthy period of time made a citizen of New Amsterdam vulnerable to loss of the burgher right. Anyone expecting to work in the city had to make an application for the burgher right within six weeks of arrival. These provisions were generally taken directly from civic law in Holland though frequent allusions to the English custom of the freemanship were mentioned in the initial laws.

Between 1657 and 1661 more than 260 persons stepped forward to claim their burgher right at town meetings. This list of burghers was the most complete enumeration of the heads of households in the tiny city. Handicraftsmen, including carpenters, cordwainers and tailors, had the largest representation. Political office seekers also made up a large contingent.[9] Total participation indicates that the early Dutch government took the burgher right very seriously. In order to attract skilled and unskilled workers to the young colony the Dutch were willing to grant monopolies to many trades.

As part of a general drive to impose stricter controls on local workers, the New Amsterdam town government clearly saw need to regulate the cartmen. Early violations included riding on the cart and, more ominously, the death of a child killed by a poorly tended carter's horse inspired laws. The cartmen were not particularly apologetic about problems. When William Kock's cart horse kicked the son of Sherriff Allard Anthony, Kock blandly explained that it was the animal's custom to do so and many people had complained about such behavior. More important was the need to fix the cartmen's prices to avoid rate-gouging and to extract necessary labor helping clean the streets, fight fires and repair the roads.[10]

Government negotiation with the cartmen set them apart from other workers in the small city. The cartmen joined the city's artisans in seeking the protection of the Dutch small burgher right, and then, after the English takeover, the freemanship. Cartmen also shared the city streets and, likely, taverns and other public spaces with artisans, but the intensity of their relationship with the city government created separate occupational and political patterns from handicraft workers. Simon Middleton, in his rich study of workers in colonial New York City, errs, I argue, by mixing the history of the cartmen and other licensed trades, such as tavern keepers, butchers and porters, with the city's artisans. This is not a small point. As Christopher Tomlins has argued, early America law was highly variable by time and place. Beginning with small, early measures intended to extract labor and to form a bond of attachment with the cartmen, the city government increasingly tightened its embrace with them. In return, the cartmen demanded and gained additional protection and patronage far beyond what artisans wanted or expected. The close bonds between officials and the cartmen evolved into structures and histories different from those of free laborers.[11]

In 1667, the English granted the request of the Dutch carters that they "be affixed in a fellowship in the manner of the weigh-house porters."[12] The city government allowed the eight "karmen" to form the fellowship but demanded that in return for the privilege the carters "attend all fires" as a responsibility. The porters, the model for organization, were formed as a fellowship in 1657. A primary difference between the two fellowships lay in the porters' mutual assistance fund. By requiring that each porter put aside a small portion of his wages into the benevolent fund, the government and the trade created an early form of workman's compensation insurance. This policy was akin to methods used by the various fellowships of porters in London and Amsterdam where benevolent societies accumulated vast amounts of capital.

The porters never gained the importance in the New World that they held in, London and Amsterdam. Rather, they remained a small occupation with regulated fees of less value than the cartmen's. Two reasons seem plausible. First, the narrow streets of the Old World were more conducive to portering than New Amsterdam's broader streets which provided easy access to carts. Secondly, portering required enormous numbers of laborers to be effective. Both London and Amsterdam had great surpluses of labor and local authorities were happy to regulate them into a trade which benefited the city and provided some sort of social control. Such labor surpluses simply did not exist in New York. Carting served the needs of the city more effectively. Accordingly, the number of carters in New York increased tenfold over the next century while the porters remained few.

Contemporary observers often remarked on the favorable wage climate in seventeenth-century coastal cities. Daniel Denton described New York as a place "where a cartman may do as well as a coachman" in London. Cities were vitally interested in attracting a class of permanent laborers who would remain in the city rather than leave during hard times. Additionally, the corporate philosophy of government embraced by local officials in

New York respected the vested interests of the cartmen and protected them against encroachers.[13]

After the initial contract with the carters in 1667 the city government continued to extract concessions from them. After agreeing to "confirm the eight carters in their places" the government gained other duties from them. The carters promised to give satisfactory labor to whoever employed them and to do public work as required. They agreed to take turns on Saturday afternoons carting the "dirt" of householders away to a public dumping ground. For each load citizens paid the cartmen "ten stivers seawant (wampum)" and no more. This remained the fee for the standard load until 1696. This early method of garbage collection was a departure from earlier requirements that citizens bring their own "dirt" to several local dumping grounds.[14] It meant the establishment of the carters as semiofficial city workers and bound the trade and city government closer together. This action by the city to "confirm" the carters became, as a result of law, an annual affair. Each year the carters sought renewal of licenses at the court of burghomasters and shepens, and, later, under English rule, the Common Council and mayor. This renewal was not necessarily automatic and each carter understood that his employment as a city carter was dependent on the good will of city magistrates. Political favor became vitally important. Eventually annual renewals became a major weapon used by politicians to enforce political loyalty.

The agreement to do "public work as desired" was an open-ended clause which soon created animosity between city officials and the carters. Within two years the city ordered the carters to make major repairs on the local fort. Initially it asked that this work be done without compensation as part of an agreement by which the cartmen would provide two days a week for public labor. After strong protest by the trade, the city relented and agreed to pay standard rates.[15] Laws requiring that the carters perform the often unpleasant task of garbage detail were established at this time; the city agreed that the carters be paid standard wages for "dirt" collection.

At the same time the city declared that the carters could not refuse a request for labor from any citizen. This was to avoid monopoly of their labor by the merchants and to insure that the city itself would be able to employ them when needed.[16]

Despite these early laws the cartmen's conduct was often uncivil. After several incidents of reckless driving in 1667, the court of burghomasters ordered that in the future accidents which harmed citizens would "cost a horse and cart." If a cartman caused someone else's death, his own life "shall be under the lapse of law." To bolster this the city began to demand bonds and references from the trade. The abusive behavior of the carters also came under criticism from city officials. Cartmen "do many times use ill and Bad language to the Burghers" complained the court in 1667. The court set dismissal from service as the penalty for not behaving "civilly."[17]

Some municipal work harnessed incivility. The trade was employed at celebrations, funerals and executions. The execution of Angel Hendrickson, a child murderer, is an example. Before being hanged, she was "carted" through the streets and jeered at by the citizens. While one drove the lady through the city, other cartmen hauled the lumber used by carpenters to build the gallows. While Mrs. Hendrickson suffered her last worldly agonies, carters and other workers gathered by her feet to drink the "wine and brandies" served by local government in partial payment for their services.[18]

Ethnic tensions, combined with discontent over the required city labor, made relations between city and cartmen uneasy in the 1670s. In 1671 a number of complaints were made about rude behavior and refusal to work. After the Common Council summoned them the cartmen "made their excuses and promised in the future to be verry delligent and preforme said orders."[19] The court accepted this excuse and reaffirmed the entire force at the same meeting. This was the first of many such meetings over the next century in which city government, responding to complaints, would interrogate the carters and then send them away without severe penalties. In some ways the carters were more necessary to city goals than the complaining citizens.

To gain greater control over the carters, the government appointed an Englishman to become the first foreman of the Dutch carters. While his installation had little effect on the immediate problems, for there were continued complaints that the trade refused to "ride timber, stone, and other materials for the city and public service," the foreman became an important link in the ties between city government and the cartmen. The foreman represented the trade in negotiations with the mayor and alderman, grew into leadership among his fellow workers and helped foster attitudes of independence.[20]

The city government moved to protect them from unwanted competition. Farmers from Long Island and New Jersey were forbidden to take temporary residence in the city in the summer months in order to drive a cart. In a move partly inspired by reports of reckless driving, the aldermen enacted a law barring "youths under twenty-one years of age" from driving carts.[21] Exceptions could be made for sons of carters helping their fathers. The law, however, effectively foreclosed the institution of apprenticeship from the occupation, separating it from the experience of English carters and limiting capitalist development.

A similar law of even greater impact was legislation enacted in 1684 barring black New Yorkers, whether slave or free, from carting and portering. The council acted on a petition from the cartmen and declared that "noe Negroe or other slave doe drive any Carte within this Citty under the Penalty of Tweenty Shillings, to be payd by the Owner of such Slave for Each Offense (Brewers Dayes or Carriages for Beer, Only Excepted)." While the law was ambiguous about the status to the tiny number of free blacks in New York, future magistrates and the white carters concluded that no blacks should drive a cart in the city.[22]

This was a reversal of Dutch practice which had few barriers to black entrance into any occupation. Closing the carting trade to blacks, who constituted nearly 20 percent of the city's population, had a devastating effect, for it denied access to a potentially lucrative, entry-level occupation requiring only general skills. Several reasons motivated this action. Cartmen, as did other tradesmen, feared the use of slaves by merchants, who owned most of them, for tasks reserved for white carters. Secondly, the negrophobia of the carters, like most white workers of the time, was undeniable. Racial attitudes, somewhat fluid up to this point, congealed into the bitter prejudice which henceforth characterized the white laborers' position toward blacks. Carting licenses in New York became permanently segregated. Last, the law permitted exploitation of blacks in the city. Though blacks could not gain carting licenses, nothing prevented cartmen from hiring them by the day. Before long a three-tiered system of employment emerged. White carters would contract for a job. Their wages, around three shillings per day, were the highest. Next came white laborers working on the job and earning about one shilling and six pence, or half the cartman's wage. Black laborers, both slave and free, also worked for the cartmen, but were paid but six pence a day, or in alcohol.[23] Within the protection of a monopolistic license the cartmen were able to control the wage climate for laborers; although the expenses of feeding the horse and maintaining a cart accounted for some of the difference, they were able to accumulate much higher wages beyond the costs of their hired help. While white laborers could possibly save enough to obtain a cart and horse, little such hope existed for the blacks. The cartmen were vigilant about protecting against the employment of enslaved people in carting. In 1684, Elsie Leisler, the wife of Jacob, the future revolutionary and a slave trader himself, petitioned the Mayor's Court on behalf of her husband for permission to employ her slave. The Leislers owned a mill and experienced hardship getting cartmen to "carry Wheat and other Corne." She sought permission to use her slave, "who is a Christian, being Baptized and Instructed in the Christian religion. The Court ruled that only white men could drive carts. This early example of what David Roediger has termed the "wages of whiteness, " created a preferential status for white cartmen in this critical occupation. [24]

Such protection characterized English efforts to forge strong ties with its Dutch carters. New York's merchants were themselves quite oriented toward monopoly. During the early years of English occupation city merchants appropriated monopolistic control over several segments of the colony's economy to benefit urban growth. Extension of this philosophy toward laborers such as the cartmen was not only a good means of control but also reflected the city government's corporate philosophy.

Nonetheless, serious breaches occurred. In 1677 the city council dismissed all twelve Dutch carters for "not obeyeing the Command and doing their Dutyes as becomes them in their places." As the record indicates, the carters were fined either three shillings or required to cart fifteen loads of dirt to the city wharf. Each cartman submitted to these conditions and "prayed to be re-admitted as cartmen."[25]

Despite this initial settlement a second dispute occurred in 1684. Master boatmen supplying firewood to the city petitioned the Common Council to complain about cartmen who were engrossing firewood. The petition was supported by numerous city merchants. The council sympathized with the petitioners and ordered that cartmen no longer be permitted to purchase firewood. It also reaffirmed Dutch regulations about the length and quality of firewood and ordered that cartmen bring all firewood to two inspection points in the city where the firewood could be "coarded." Measurers were appointed and fees were collected from the cartmen for this service. This meant that not only would the cartmen be responsible for inspection fees but would also have to make an extra trip without compensation to the inspection site. It also foreclosed the possibility of the cartmen capitalizing on the city's constant need for firewood. A second new regulation brought further discontent when the Common Council ordered that carters drop whatever work they were doing to attend to the unloading of any shipment of grain, corn, or other perishable goods protected under the Bolting Act of 1680 which gave New York City a monopoly over milling grain in the colony.[26]

The cartmen immediately went on strike in protest. Just as quickly the Common Council "suspended and Discharged them from being any longer Carrmen." Public notice was given that any and all persons "within this citty have the free Lyberty and Lycense to Serve for Hyre or Wages as Carmen (The said Carmen and Slaves excepted) till further ordered." Significantly, there were no takers. A week later the strikers returned after payment of a nominal fine of six shillings and agreed to conform to the "Lawes and Orders Establisht."[27]

What these incidents demonstrate was not a clear victory for the city government, as a previous historian has perceived, but the increasing interdependence of city government and cartmen.[28] By continuing to define and enlarge the carters' responsibilities, city officials now viewed the carters as quasi-civic employees. By suspending the entire force, city government served notice that the form of organization was going to work even if an entirely new membership was required in the fellowship. The inability of the cartmen to find work or to act as carters outside the city system meant that they would at least have to pay lip service to municipal ordinances. The scarcity of labor and the strength of the carters' organization prevented wholesale firings.

The strikers were not transient employees. Rather, they were long-term, closely-knit workers whose service to city government extended beyond carting. Analysis of tax lists of 1677 reveals that cartmen lived in a small community on Smith's Street Lane, a back alley containing some of the poorest housing in the city. There, Peter Wessels, John Bosh, Ambrosius Warren, Thomas Vardon, Barrent Gerritse, John Langstraet and John Coursen, nicknamed "Cherry Tree," lived in shabby dwellings evaluated by tax assessors as among the poorest in the city. The average tax of the seven was five shillings, just above the lowest recorded rate of four shillings.[29] Other cartmen around the city had similar holdings. John Myenderrsse's home on the Bever's Gracht was taxed for four shillings as was John Teunis' on the Water Side. Sigmundus Lucas' tax payment of four shillings was dwarfed by those of his wealthier neighbors on High Street whose rates were triple his. One cartman, William Cooke, owned two houses on the water Side and rented one of them. Despite this landlord status his two homes together were taxed for only ten shillings.[30]

As was often the case in New York, Smith Street Lane became known by the occupation of its residents. Soon it was known colloquially as the "Carmen's Street," just as nearby streets were known as the Brewer's Street and the Marketfield Street by the work of their inhabitants. The Dutch carters living on Smith Street Lane went to the nearby Niew Straat Dutch Reform Church.[31]

Most of the strikers continued their careers as carters. Many received government appointments over the years. Conradus Van Der Beake was first appointed a carter in 1680. He was fired but then reappointed in 1684. In 1697 he was elected to be Constable of the West Ward, a position he held through 1702. That year he was appointed Corn Measurer. As did many of his fellows, he continued as a cartman while holding this low-level government job. Teunis Quick became Constable of the North Ward after nine years as a cartman. He continued in his position for a number of years and later was elected Collector and then, in 1724, after over thirty years as a carter, was given the post of Overseer of the Public Drain.[32]

John Langstraet was the earliest leader among the cartmen. A long-term member of the city watch, he first joined the trade in the early 1670s. He was dismissed during the strikes but was reinstated both times. He, his wife and four children lived in a modest home on Smith Street Lane and attended the nearby Niew Straat Dutch Reformed Church. Later he moved to the West Ward.[33]

At the same time the cartmen were battling the city government, New Yorkers were granted a new charter which greatly broadened their liberties. An assembly was created, along with voting qualifications. Freemanship status was granted to all English newcomers and continued for Dutch citizens. Despite these gains, tensions remained strong. Dutch merchants resented Governor Andros' favoritism of Englishmen. The Common Council was a battleground throughout the 1680s as factions vied for power. Animosities in New York provoked a rebellion in 1689. That year Jacob Leisler, a prosperous German merchant, seized power in New York in the aftermath of the Glorious Revolution in England. The confusion over legitimate authority in America after the Glorious Revolution allowed Leisler to retain power for two years. During that time Leisler led reform movements which attempted to break up land and trade monopolies held by wealthy Anglo-New Yorkers, reform the tax system and improve the lot of the common man. Leisler's leadership became the symbol of resistance for aggrieved New Yorkers.

The Leisler Rebellion of 1689–91 was perhaps the most significant event of late seventeenth-century New York. Historians are still undecided whether it was caused by ethnic tensions between Dutch and English, by fear of Papist plots, by class tensions, by rivalries between merchants, or by anger over the elimination of the representative assembly by Governor Andros. Whatever the cause, the rebellion heightened political awareness of the common man and increased the need for stabilizing forces within New York society. Leisler's Rebellion persuaded royal governors and leaders to employ Whig paternalism to pacify restless colonials.[34]

During the rebellion, John Langstraet had an opportunity to display the loyalty felt by many Dutch laborers toward the self-appointed governor, Jacob Leisler. One day, as Leisler was walking in the street near Fort George, he was set upon by over a dozen merchants. Wielding sharply edged coopers' adzes, the band attacked Leisler, shouting "Kill him, kill him!!" Langstraet, sitting on the tail of his cart along the curb, immediately jumped into the fray, pushed aside the mob and commanded, "I will not suffer this to happen." Langstraet's quick defense allowed Leisler to draw his sword and then carefully back away from the would-be assassins.[35]

Although Leisler's Rebellion ended the following Spring with his execution, the new leaders, wishing to conciliate the Dutch carters, made Langstraet the new foreman. Whether this was in recognition of his heroism, which earned him great fame, or long service as a cartman, we do not know. Langstraet remained the leader of the trade until his death in 1703.[36]

Leisler's Rebellion continued to seethe long after his death in 1691 and the outnumbered English government took pains to alleviate tensions. The same year the city government agreed to a number of changes in the cartmen's laws. The government increased the number of cartmen to 24 and appointed Obadiah Hietselbie, a 20-year veteran of the streets, as co-captain. The cartmen agreed to pay six shillings annually to the mayor for licensing, which initiated a practice that would bring lucrative profits to His Honor and deep resentment from the trade. Each cartman agreed to drive only his cart; leasing of carts was forbidden. This law reaffirmed individual ownership and removed the possibility of capitalistic exploitation. For example, this law prevented the merchants from purchasing a number of carts and hiring local cartmen to work on a wage basis. Carters were also required to rotate the duties of "dirt" removal and were paid three pence for each load. The carters were ordered to alternate their daily activities between the docks and the commercial districts.[37]

In an important victory for the cartmen, the city authorities voted to cease suspensions for petty infractions. Although the mayor retained power to remove the entire force for cause, small violations were now to be punished by nominal fines. This greatly relieved the constant anxiety over displacement and attested to the city's increased reliance on the cartmen as its laborers. It also reflected the government's inability to replace striking carters in 1684. All of these laws came directly from English regulations.

Despite the death of Leisler, his followers remained politically active and were successful in winning control of the Common Council in 1692 and 1693. To counter this the English government began to politicize the freemanship and enfranchise more pliable voters. Just before the hotly contested council election of 1695, a rumor spread that a press of sailors and cartmen was imminent. The night before the election John Langstraet led his band of cartmen down to the City Hall to receive the freemanship.[38]

Soon New Yorkers universally adopted the freemanship. The mayoralty of William Merritt from 1695 to 1698 saw the greatest number of new freemen since the institution of the small burgher right forty years before. Three hundred sixty-five New Yorkers, representing 28 trades ranging from merchants and gentlemen at the apex of society down to the cartmen, blacksmiths and laborers, gained the rights of freemen. Cordwainers and carpenters were the largest groups, showing the popularity of the small-scale crafts in the city. Large numbers of workers, however, came from the mercantile sector. Coopers, blockmasters, sailmakers and mariners formed increasing percentages of the freemanship rolls. Only the blacks of the city were denied representation.[39]

The status of the freemanship not only protected the company of cartmen but served as an ideology. As a freeman, the cartman could proudly identify himself as a citizen of the city, capable of resisting change harmful to his interests. The freemanship protected him from impressment. As a freeman he could vote in municipal and assembly elections regardless of the value of his freehold. His pride also encompassed his belief in his racial superiority as blacks were never allowed the freedom of the city. In short, the freemanship elevated him above potential competition and placed him on an equal footing, politically, with higher ranks in society.

As a result of the Leisler Rebellion and the increased number of freemen, local politics took on a more competitive cast. In the next few years seminal political parties formed around the tensions arising from the revolt. Contested elections, signs of fraud and voter coercion demonstrated a stronger political struggle within the city.[40]

In order to counteract the political strengths of the pro-Leisler laboring classes, the English authorities again used the freemanship to pack the electorate with more pliable voters. In 1702 Lord Cornbury registered nineteen of his "gentlemen and servants" as freemen. At the same time 203 members of the officers and soldiers of His Majesty's Garrison were given the right to work and vote in the city.[41] This tactic, which would later give rise to much resentment during the prerevolutionary days, allowed idle soldiers to work in the streets at reduced rates and to vote according to their commanders' pleasure. The freemanship was thus directly tied to the political battles of the day. Rather than abandon it, however, and lose the social stability it provided, the English authorities diluted the freemanship by awarding grants to transient soldiers.

The privileges of a freeman provided for legal equality before the Mayor's Court. Presided over by the mayor and aldermen, this court decided small disputes. The suit by John Coursen, alias "Cherry Tree," a cartman from 1676 until 1697, demonstrates use of the court to satisfy grievances by laborers against merchants. In August 1688 Coursen carted 83 loads of chipped stone for merchant Hendrick Dominick. His bill for six pounds went unanswered. By October Coursen initiated a suit to gain his wages. The court determined that Dominick "did craftily and evilly deceive the said carter of the sum" and ordered the merchant to pay or face imprisonment. Before the law, carters and merchants were equals.[42]

Patronage became an effective means of pacifying the rebelious cartmen. The establishment by the Church of England of Trinity Church in 1696 caused great apprehension among Dutch carters and artisans. Yet Trinity also became a steady source of employment during and after construction of the church. The annual bookkeeping of the church reveals large sums paid to cartmen for riding timber, stone, sand and other materials.[43]

By the close of the seventeenth century, major elements in the relationship between cartmen and city government were in place. Laws were codified which would last for the next century and a half. Patronage patterns were established to reward loyal carters. The freemanship became a mark of status accessible and profitable to cartmen as well as merchants. City government showed its determination to protect the white cartmen from the competition of black New Yorkers or of farmers coming in from New Jersey.

The cartmen's grip on local transportation became firm in the latter part of the seventeenth century. They were able to exclude blacks and farmers, and secured a virtual monopoly of local transportation. Meanwhile the cartmen secured unchallenged hegemony over municipal labor for cartage required by the merchants and at the marketplaces which developed around the city. All these victories were part of traditions which would dominate local transportation for the next 150 years.

CHAPTER THREE

Affirmation of the Bond, 1700–1745

The economic interests of New York City at the onset of the eighteenth century lay mostly in commerce and trade rather than in land and manufacture. Commerce formed the basis for wealth and political control in the city.[1] Occupations involved in trade, such as porters and cartmen and the inspectors and measurers of commodities, continued to hold the exclusive monopolies designed in the seventeenth century by city government to retain their loyalty. Local government of the eighteenth century tended to look with favor toward trades in proportion to their contribution to the economic health of the city.[2]

The cartmen had been given exclusive protection by the mayor and Common Council and in order to ease the stress exhibited in the late seventeenth century, city officials used patronage to find a common ground with the cartmen. This use of patronage coincided with the carters' goal of continued monopoly. The relative stability of politics in the first half of the century lent itself to the attainment of these goals. The government used its powers to ease tensions in a number of ways. It granted the freemanship to each carter by making it a virtually automatic part of licensing. Of the 101 carters licensed between 1700 and 1745, 90 were freemen. Of the fifteen carters whose careers extended from the seventeenth to the eighteenth century, all were freemen. Nonfreemen had very short careers as carters.[3]

New York City liberalized access to the freemanships in 1701. Under new legislation artisans and laborers who qualified as legal residents working in the city became freemen after paying a six shilling fee. The six shilling price of a license included the freeman fee. The Common Council awarded the freemanship without charge to poorer workers. To avoid undue political influence, however, the New York Common Council instituted a three-month waiting period before suffrage eligibility could take effect.[4]

Although historians view the first half of the eighteenth century as a time of movement toward laissez-faire, the freemanship and its exclusive privileges remained paramount in New York City.[5] Over 2000 New Yorkers received the right between 1700 and 1745, a substantial portion of white male adults. As many as 91 different trades were represented on the freemanship rolls.[6]

Politically the freemen remained strong. Although the Montgomerie Charter of 1731 allowed freeholders to be elected to public office without need of the freemanship, politicians still paid heed to freemen. At the height of the Cosby Crisis of 1734–1735, the governor regularly invited freemen "from all ranks of society" to the fort and mansion for drinks. Patronage was readily available to freemen.[7]

During their relatively prosperous second decade of the eighteenth century, 36 carters registered as freemen. Of these, 13 received it gratis as "poor men." From 1720 to 1746 nineteen of fifty-five "free" cartmen thus became citizens. Few of these were of Dutch ancestry; indeed only six of the 55 new carters were Dutch. While the expanding economy required more carters, city government discriminated in favor of Anglo-Americans, and, in its desire to provide a means to work for even the poorest of English citizens, offered monopolistic trade protection and political suffrage. As New York City embraced slavery in the early eighteenth century, prohibitions against the enslaved and the dwindling number of free blacks from carting continued. While no law specifically mandated the gender of carters, no female New Yorkers tried to break into the trade. As Serena Zabin has shown, female New Yorkers did engage in a variety of informal, often illicit trades in the early eighteenth century, ranging from tavern keeping to hawking fruits and vegetables in the streets, pawning used clothing and fencing goods. All of these jobs required some physical labor. Poorer women, especially those with rural backgrounds, could handle a cart and horse. White male carters were always vigilant about excluding enslaved black men. Women driving carts was apparently unthinkable.[8]

The government also showed its concern for the economic well-being of its carters by raising the maximum fees for common loads during recessions. In 1729, in the midst of the worst depression before the collapse of the mid-1760s, the Common Council raised this fee to four and a half pence per load. A previous raise occurred during the slump of 1717–1718. The city also expanded its regulation and protection. of the cartmen. The "Lawes Governing Carts and Cartmen," were issued and distributed among the public. These codes, issued in 1729, entailed eleven provisions which carefully established the rights and responsibilities of carters. Penalties for disobeying the statutes were also listed. Following the laws were long lists of over 100 commodities and respective maximum fees for carting with differentials for weight and distance.

Several of the eleven provisions are noteworthy. The first noted that the mayor "has undoubted right by charter to appoint and license carters and also to remove and displace ... carters." While, heretofore, council and mayor had divided this duty, the exclusive powers of the new charter gave him additional rights of patronage and potential income. For the next eight decades New York's mayors enriched themselves on the excise taxes received from the license renewals of cartmen and tavernkeepers. The right to "displace" carters gave ample political powers to the mayor which future magistrates would use to enforce political loyalty.

In a second provision the council described what would be the standard cart for the next century. In order to insure a fair load, the council ordered that each cart be at least two feet eight inches wide and to have rungs at least three feet high. There was no stipulation of length. By requiring minimum sizes the council sought to insure that New Yorkers received equitable loads, particularly of firewood. A cord of wood was determined to be four cartloads.

A third provision required that each cart display the license number of the driver in bold red paint on a white background, repeating an important London regulation. The majority of other laws were repetitions of earlier codes restricting night driving, riding on carts and requirements of service. Black and minors were again forbidden to drive carts for hire.[9]

The strongest language in the laws was reserved for firewood and hay carting. Elaborate weights and measures were established to protect New Yorkers against forestalling, encroaching, or short-weighing. The Common Council set up several places for measurement and announced fees, payable by the carters, for inspection. Cartmen faced a whopping forty shilling fine for violations. The severity of this law demonstrated the council's concerns over the desperate firewood situation. Although freemen still had the right to cut wood from the common lands on Manhattan Island beyond the city, the island was rapidly becoming denuded of trees. In harsh winters cartmen who gained control of firewood were in a position to make unconscionable profits. The council enumerated fair price laws to prohibit such profiteering. The severity of the council's laws and the exorbitant fines indicates the great local concern over potential abuses.[10]

The lengthy list of fees indicates, however, that the council clearly considered the carters to be the primary carriers of commodities in the city. Fees were calculated in a variety of ways in addition to weight and distance. The "common load," which included grain, firewood and any other unlisted "goods, wares and merchandizes," was listed first. Cartage for the common load in 1731 was four and a half pence per half mile. Items of local commerce, including lime, bricks, staves, hoops, beef, port, pitch, beer, flour and any "other goods in tite Barrels allowing four Barrels to each load," were six pence for cartage. Cartmen fortunate enough to carry gunpowder to or from the powder house received eighteen pence per load. Commercial imported goods, such as hogsheads of rum, pipes of wine and molasses, cost the same. Large loads of sugar, rum, molasses and wine could cost up to two shillings for cartage. By far the most lucrative fees involved the transportation of trade merchandise. Cartmen who secured favor with importers could count on good profits when shipping was prosperous. The lesser fees for carting dirt and for delivering firewood may have been to alleviate poor sanitation and to prevent rate-gouging in the winter time. Haycarting, on the other hand, paid quite well; cartage of a load of loose hay provided a fee of eighteen pence.[11]

At this time cartmen had complete freedom of the streets and could wander in search of work where they pleased. Most preferred to await work near the markets, like the Oswego on Broadway or the Fly Market in the Dock Ward. Carters who specialized in wood or hay delivery would be found near the ferry landings in the North Ward or along the docks of the Montgomerie Ward. The commercial streets of the South Ward attracted carters. In the compact "walking city" a citizen who wished to find a favored carter would not have to look far. If the customer was not particular he merely had to walk into the street and cry "Cartman, Cartman," to find service.[12]

A sense of the wages paid cartmen in the first half of the eighteenth century may be gained from the financial records of Trinity Church. Working in the land known as the Church's Farm, cartmen performed numerous jobs for Trinity including hauling sand and oyster shells for landfill and "ryding" bricks, nails and timber for construction of wharves and streets. The records of payments made by Trinity Church indicate frequent employment of carters at wages around three shillings per day. Two cartmen were together paid six shillings on September 12, 1721. A few weeks later the church groundskeeper paid a cartman three shillings six pence for "ryding seven loads of boards and two of timber." Single jobs for carting "a load of boards" paid the standard rate of nine pence per load.

The Trinity Church records indicate use by cartmen of black help. In 1721 the Church paid a cartman "one shilling six pence and rum for the negroes." Another account noted payment of one shilling one pence for a cartman and "a Negro from Smith Street's Lane." By themselves blacks earned one shilling six pence per day; payment "for a Whiteman" for three days' labor was nine shillings.[13]

At this time a loaf of "the finest flour to weigh two pounds thirteen ounces" sold for four pence halfpenny. A cheaper loaf was available for "three halfe pence." Although carters were not getting rich working for Trinity Church, even one load was more than enough for daily bread.[14]

Some carters made long-term agreements with local families to provide them with firewood, hay and other necessities. The standard procedure was for the carter to extend credit to the family which would reimburse him for the cost of the commodity plus cartage. This personalized service was not possible without a strong degree of mutual trust. Still other carters became regular carriers for merchants. Here again mutuality was all important. Merchants secured safe, efficient movement of their goods. Cartmen obtained regular income plus the potential for loans and personal references.[15]

The harmony between carters and the city government fostered stability in the trade. Available records indicate that once a man took the freemanship as a carter he could expect a lengthy career. Of the 101 carters licensed between 1700 and 1745, 40 had careers lasting 30 years or more. Only a handful worked fewer than five years. Some, like Servaes Vlierboom, worked more than 40. He obtained his first license in 1695. Forty-one years later the council minutes note that Jacob Pitt, Abraham Blanck and Vlier-boom, "three ancient and infirm cartmen be licensed to sitt upon the Shafts of their Carts and drive the same for their ease and relief." Pitt and Blanck were initially licensed in 1719.[16]

Carting became a family profession at this time as a number of the city cartmen passed the occupation on to their sons. These included Casparus Blanck, Jr., Cornelius Cousine, Armiont Hendricks, Jacobus DeLaMon-tagne, Teunis De Voor, Abraham Palding, Henry Parcell, Lucas Stouten-burgh and Jacob Banker.[17] Some carters were related by marriage. Abraham Brower married Elizabeth Ackerman in 1723 and soon took out a cart-man's license. His wife was the sister of cartmen John and Heribus Ack-erman.[18] Abraham and Elizabeth gave birth to David, Abraham, Aldrick, Nicholas and Gerret Brower who all carted in the 1750s and 1760s.[19] Aert and John Middaugh were brothers and cousins of Claus Bogert.[20] David Ackerman was related by marriage to David Waldron, Isaac Blauveldt and Dirck Brinckerhoff.[21] Brinckerhoff was first employed as a shopkeeper but turned to carting in the 1740s. His son, Dirck, Jr., was a carter in the 1770s and in postrevolutionary New York. The Brinckerhoffs were also related to the Bantas, one of the largest of the cartman families of New York.[22]

Servaes Vlierboom was related by blood and marriage to at least five other cartmen of his time. Born in New York City on July 22, 1674, Servaes married Geertruyd Lesting, daughter of cartman Peter Lesting, in 1697. The Vlierbooms were leading members of the Lutheran church and numer-ous weddings and baptisms took place in their home in the North Ward. His son, Pieter, born in 1704, no doubt helped his father in his early years before becoming a cartman in 1725. Servaes Vlierboom's cousins included Cornelius Cousine and Teunis Quick, both cartmen. His sister, Maria Vli-erboom, married cartman Reynier Meynartszen in 1696. Except for Mey-nartszen and Lesting, Servaes Vlierboom's cartman relatives were still work-ing the streets when he died in 1743.[23]

Nepotism was frequent in other city posts as well. Carter Jacobus DeLaMontagne walked the city streets each night crying out each hour as a city bellman. At the same time the city appointed Dirck Cook, cartman, and Johannes DeLaMontagne, Jr., to the same post. Jacobus' nephew, John, also became a bellman. Jacobus, Johannes and John were all members of the watch which added a further supplement to their incomes.[24]

One family, the Crannells, controlled the watchmen. Robert Crannell was given a position as Supervisor of the Watch in 1731. At his death two years later his son Robert Crannell, Jr., assumed the post. His son, Bartholomew, gained the post of Supervisor of the Watch House and took over as Head of the Watch at his father's death. Robert Crannell, III, was a public measurer.[25] As these appointments indicate, nepotism, prominent in government appointments of later eras, was also characteristic of the first half of the eighteenth century. Cartmen and other low-level laborers could expect continuity in employment for themselves and for their heirs. And, as the numerous interrelationships demonstrate, a body of government employees, of which the cartmen were the most numerous, was slowly taking shape.

Because only one carter left a will in this period, it is difficult to determine variations in wealth among them. Cornelius Quackenbush left but 20 shillings to his son "as bar against any pretence to his Birth right." The remainder went to his wife Annattie and his other son Benjamin. Both sons were carters.[26] Other than that cartman wealth must be reconstructed by inference. Of the 101 carters given the freemanship between 1700 and 1746, 42 received it "as poor men."[27] That nearly half of the carters of the time came from such humble stock indicates that it was an entry-level position. Though compensatory income could be gained from such posts as watchman, inspectors and measurers, the gradual growth of the economy did not, apparently, foster the kind of property accumulation which would become apparent after the 1750s.

Cartmen tended to live in the poorer wards. The census of 1703 lists eleven identifiable cartmen. Seven lived in the newer and more modest West Ward along the North River. John Langstraet, captain of the cartmen, lived in the East Ward while Peter Wessels, the sole slaveowner among cartmen, lived in the prosperous South Ward. Three others lived in the lower class North Ward. Thirty years later the pattern remained much the same. Most carters lived in either the North Ward (36 percent), the now downtrodden East Ward (18 percent), or in the West Ward (21 percent). None lived in the more elite southern wards.[28]

The first half of the eighteenth century saw the affirmation of the bond between cartmen and the City of New York. The monopolistic grip held by the cartmen over intra-city transportation was tightened by city laws making them the principal urban carriers. Price controls continued. The city also further bound the cartmen by extensive use of the English tradition of the freemanship. The right had great economic importance and, later, allowed the cartmen to exert their political powers, as well.

Cartmen began to assume specialized roles in this era as the economy and society began to diversify. Some worked the docks, others brought hay and firewood to families and the community at large, while some began to work for the city on various projects including street preparation and filling, and garbage removal. Laws governing the carters were codified and widened. By 1745 the number and importance of the city cartmen was growing in significance.

CHAPTER FOUR

Expansion and Prosperity, 1745–1760

Between 1745 and 1760 New York City experienced unprecedented growth in virtually every area of its economy and society. Aided by a succession of wars in which the city played a key role as a supply depot for British troops, New York grew from a small coastal port into a thriving international center. During this period it was able to draw even with and eventually surpass Boston in attracting European trade. It was helped immeasurably when it became the American terminus of the British transatlantic mail boat. Unlike Boston, New York was able to benefit from the colonial wars without excessive internal strife, burdensome taxes, or contributing much of its working population to the British army. Moreover, British successes inland enabled the development of a deeper and more populous hinterland which further stimulated the city's position as an entrepôt for arriving European immigrants and commodities. New York's merchants became sophisticated handlers of a variety of commodities and were particularly expert at the intricacies of underwriting and marine insurance.[1] New York's prosperity mandated increased supplies of food and fuel from its rural environs, all developments that made use of the cartmen's labors.

The wartime economy was abetted by the heavy involvement of New York merchants in privateering. Although New York continued to lag behind Philadelphia, Boston and even Annapolis, Newport and New Haven in shipbuilding and construction, general construction flourished as never before. Even in the intervening periods of peace, New York continued to prosper. At the close of the 1750s New York appeared at the threshold of even greater gains.

The prosperity which made Governor George Clarke exclaim in 1741 that New York "was never in so flourishing a condition as it is now" spread throughout the ranks of society and was at least partially responsible for the increase in population from 11,000 in 1742 to 18,000 in 1760.[2] Prosperity and growth generated great changes among both the elite and the laboring classes. Imported carriages enabled the wealthy to parade through the streets beyond the touch of the common folk. Merchant John Watts noted that "not long since such an Importation of coaches Chariots appeared in the streets, as surprized every Body."

High profits and full employment brought changes in the attitudes of employers. A heightened sense of self-interest competed with the established corporate loyalties. John Holt's *New-York Gazette* commented at the time that "self-interest is the grand design of all human action.... It is unreasonable to expect service of a man who must act contrary to his own interests to perform it." Growing ambition for bigger profits impelled merchants to prefer trading with the French enemy to dealing with the British. In like spirit the bakers sought a two shilling rise in the assize of bread on learning of an impending war contract. Despite these changes the city government and its cartmen remained wedded to monopolistic control of regulations.[3]

The political scene remained tranquil. Few controversies disturbed the political calm of the prospering city. Major disputes which heralded later conflict were over continued problems of impressment and of the British troops lodged in the city who took work away from city mechanics during wartime lulls. Tensions turned into riots in 1758. Local workers turned to the city government in expectation of protection and maintenance of traditional values. The same year riots occurred when the British navy raided New York to impress Americans as sailors. One such raid in 1757 netted over 800 New Yorkers. Only after complaints by city officials were several hundred released. The ability of local politicians to work out temporary solutions may have added to the tendency toward longer terms for charter officers in this period.[4]

Of all the laboring groups none was so visibly affected as the cartmen. The general prosperity of the city was reflected in the larger sums of money and property garnered by a few cartmen. For the whole of the trade, benefits included an increase in the common load fee to nine pence in 1749, while fees for many commodities common to shipping and trading ranged much higher.[5]

The major political change in this period was the coming to power of a strong mayor. John Cruger, Jr., a wealthy aristocrat who combined three careers as politician, merchant and lawyer, became mayor in 1756.[6] He quickly expanded the number of cartmen and absorbed many of the powers over the carters previously assumed by the Common Council. While that body continued to regulate and establish rates, the mayor's office became the center of patronage. Cruger granted freemanships to the carters and collected fees as his salary. With the mayor controlling entrance into the trade, the council lost a good deal of leverage. As council elections hinged on just a few votes in the 1740s and 1750s, the political powers of the freemanship may have prompted the *Independent Reflector* to accuse the aldermen caustically of "being in more awe of a Band of Cartmen than of an armed Host . . . the reason is not so much out of natural timidity as a more political one."[7] The tenfold increase in the number of carters could only have compounded the anxieties of the council.

The demand for labor caused Mayor John Cruger, Jr., to begin expanding the trade in 1756. During previous decades the total number of cartmen ranged between 30 and 40. During his nine-year term in office Cruger licensed 386 new carters. This nearly tenfold increase far exceeded the general population growth in the city and reflects the strong desire of local merchants, of whom Cruger was a powerful one, to insure efficient, safe and available cartage for the booming shipping industry. As William Livingston remarked, New York had a strong advantage over other cities in that cartage to and from the waterfront was never more than a quarter of a mile.[8] Furthermore, Cruger, an ally of the dominant Delancey faction of the assembly, had great amounts of patronage at his disposal. Offering a laborer a cartmen's license and the freemanship created a great loyalty and could have large political benefits.[9] Cruger granted the freemanship right to each new carter. The vast majority of these freemanships and licenses occurred in the period of prosperity and relative political calm between 1756 and 1761. The freemanship was a strong corporate link between city government and workers, not an anachronism useful only in times of political crisis. Nor would politicians like Cruger have created a block of 386 potential voters without confidence in their loyalty. The bonds between city officials and cartmen remained unaltered despite the large increase in their numbers.

Between 1756 and 1765 Mayor John Cruger, Jr., enrolled every one of the 386 new carters as freemen. Many of these carters are listed in "Burghers and Freemen," but under the occupation of "laborer." Only by comparing the "Burghers and Freemen" lists with "Cruger's License Book" can the full number of carters be known. The carters were by far the largest occupational group "made free" by Mayor Cruger.[10] The cordwainers were the next largest group who, benefitting from large orders of shoes for the British army, registered 60 freemen in this period Carpenters of all sorts were the next with 47.[11]

Another effect of the growing need for workers in the "carrying trade" was the "return" of Dutch laborers. After a half-century of near exile from the ranks of licensed carters, Dutch workers under Cruger accounted for about 30 percent. Another ethnic group, the Irish, made its initial impact on the trade, coming to about five percent of all cartmen. The rest were Anglo-American. The implication of this change is less a liberalization of restrictions than a concession to necessity. The rapid expansion in the trade demanded more men than, the Anglo-American population could supply. That the greatest increase of newcomers to the trade came from the first European settler group demonstrates the commitment of the city corporation to provide employment to its citizenry. That the city did not turn to large numbers of free blacks and slaves demonstrates its unwillingness to spark trouble from its white laborers.

Continuities are apparent in the Common Council's fee increases for cartage. The council raised the standard rate for garbage collection above that of a common load. The council also increased cartage rates for over one hundred commodities listed in government-printed chapbooks distributed throughout the city. In so doing, the council confirmed previously enacted regulations and gave notice that it intended the carters to be the sole conveyors of commodities in the city. Regulations were also extended to cover the sleds or drays used by carters in the wintertime.[12]

Slowly but surely the city moved in the direction of regulating every conceivable aspect of the cartmen's function. Despite the increased prosperity and the drift toward self-interest in other trades, the city government made it plain that it considered carting too valuable a function to remain unregulated. Nor is there any evidence that carters chafed under these regulations. Rather, the laws reaffirmed the close personal and corporate ties between the trade and city officials and strengthened the carters' unquestioned control over intra-city transportation.

The essential position of the cartmen in the economic life of the city, joined with their unique political power, gave them an unusual status. Their rank in society was actually much higher than historians have appreciated. In recent studies of the ranks of occupations in eighteenth-century port cities, the cartmen have been placed below journeymen artisans and just above transients, the unemployed, free blacks and others who made up the emerging proletariat of the cities.[13] Their lives held many uncertainties. Only their possessions of a cart and horse gave the carters status above the bottom of society. A bad year, illness, or injury could easily tear away these valued possessions. And, as Eric Foner has observed, the social gap between artisans and laborers of the "meaner" sort was quite as wide as that between merchants and artisans.[14] With such views in mind the carters appear much despised by their social betters, buffeted by the imperious demands of the merchant class and whipped by expectations of deference and the rise and fall of economy and personal fortune.

In fact, the trade had many variations in income. Some carters achieved sizable estates working solely for the merchants. Abraham Blanck, who frequently worked for Evert Bancker, left an estate of £250 plus four houses and lots. His four sons, all cartmen, divided the estate equally. One son, Abraham, was also a tavernkeeper.[15] Jacob Banta owned lots on Fair Street and on King George Street which he left to his cartmen sons, Jacob, Peter and Henry.[16] Johannes Banta's daughter married Teunis Vreeland, who received his license in 1760 and purchased land on Greenwich Street.[17] Barent Barheit left houses on Beekman Street, Huddlestone Street and Fair Street as well as two muskets and two slaves.[18] More typical, perhaps, was the estate of Israel Chadwick, who left a house and a few pounds to his wife and children.[19]

Political power enhanced their position in society. Many carters were freeholders or qualified to vote in assembly elections by possession of forty pounds in real estate. By comparing the identifiable freeholders in poll lists of 1768 and 1769 with Cruger's License Book, it can be determined that of 94 carters voting in 1768, 33 or slightly more than one-third, were free-holders.[20] In 1769, 32 of 75 voting cartmen were freeholders.[21] From this it may be projected that about one-third of all carters amassed sufficient wealth in their lifetime to own their own homes and to be freeholders.

Another positive factor in their status was the permanent quality of the carters in the local scene. Cartmen often had lengthy careers. The generation of the 1750s, for its increased size, was no exception to this rule. At least 14 carters who began their careers in the 1750s were still at work in the 1790s.[22] Cartmen Marmaduke Earle, Dirck Brinckerhoff, Jr., Peter Banta, Albert Ammerman, Abraham Martling, Sr., worked through wars and political changes. Their faces must have seemed perennial to New Yorkers. Indeed, some carters formed personal relationships with their customers which lasted a long time. Abraham Martling, for example, borrowed money from the merchant family of Banckers. Barent Sebring, blacksmith, witnessed the will of Cornelius Quackenbush. Merchant Abraham Messier performed a similar duty for carter Peter Stymets.[23]

During the last years of the prosperous decades of the 1750s numerous carters leased land on which they built homes, thus developing a community which added to the air of permanence in their status. By 1760 Mayor John Cruger, Jr., licensed 225 carters. Of these, 75, or one-third, were tenants of the powerful, wealthy Trinity Church. Cartmen who signed leases with Trinity joined carpenters, gardeners and laborers in settling the Church's Farm which quickly became the most populous portion of the North Ward. Not only did the lease plan give remarkable security to the carters at nominal rates, but Trinity was also open to sales of the lots and even permitted subletting. Some cartmen, flush with prosperity, leased two or three lots and used the extra land for speculation.[24]

A subculture quickly emerged in the Church's Farm. As carters put up their new homes many announced their occupation by placing wooden signs signifying cart and horse in front of their houses. Abraham Montanje's tavern on Broadway across from the Fields became an informal neighborhood headquarters for the cartmen. The tavern had a spacious open courtyard where cartmen could hitch their wagons and horses. Once the courtyard overflowed, carters left their horses and carts in the street. The tavern was a natural retreat for convivial conversation at the end of a day's work. By this time local politicians had learned to drop by

taverns like Montanje's and stand a round or two. This means of garner-
ing interest in political candidacies became a universally observed custom
in New York City and lasted over a century. The tavern also became a
center for political and social celebrations and also functioned as a re-
cruitment office for employers and, later, for the military. Patrons received
their mail at the tavern. In short, it acted as the central meeting place for
the emerging neighborhood.[25]

The Church's Farm was accessible to both the Oswego Market on
Broadway and Montanje's and to the docks and piers of the North (Hudson) River. The broad regular streets were conducive to cart races by the
cartmen who each morning hitched up their wagons and drove in teams
down toward the commercial district.

Few of the streets of the Church's Farm were paved and the roadbed
quickly became a quagmire of mud, garbage and manure. Unlike more east-
ern wards where the slope of the land provided some natural drainage, the
Farm's swampy lands retained the fetid stench of the streets. Dogs, horses
and pigs performed garbage disposal. The homes constructed by the carters
tended to be inexpensive single-family dwellings. In harsher weather horses
were frequently stabled on the premises. The presence of prostitutes, sailors
and disorderly slaves gave the neighborhood a raucous air that provoked
complaints from farmers and merchants who traveled through the streets of
the ward to and from the docks on the North River.

In just a few years the cartmen and other laborers created a classic laboring class neighborhood. Trinity Church established branches within the
Farm area for the worship of the tenants, but the tavern remained the center of culture. The free and easy tavern life included gambling, bull-baiting,
wax-work shows, cart-races, or an occasional spectacular event such as the
display of a leopard at Montanje's.[26]

The growing occupational segregation of the city may be seen in the
divergence of carters from the politicians and merchants who were their
putative masters. While cartmen lived on Church's Farm, John Cruger lived
on fashionable Smith Street where his neighbors included such members
of the elite as the Clarksons, Phillipses and Ludlows. Cruger's father, John,
Sr., lived opposite the fort where his neighbors included the Livingstons,
Morrises, DeLanceys and Bayards.[27] The cartmen were creating their own
cultural environment far from the elite addresses of their masters.

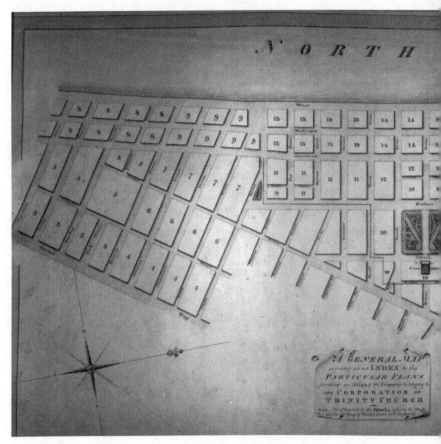

"The Trinity Church Farm," 1815, Trinity Church Archives. The Farm extended from the church up the west side of Manhattan to Greenwich Village. Courtesy of Parish of Trinity Church.

The 75 cartmen were by far the largest occupational group in the Church's Farm in 1765. The remaining lots were scattered among carpenters, stonecutters, laborers, gardeners working in the estates just beyond the city, butchers and a few merchants who acquired property as potential investment.[28]

The preponderence of the cartmen in the area indicates that the Church's Farm was an early forerunner of the later "Cartmen's Wards" of the 1790s. When the city drew its wards in 1791 the Church's Farm became part of the new Sixth Ward, which newspapers of the 1790s referred to as the "Cartmen's" because of the large numbers of the trade residing there.[29] The length of the Church's Farm leases provided stability necessary for an

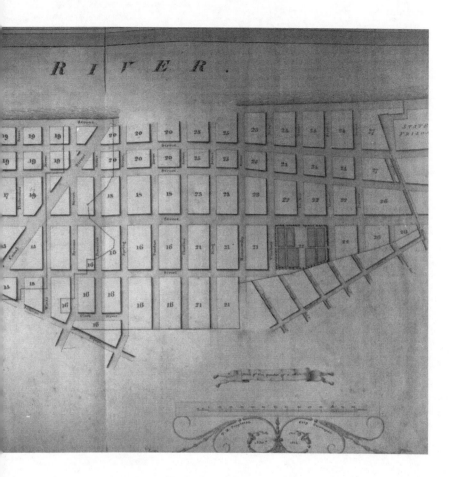

occupational ghetto and combined with the long careers and general trade
characteristics to make the area a cartman community.

The record books of Trinity Church give the most complete information on patterns of the laboring class housing in the 1750s. No other
such complete information is known to exist. There is scanty evidence
from wills that cartmen owned property elsewhere. As mentioned, Abraham Blanck, Jacob Banta and Thomas Montanje all owned property in
the East Ward, but beyond those few it is difficult to describe with any
accuracy property-holding by cartmen in this period. Comparison of the
names of the freeholders on the poll lists of 1768 and 1769 with the tenants of Trinity Church indicates that carters did own or lease land elsewhere. Of the 33. freeholders voting in the elections of 1768 and 1769,
19 were residents of the Trinity Church Farm. This means that 14 held

property or leases elsewhere in the city. Available records do not, however, reveal where.[30]

The 1740s and 1750s saw an unprecedented expansion of the economy and society of New York City and an accompanying growth in the cartmen's trade. Despite the dramatic increase in their numbers from around 40 in the 1730s to 386 by 1765, cartmen maintained their bonds with city government. The emergence of a strong mayor, John Cruger, Jr., who perpetuated most of the powers of regulation over the carters, meant that the laws and philosophy behind them remained unaltered. Social bonds between cartmen and the merchant class complemented these legal ties. Cruger's grants of the freemanship to all the cartmen meant continued importance of the right.

The opening the Church's Farm to development provided many carters with inexpensive land with long-term leases. The emergence of a cartmen's community enhanced the trade's strong sense of civic identification. This was further augmented by the lengthy careers of many carters. Many stayed on the job for 20 years or more and continued the patterns of occupational stability. The freemanship glued all of these traits together. These characteristics of cartmen life in New York City bore heavily on their conduct in the prerevolutionary events.

CHAPTER FIVE

The Cartmen in the Era
of Revolution, 1760–1783

Prosperity in New York City came to an abrupt halt with the close of the Seven Years War in 1763. The defeat of the French meant an end to the lucrative war contracts and over-stocked inventories. The withdrawal of most British troops caused a decline in the earnings of small merchants and artisans. The remaining troops distressed local tradesmen because of the tax required to support them and because the troops often took part-time work and undercut wages of local laborers. As work began to dry up in the city, many artisans began drifting out in search of work elsewhere. Runaway indentured servants and British deserters arrived from the countryside in a futile quest for employment. Credit became much tighter and bankruptcies soared. Prices of meat, wood and grain rocketed.[1]

The economic slump in New York was exacerbated by the British government's decision to extract much-needed revenue from the colonies through taxes. Reaction to British plans created a political turmoil which soon transformed the shape of politics in the city forever. Before the 1760s, whether dominated by various families or by factious interests, New York City politics remained the arena of the merchant elite. The thought of plebeians "standing" for nomination to the colonial assembly would have struck everyone in New York as ridiculous. By the end of the 1760s, however, the often-turbulent reaction to British tax measures and to local disputes over employment of English soldiers created a new type of politician. Men like Alexander MacDougall, John Lamb and Isaac Sears, of "humble" though not "mean" origins, became adept at manipulating both the ambitions of the political elite and the grievances of the common people, thereby creating followings of their own. Elite politicians such as James DeLancey and members of the Livingston and Schuyler families learned to negotiate favor with MacDougall, Sears and Lamb in order to obtain the votes of their followers. Though the time of successful middle-class or mechanic candidates was still in the future, the new political leaders used the crisis to further their own ambitions.[2]

The common folk were not passive in the midst of this change. Whether organized into the Sons of Liberty or acting as a spontaneous mob intent on correcting a perceived grievance, the common people became an important force for change in the growing resistance to British control. The "mob" induced the assembly in 1765 to react against British taxes as a means to placate popular opinion. The 1760s were marked by increased participation of the common people in New York's elections. Endowed with greater suffrage in most colonies, New Yorkers became more active in the assertion of their rights.

For carters, the first few years of the 1760s were much like previous ones. Mayor John Cruger, Jr., licensed fewer new carters between 1760 and 1763; the 77 licensed in this period brought the total since 1756 to 302. He appointed James Lowns and Rynier Hopper to be foremen of the carters.[3] The Common Council continued to offer cartmen sinecures in this era. For example, Rynear Nack gained the post of public measurer.[4] The council awarded a contract to Hugh Ross for "digging and carting 550 loads of ground from out of King George Street," for which he was paid six pounds. John Emmott was paid three pounds for working on the same project. Dirck Ammerman received twenty pounds for filling up Peck's Slip.[5]

Other carters earned income from the British. The account book of H. M. Office of Ordinances indicates often lucrative employment. John Steel, John Van Wart and James McKenney carted wood and gunpowder for the British and received quarterly payments of £21 each. David Provost received £90 for wood delivery in 1760.[6]

Money could be made selling wood to the city government. Evert Bancker, quartermaster of the city and the colonial militia, hired 20 cartmen per year to supply firewood. Carters purchased wood from boatmen from New Jersey and resold it to Bancker at the fixed rates. The profit for the carters came from "ryding" the wood.[7]

On the other hand, the Common Council moved to insure that carters did not unduly profit from wood sales in hard times. In the winter of 1762, the council, announced that the standard rate was payable for one cord per four loads. Anything less indicated fraud by the carters. The council kept the common load fee at the level fixed in 1749, but raised the fine for "forestalling and engrossing" to five pounds per violation.[8]

Compared to assembly and popular policies, municipal politics remained stable as city councilmen stayed in office in the 1760s three times as long as in the 1730s. Only two mayors, John Cruger, Jr., and Whitehead Hicks, held office between 1756 and 1776.[9] The consensus established in the charter elections carried over into the first assembly election of the decade, held in 1761. The assembly elections of this decade are considered crucial by historians because they demonstrated the changes in New York politics from feuds among the important elite families, the Livingstons and DeLanceys, into true partisan contests. Politics in the 1760s evolved from family factionalism into ideological disputes about the control of the British government over the economic and social life of New York. The elections also demonstrate the increased involvement and importance of the common man in the political process. More voted as ambitious politicians made direct appeals to them.[10]

Colonial elections in New York used the *viva voce* method which insured that preferences became public knowledge. Not surprisingly, the greatest cartmen support was for Cruger. Their 55 votes helped him pile up the largest winning total and constituted a solid five percent of his electorate. Cruger was in a unique position to expect loyalty. As mayor he gave the carters the right to work and, often, to vote. As a local merchant he and his brother were frequent employers of cartmen. As Commissary-General of the Colony of New York, he employed carters to carry supplies to distant forts and expeditions; soon after his election, Cruger hired carters who supported him to deliver goods to the militia in Albany.[11]

The cartmen votes were small but significant additions to the totals of their candidates. Wealthy merchants Leonard Lispenard and Philip Livingston came next receiving 46 or 65 percent of the cartmen votes. The remainder were split among William Bayard, of the victorious Livingston faction, newcomer James DeLancey, Jr., and a lawyer, John Morin Scott. The relative bunching of votes indicated that, except for Cruger, there were no clear cartman favorites. Even Scott, the lawyer, whose continued candidacy scandalized the merchants, received support from the carters.

By 1761 Cruger had licensed 225 carters. Of these, 74, or slightly less than a third, voted. The reason for this apathetic response is not known. The relative calm of politics may have made carters disinterested or perhaps voting remained a method of repayment for economic favors rather than a vehicle for social change. The potential size of the cartmen's vote, however, meant that politicians would learn to appeal to them.

As the 1760s wore on a deteriorating economy and worsening political strife caused radicalization of local politics. The Sugar Act of 1764 adversely affected three branches of colonial commerce—molasses, wines and inter-colonial trade—and caused hardship among New York City sailors and certainly those cartmen working for merchants involved in the trade. British impressment raids in 1764 and 1765 further irritated the populace.

The worst outbreak of anger between common people of the city and the British came in the Stamp Act Crisis of November 1765. The plan of the British to attach a tax on many commercial exchanges met with unified displeasure throughout the ranks of society. In November 1765 about 1200 freemen and freeholders used a committee of 12 to instruct Assembly-men Cruger, Livingston, Lispenard and Bayard to single out two essential rights in a bill of grievances: "No taxation without consent and trial by jury." One historian suggests that the assembly reacted to stem the more radical wishes of the "mob." Anger of the "people in the street" became apparent in the streets.[12]

The tense city erupted in November 1765. Lt. Governor Cadwallader Colden invited disaster by extensive preparations for the defense of Fort George, where the stamps were stored. The crowd "carted" an effigy of Colden around the city. The crowds continued to grow as the rioters came down from the Church's Farm, smashing windows en route and finally stopping to sack Colden's barn and burn his carriage.[13]

The Stamp Act Riots were important because they solidified the Liberty Boys, the political organization of the common people. The riots led to the closing of the port of New York in reaction to the Stamp Act. Two hundred New York merchants signed a Non-Importation Agreement until the British repealed the Stamp Act. This fusion of elite and popular sentiment eventually convinced the British government to repeal the Stamp

Act. This success made the riots legendary among city folk who erected a Liberty Pole opposite Montanje's tavern and the Oswego Market[14] in a large open space known as the Fields. The Fields soon became a popular meeting place and would remain so for the next 40 years. Two taverns on the Fields, Montanje's and Bardin's, were headquarters where the "Riotous Liberty Boys met in 1765 and 66." A relative of several cartmen, Montanje lived in the Church's Farm and had political ambitions of his own. He desired an appointment as a potash inspector and hoped that through some contact with local politicians his goal could be secured.[15]

The memory of the Stamp Act Riots brought business to Montanje. Each year the Sons of Liberty held suppers there to commemorate their successes. Montanje's tavern became a favored watering-hole for carters and Liberty Boys. Taverns, always spots for male conviviality and commerce, now became more practical sites for the practical organization of politics and for the stewing mix of grievances that led to the American Revolution. As workers who were deeply invested in local politics and as staunch members of a laboring community, the cartmen were prominent in debates at the taverns.[16]

Success of the demonstrations against the Stamp Act greatly helped local politicians. Isaac Sears and Alexander MacDougall increased their reputations as leaders of the Sons of Liberty. James DeLancey, Jr., established his political reputation by his outspoken criticism of the British.

Local workers saw new meaning in their own political involvement. The carters joined other tradesmen in the large turnout of common people in the assembly election of 1768. This contest, characterized by Patricia Bonomi as the first large-scale partisan election in New York, was fought on several levels.[17] The combined forces of James DeLancey, Alexander MacDougall and Isaac Sears used the growing anti-British feeling among New Yorkers to portray their faction as more responsive to local grievances. DeLancey joined forces with the Sons of Liberty as a source of support for his candidacy and those of James Jauncey and Jacob Walton. Despite the continued popularity of Philip Livingston, his faction was hampered by the presence of a lawyer, John Morin Scott. The DeLanceyites, now in the role of "popular Whigs," concentrated on destroying the candidacy of Scott. William Bayard, who was quite aged, and Amos Dodge, a carpenter and the first mechanic candidate, were not considered serious contenders.[18]

A score of campaign pamphlets and newspaper articles attacked Scott's profession. "The Voter's new catechism," published on March 3, 1768, asked rhetorically if the "blessed Parliament has any lawyers." It accused lawyers of "thriving on our misfortunes" and that lawyers were "maintained and enriched entirely on our labour and property." It asked the consequence of the actions of those lawyers who refused to go along with business without stamps during the Stamp Act Crisis; "All business stopped," thundered the editorial.[19] DeLancey and his cohorts, keying on the candidacy of Scott, attempted to link lawyers with hardships among the common people.

Other political devices concentrated on the interdependence of laborers and merchants. A card handed out in the streets stressed first that the "leather-aprons (a very respectable body) are clearly of the opinion that trade . . . and not law supports our families." This card also noted that "honest Jolt the Cartman says he never got six-pence by riding law books tho' he gets many pounds from the merchants." The card concluded by stating, "We all say . . . No lawyers in the Assembly." This card is significant to this study in several ways. First, it reaffirmed the traditional bonds between merchants and cartmen. Second, it was a direct appeal to the cartmen's pocketbooks. Third, it was couched in the language of the trade itself, a practice which would become common in the 1790s, but was innovative in the 1760s. The opposition could only make weak replies that "lawyers were as honest and competent as any merchant."[20]

Except for support for Philip Livingston, the wealthy and popular merchant, the carters voted heavily for DeLancey, Walton and especially for Jauncey. Nearly 70 percent of the 65 voting carters supported Jauncey. DeLancey and Walton both received over 50 votes from the cartmen while Scott lagged far behind with only 40 cartmen votes. Had they given their support to Scott, Jauncey would have been defeated. Few carters gave any attention to Bayard or Dodge; only one of ten cartman votes supported Dodge.[21]

The election of 1768 showed the increased value of political appeals to the carters and other laboring groups. Though only one in four carters turned out, every vote counted in this hard-fought election and politicians used stronger appeals the next time.

The assembly of 1768 was a short-lived one and a new ballot was called in the Spring 1769. This time the moderate Whigs found an issue with which to attack DeLancey. His Anglican church affiliation became a liability because many New Yorkers feared the establishment of an Anglican bishopric in the colonies. DeLancey and the popular Whigs had done little in the assembly to please the Sons of Liberty. DeLancey attempted to gain popularity for his ticket by adding John Cruger, who left electoral politics the year before to become the first President of the new Chamber of Commerce.[22]

In an attempt to fight off attacks from the moderate Whigs, DeLancey and Jauncey used a tactic successful the year before. They distributed a broadside in the streets on January 16, 1769 containing an affidavit before the assembly concerning the benevolent behavior of James Jauncey. In the message cartman Obadiah Wells told a story of Jauncey's long-standing philanthropy. It appeared that Jauncey had, for a number of years, used Wells to distribute anonymously several hundred pounds each year in cash, wood, food, and other necessities. Wells testified that Jauncey hired him to distribute "considerable sums of money and large quantities of fire-wood, Beef, Pork, wine, butter, Sugar, Blanketts, clothing . . . to the sick and poor of the . . . City, but especially such as lived about the Fresh Water, and on the Meadows and on Church-land." The deposition ended with a plea to vote for Jauncey, Cruger, DeLancey and Walton.[23]

Shortly after, another broadside entitled "A Contrast" compared the merchant, "who cannot enrich himself without benefitting those amongst who he resides," and the lawyer, who by "chicannery has been the instrument of bringing multitudes to distress, disease and penury . . . grinding the face of the poor."[24] However, in 1769 the Sons of Liberty did not have the positive impact of the previous year.[25] Although DeLancey and his allies returned to the assembly as Philip Livingston went down to defeat with Scott, Van Wyck and Brockholst Livingston, the margins of victory were much closer than before. Indeed, the overall vote was lower. The cartmen appeared to be badly split among the candidates. DeLancey, with 40 or 51 percent of cartmen ballots, received the greatest number. The remainder of the candidates followed closely behind; Van Wyck finished last among carters, but still retained 31 or 41 percent of their votes. Five candidates, John Cruger, Walton, Jauncey, Philip Livingston and Scott, received 37 of the 75 cartmen votes.[26]

The cartmen split their vote almost evenly without a clear favorite among the eight candidates. DeLancey polled best among carters; Jauncey for all his benevolent acts did no better than third. The cartmen vote was important for each candidate, however, as the percentage of cartman support varied between four and six percent of each's total. Cartmen also voted in blocs. Thirty-two carters voted solidly for the DeLancey, Cruger, Jauncey and Walton ticket while 26 voted exclusively for the Livingstons, Scott and Van Wyck. The splits among the carters refute the belief that laboring men at this time were steadily moving toward popular Whiggery. The cartmen were divied between the moderate and popular Whigs.

One reason for the low cartman turnout may have been due to bullying at the polls. Oliver DeLancey and the treasurers of Trinity Church stood by the polls to insure church tenants voted the correct way. Many carters were tied to Trinity Church, the principal Anglican institution in the city. Not only did 75 cartmen live on the Church's Farm, but, 84, or 21 percent, of the 386 licensed carters between 1756 and 1765 were married in the church.[27]

Trinity employed cartmen. The financial records of the church reveal that several carters were favored with constant employment. John Storm, who voted for DeLancey, was paid one pound, six shillings for "1 cord of wood plus cartage." Later, Storm was hired to "cart 60 loads of earth" for which he was paid twelve shillings. A third contract required "carting 370 loads of earth" for dock building and paying three pounds, 14 shillings. Abraham Ackerman received a similar contract.[28] He also voted for DeLancey. This data, perhaps insufficient for a generalization, suggests that cartmen business ties affected their voting patterns.

After these elections tensions remained high in the city. Chief among complaints was the growing bitterness over the presence of British troops. The troops were seen as costing money and jobs. The soldiers in turn resented the hostility of local citizens. Their attention became fixed on the Liberty Pole erected in the Fields across the street from Montanje's which commemorated the success of the Stamp Act Riots.

On Saturday night, January 19, 1770, the poor relations between the troops and the patriots at Montanje's exploded. The troops attempted to cut down the pole. When their intentions were discovered a riot occurred.[29] The troops drove the patriots back into Montanje's. They then proceeded to sack the tavern, breaking windows, overturning tables and driving out everyone except Montanje himself who was found cowering in the kitchen. The pole was torn down and cut into little pieces which

Pencil sketch by Pierre Eugene du Simitiere, 1770, Library Company of Philadelphia. Pictured are Montanje's tavern on the left, the jail in the middle, and the Soldiers' Barracks on the right. In the left foreground is the Liberty Pole.

were deposited on the steps of the tavern. Clashes ensued in the streets. Not until Mayor Whitehead Hicks was able to secure an agreement to have the troops quartered in the fort was the tense atmosphere relaxed. Hicks also asked and received permission to erect a new pole.[30]

This incident was deeply troubling to the cartmen. The tavern was one of their headquarters. Across the street was the Oswego Market where many worked. In the streets behind lay their homes. The pole symbolized the growing political independence of the laboring man in the city and his increasing hostility toward troops and parliament. During the riot Pierre Eugene du Simitiere sketched cartmen and other citizens driving a "devil's cart" through the streets to express their anger at the soldiers.

This hostility grew steadily in New York in the first half of the 1770s. The Liberty Boys broke with DeLancey in 1770, just months after his victory in the assembly. A bitter controversy broke that same year over a proposal to introduce the Pennsylvania secret ballot.

More local issues added to the tense atmosphere. Cartmen learned that the Common Council could also be an oppressive instrument in the Oswego Market incident of 1771. The market, built in 1721, was, like Montanje's, a central part of the cartman's daily experience. One of the largest markets, it served all the city and was a measuring point for wood and hay. Yet it was a health hazard. Located in the middle of Broadway just below the Fields, the market not only obstructed traffic but also produced complaints of rats, the stench of spoiled meat and rotting vegetables. Add the fierce odor of cartmen's horses and the resolution of the council to have the Oswego Market destroyed seemed reasonable. The best site, decided the council, was a corporation-owned plot of land on the North River above the residential part of the city.[31]

Cartmen immediately objected to the proposed change. One hundred twenty-five cartmen presented the Common Council with a petition endorsed by such Liberty Boys as John Lamb, Marinus Willett, Gabriel Furman and Abraham Montanje himself. The cartmen complained that they would lose the "business of Ryding the different commodities brought in from the Jerseys who pay no taxes" if the new market replaced the Oswego.[32] The complaint by the cartmen was matched by a similar plea from licensed butchers of the city. They, like the cartmen, worried about accessibility of the North River site to their customers. The Oswego, they argued, was "nearer to the growing part of the city and more accessible to the Farmers, Gardeners and others who come from the Bowery."[33] Both carters and butchers petitioned the council to consider a new market on the northern edges of the Fields. After an extended debate the council rejected both pleas by a decisive vote of eleven to four.[34]

Undaunted by this dismissal, the cartmen offered a new series of petitions. In one, placed after the Oswego Market had been torn down and replaced by a new building on the North River, 100 cartmen repeated the request for a market on the Fields. They even offered to build it at their own expense and using their own labor.[35]

The dispute was finally resolved by the failure of the North River Market. Butchers and cartmen boycotted it and within a short time the council announced construction of another market at the corner of Maiden Lane and Broadway, named in honor of the old Oswego Market. Butchers and cartmen flocked to the new Oswego and ignored the North River or Bear Market. This incident demonstrates the importance of custom among the trades. Destruction of a part of their community and reordering of their work lives were unacceptable to such traditional groups. The issue was important enough virtually to unite cartmen and contrasted strongly with their division in the political realm.[36]

The following year the council made partial amends by raising the common load to a shilling a ride, the first such increase since 1749. It acknowledged the increasing violence in the city by adding a regulation that no cartman be allowed to carry pouches of gunpowder with them "on account of the extreme danger."[37]

A series of incidents demonstrates the carters' growing hostility toward their social betters. Merchant William Kelly was burned in effigy for attempting to avoid the Non-Importation Act of 1773. His effigy was "carted" around town and then burned in front of his home. Samuel Hake became so enraged at silversmith Samuel Casey for avoiding payment for cartage of timber that he petitioned the Mayor's Court successfully to have Casey arrested and imprisoned.

Another incident showing the trade's lack of deference was the dispute between a Mr. Page, a minister, and cartman Bartholomew Van Brockle. The latter apparently became disillusioned with the preacher after contributing money to his church. He publicized his anger in the streets by distributing letters from the Bishop of London which questioned Page's behavior. Page complained of slander by a "common carman." Van Brockle responded that, "it is better to be a common carter than a deceitful minister."[38]

Throughout the early 1770s the Liberty Boys continued to hold annual suppers at Montanje's. As the political crisis deepened, various other groups formed. Committees of Correspondence interacted with other Sons of Liberty organizations in other cities. By 1774 the laboring men in New York City organized Committees of Mechanics to represent their interests within the emerging colonial cause. No cartmen were included in these committees, however, which foreshadowed the split between mechanics and carters after the revolution.[39]

The American Revolution arrived later in New York than in Boston or Philadelphia. By 1776, however, colonial militias were marching in the streets. The rapidly unfolding events of that year required quick choices by cartmen and other citizens. When war finally arrived the carters displayed divisions shown in the elections of the 1760s. Scholars are still deciding the reasons why some laborers adopted the patriot cause and others remained loyal to the King. Using the lists of Loyalists compiled by Robert Kelby, it is possible to make some suggestions about the cartmen. Of the 386 licensed by Cruger, 50, or 13 percent, appear on Kelby's List. By the same method, comparison of the license records with the lists of New York State patriot soldiers shows that 105, or 29 percent, left the city to join the Revolution. According to the accepted view of New York City loyalism, most who remained in the city were from the upper classes. Only about 10 percent of the city Loyalists were worth less than £500. Wallace Brown identified the active Loyalists of New York City as wealthy recent immigrants from the British Isles who tended to be merchants or shopkeepers.[40]

Yet many humble carters joined the British side. The reasons why some carters stayed vary. Rynier Hopper had been a foreman since 1758. Paulus Banta and Abraham Brower were of long-standing New York families involved in carting, as were Elias Bailey, John Couwenhoven, John Bennett, Thomas Palmer and Stephen Allen.[41] Still others retained other old ties. Twenty, or 50 percent, of the carters who voted for James DeLancey served in a regiment commanded by his loyalist brother, Brigadier General Oliver DeLancey.

Similar continuities are apparent with patriot carters. Many joined to form regiments headed by local politicians. Marinus Willett and John Lamb headed regiments containing carters. Alexander Lamb, Jr., son of the door-keeper of the assembly, rose as high as quartermaster. Lamb would emerge as a postwar cartmen leader.[42]

Many cartmen who served in the New York State troops included members of old cartman families. John Ackerman, Abraham Martling, Henry Palding, Gersham Sherwood, Isaac DeLaMeter, John Day, John Hitchcock and John Galespy all came from second generation cartman families. Albert Ammerman, John Bell, John Brinckerhoff, Duncan Campbell, Vincent Carter and Isaac Blauveldt had carted since the late 1750s. Their ties with the city were strong. A few, including Alexander Lamb and Dirck Ammerman, were fairly young but still had life-long ties with the city.[43]

The British occupation of New York City during the Revolutionary War had a disastrous effect on the city. Two major fires destroyed much of the housing stock. Churches and public buildings were commandeered for use as barracks, storehouses and prisons. The population of the city dropped from 25,000 to 5000 in 1776. Local government soon became highly corrupt and was eventually replaced by military command.

Drawn by du Simitiere just after the Golden Hill Riots of 1770, this caricature shows cartmen displaying their ire over the soldiers' attack on Montanje's. Library Company of Philadelphia.

Regulation and licensing of cartmen, butchers and tavernkeepers continued throughout the conflict. Neither inspection nor price control was very effective. Loyalist cartmen and British officers combined to create schemes involving large profits. The rampant inflation of the war destroyed the prewar regulation of cartage. Although the common load rate was increased to two shillings, six pence in 1778 it had little to do with the reality of prices. An official commission formed to legislate fair rates heard testimony from merchants and citizens that carters were earning from forty to one hundred shillings per day. The standard rate of pay before the Revolution was three to four shillings per day. Wartime conditions enabled cartmen to make undue profits.[44]

The behavior of the cartmen who stayed behind in New York City points to the advance in trade organization. As the mechanics had in 1774, the cartmen formed a committee to represent the trade in the negotiations with the Chamber of Commerce, which was acting on behalf of the merchants of the city. The Chamber of Commerce listened to the committee explain that "provisions and provender" were more expensive and an increase in the regulated fees was necessary. Their request was approved.[45]

The difficulty of attracting and keeping an adequate supply of carters as well as the near-anarchy present in the city may have had something to do with the Chamber of Commerce's attention to the carters. The perilous situation is reflected in the announcement in 1778 that "all persons wishing to cart shall register at the police office and receive a license gratis. Those continuing to cart without license will be arrested and imprisoned."[46]

The police backed up their attempts to rein in the carters by imposing heavy fines. Teunis Somerindyke and George Moore were fined five pounds for "riding on their carts." Moses and James Egbert, Jacob Ewel and Peter Van Blarcum were fined 40 shillings each in 1780 for extortion.[47]

As the war continued to take its toll on New York City, the scarcity of laborers forced the British to break the color line by giving local blacks carting licenses. Though often cheated out of their wages and laboring under harsh conditions these black carters, about 50 in number, were the first to crack the previously segregated trade. The American victory, however, cost them any chance of retaining their jobs.[48]

Measurement of wood broke down completely. The misery caused by fires, invasions and bad winters was not alleviated by corruption in the quartermaster's office. The four loads required for a cord of firewood before the war now became three. Cartmen spoke of such loads as "barrack-master's cord." The local wood inspector boasted that he visited the inspection site but once during the war but continued to collect a salary of a guinea a day. By 1779 one prominent citizen was forced to be content with a load of green twigs for which he paid the cartman a sizable sum.[49]

Much of the employment for carters came from military operations. The British used carters to drive military carts around the city and out to Long Island. While the established rates were one shilling, six pence, actual charges ranged much higher. According to the constant complaints of the military controller, costs per quarter amounted to over £400 for a force of 30 to 50 carters.[50]

It is not surprising then to find that some carters were able to acquire great wealth during the war. Abraham Parcell was able to leave his heirs three houses in the city, over £250 of sterling and a 600-acre farm in New Jersey. This was a considerable improvement in wealth for a man who was unable to qualify for the vote as a £40 freeholder in 1769. Other carters put in claims after the war which attest to economic gain. Thomas Ryan estimated his wealth to the Commission on Claims at better than £378 Thomas Mills claimed £500 plus two houses in Manhattan. These scanty records suggest that some loyalist carters gained large profits during the war. Others were so poor that they remained in New York City after the evacuation by the British.[51]

The revolutionary years saw great change for the cartmen. Their numbers soared with the growing economy. The freemanships given them by Mayor Cruger turned into political capital during the heated elections of the late 1760s. Politicians learned to appeal to the carters, usually on the theme of the interdependence of merchants and the trade. Later, the unified trade reaction to the closing of the Oswego Market, abetted by the Liberty Boys, was a direct confrontation of the city's and the carters' wishes. The city won a temporary victory but may have severely alienated the trade.

For all of the political changes, regulation remained constant. Cartmen and citizens preferred the old laws inherited from English practice. This was as true in the prosperous years of the 1750s as in the anarchic war-torn days of the Revolution. The Chamber of Commerce took over where the Common Council left off as the negotiator with first the cartmen, then, a Committee of Cartmen, an evolution in the trade consciousness which would continue to grow after the war.

CHAPTER SIX

The Postwar Years, 1783–1788

When the British troops and Loyalists departed in defeat from New York City in the last months of 1783, they left behind a partially ruined city. Seven years of war cost the city dearly. Fortifications and barricades blocked streets and roads. Two major fires, one in 1776 and a second in 1778, gutted many houses. There was a scarcity of food and fuel. Crumbling wharves, the ruinous state of public and private buildings used by the British as garrisons and prisons and the ubiquitous filth all contributed to the general misery. Inflation, which sent prices for essential goods to unprecedented levels during wartime, remained rampant. There were reports of price-gouging by laborers, especially by cartmen. Despite the attempt of the British to continue regulation of cartmen throughout the war, many abuses were cited by Loyalists and incoming Patriots.[1]

Although the government of the city was no longer ruled by colonial charter, but rather by laws enacted in the Constitutional Convention of 1777, there was little real change in structure.[2] The mayor retained his powers of patronage including licensing of cartmen, tavernkeepers and a host of other trades. His mode of selection had changed, however, from appointed by the royal governor to one by a Council of Appointment composed of the governor, two senators and two assemblymen. The Common Council, the legislative body of the city, was elected now by citizens either holding a £20 freehold or possessing the freemanship of the city. The council continued to exert its powers over local taxation and regulation of trades like the cartmen, butchers, bakers and porters, as well as its powers of appointment over a small army of lower-echelon city officials including the weighmasters, packers, gaugers, measurers and marshals. Together the mayor and council acted as the local judiciary.[3]

The retention of colonial laws does not appear to have caused much consternation among the citizenry. Marinus Willett wrote to John Jay that regulation was necessary as "an honest tradesman is as rare as the Phoenix."[4] Even before calling for new chapter elections, a temporary council set up by the Constitutional Convention of New York State moved quickly to reestablish order. It regulated essential products including bread, meat and firewood just as in the colonial era. At its first meeting the temporary council announced the reinstatement of laws governing cartmen. New maximum rates were set which rolled back the inflationary fees enacted by the British during the war. Heavy fines for engrossing firewood and hay, for refusing to provide service and for price-gouging all emphasized the council's determination to insure that cartmen worked equally and fairly for all citizens and respected the notion of a just price.[5]

The necessity of quick action by the council was justified by the complaints of departing Loyalists and arriving Patriots. Regulation also insured a sense of order in the chaotic city. The council needed the services of a stable, efficient and dependable force of cartmen to take part in the planned reconstruction of society. Although trade was in disarray because the British either dumped goods upon local merchants and refused to allow Americans to trade with the West Indies, commerce was still considered the key to prosperity.

The council decreed that city charter and assembly elections should take place as soon as possible and ballots were scheduled for late December, 1783. The issues put forth had a familiar ring to them. Broadsides distributed in the streets argued for a merchant-oriented ticket. "Juvenis" explained that "the prosperity of the mechanic depends upon every merchant, and if the latter is unsuccessful, the former cannot be successful." "A Friend to Mechanics" urged that it was better to elect "discreet men, rather than violent." These pleas for a moderate Whig government were answered by "A Battered Soldier" who warned the public that those who wanted conservative Whigs in power would pander to the Tories. Whig mechanics and cartmen would then become "Hewers of Wood and Drawers of Water, to the Tories of the State."[6]

On December 27, 1783, the General Meeting of Mechanics nominated a popular Whig assembly ticket including such leaders as John Lamb, Marinus Willett, John Stagg, and Isaac Sears and a semipopular Whig senate slate including Alexander MacDougall, John Morin Scott, Isaac Stoutenburgh, William Floyd and conservative Whig, James Duane. The ticket proposed by the Committee of Mechanics won by a four to one landslide, thus marking the ascent of the mechanics to political power in the city. Thereafter, as Staughton Lynd has demonstrated, they became a power to be reckoned with in the city and continued to nominate their own slates. Because this vote was by a show of hands and no records were kept, it is not possible to know the extent of cartman participation.[7]

The Committee of Mechanics stayed active in New York City politics and made frequent suggestions to the assemblymen. One burning issue in the Spring of 1784 concerned the allocation of city licenses. Even before the American occupation of the city, a petition to Governor George Clinton asked that Tories be denied licenses in favor of "men who exerted themselves for the patriot cause." In February and March, 1784, the "late exiled Mechanics Grocers, Retailers and Innholders" protested licenses given to Tories. The Sons of Liberty called for the assembly to exclude Tories from the "advantages of trade and commerce." The cartmen were not mentioned in these petitions, but, given their prewar desire for monopoly, there can be little doubt that patriot cartmen agreed with them.[8]

In March the new Common Council and mayor began to reassemble the carters. On March 9, 1784, the council passed a law relative to the admission of freemen. The only real change in the law was the substitution of American nationality for British.[9] A week later the city appointed a number of commissioners of streets, several of whom, Thomas Ivers, Benjamin Blagge and John Stagg were councilmen, to hire as many cartmen as necessary to rebuild the city.[10] For the next two months much council time was taken up with the admission of 267 cartmen as freemen. A notice in the *Independent Gazette* of June 8, 1784 asked that all who applied for licenses come to the tavern of John Simmons, "prepared with references and securities." By the end of 1785, 54 more cartmen were admitted as freemen for a total of 321.[11] During that year, Mayor James Duane and the council agreed that no more cartmen would be licensed except in special cases. Duane, a conservative Whig, identified with the Livingston family, was opposed to liberalization of voting qualifications and thus his part in granting the free-manship to several hundred carters indicates how badly the city govern-ment needed their services.[12]

The men who received freemanships and licenses to drive a cart in 1784 were of varying backgrounds. Many were returning veterans. By compar-ing the list of New York State troops with the body of freemanship carters, at least 116 of the 325, or 35 percent can be identified as veterans. Another 94 cartmen came across the river from New Jersey. Nearly all of these were veterans of the Bergen County New Jersey militia.[13] A few, including Wil-liam Anderson, Moses Ely and Jonathan Concklin, had been waggoners, but the rest were farmers turned soldiers. During the war Bergen County had been a constant theater of conflict. Many of these farmers lost their homes and livestock to war's devastation. With little to return to or needing cash to rebuild their farms, over 200 veterans poured into New York City to work as cartmen. Some stayed but a few years, while others spent the rest of their lives in New York.

Petitions to the Common Council and mayor often mentioned veter-ans' status. Isaac Woolcocks mentioned "having been engaged in the army during the late war." Ten other carters endorsed his petition. Nine others supported John Craig's petition by noting that he "has served his country well during the war with activity and bravery when time prevented him a trade." Marinus Willett endorsed the petition of Samuel Arnot which de-scribed his "having been engaged in the late War in the expedition to Can-ada in Captain Willett's Company." Cartmen favored leniency toward some Tories who treated soldiers well. John Hendrick's application noted that he had four children, was licensed as a carter in 1773 and "has for a long time been in a helpless condition." The key point in his application was that he had shown "Liberality to the American prisoners confined in the city dur-ing the late war." This petition was signed by Nicholas Bayard, Anthony Lispenard and by cartmen Alexander Lamb and Andrew Lossye.[14]

Other cartmen whose veteran status helped them obtain licenses in-cluded John Ackerman, Peter Bogart, Francis Colegrove, Abraham Brower, John Day, George Gillespie, Nathan June, Cornelius Palding, James Van Blarcum and Isaac Wilcox. Special legislation was also drawn up in the Common Council to protect the freemanship rights of Marmaduke Earle, Charles Brower, Charles Stymets, James Demarest and David Ross who had left the city to fight on the Whig side and returned after peace to reclaim their licenses. Dirck Brinkerhoff, Jr., a former shopkeeper, and Henry Lines, a former cordwainer, were prewar artisans who became cartmen in order to support themselves.[15] Paulus Banta was allowed to continue to cart even though he remained in the city during the war.[16] That he was a third-generation cartman no doubt helped his situation.

As soldiers, these future cartmen had performed various tasks. Moses Ely of Newark, New Jersey, for example, volunteered for the Continental Army in 1776 at the age of 20. During the first years of the war, he helped build fortifications in New York City and on Long Island. Later he worked as a teamster in the New Jersey militia. In late 1783 he brought his wife and children, including future cartman, John Ely, to New York City. Moses Ely worked as a cartman in New York City for the next 50 years.[17]

Enoch Hoyt was born in Connecticut in 1759 and first enlisted in the Westchester militia in 1775. The following year he served as a "minuteman" in New York City where, like Moses Ely, he built fortifications. That same year he fought in the Battles of Long Island, Kip's Bay and Kingsbridge. From 1777 until the close of the war he served as a teamster in the Westchester militia. Then he and his wife, pregnant with the first of six children, purchased land in the Sixth Ward of New York City. Early in March, 1783, Hoyt obtained a cartman's license. He stayed on the job until 1844, 61 years later. When Hoyt applied for a pension for his Revolutionary War service, five cartmen testified to the veracity of his history.[18]

Abraham D. Brower used his experience in the military to further his career as a carter. Born in 1763 in Bergen County just across the Hudson River from New York City, Brower served in the militia as a forager with responsibilities to garner firewood and hay for the troops. Brower fought in the Battle of Paulus Hook and, more importantly for his career, took part in the destruction of the blockhouse near Fort Lee, New Jersey. The blockhouse was built by a group of loyalist woodcutters who sold their wood to the British in New York City. Fiercely loyal, these woodcutters battled an overwhelming force of patriots in late 1782. Their defeat and eventual exile created a rare opportunity for Brower and men like him. After the war he moved to New York City, took up the carting trade and soon had a prosperous business delivering firewood sold to him by former neighbors in Bergen County.[19]

Entire families came into New York City after the war from upstate New York and New Jersey. John Casparus and Benjamin Westervelt, brothers from Dutchess County, New York, served in the militia there and spent much of the war guarding the Hudson River and collecting firewood. Together they moved with their families in 1784 to New York City where the brothers became freemen and carters.[20]

John, Peter and Abraham Riker were from Newark, New Jersey, where they owned a blacksmith's shop before the war. They served as foremen and carters in the Continental Army throughout the war. In 1784 they joined the flood of refugees into New York City. They, however, arrived with skills and military connections and were thus able to obtain cartmen's licenses.[21]

One of the most famous postwar cartmen was Abraham B. Martling, Jr. The son of one carter and the nephew of another, "Brom" Martling was born in Rockland County in 1757. He served in that county's militia during the war and afterwards came to New York City to live with his father and become a carter. Soon he had earned enough money from his jobs as a carter and scavenger to open a tavern on Queen Street. He maintained his licenses even though, as we shall see, Martling and his tavern became notorious in the early nineteenth century.[22]

That two-thirds of the cartmen were veterans is important in comprehending their social and political expectations. They wanted employment. The city's need to rebuild itself was a happy coincidence. The freemanship offered suffrage, a sense of citizenship, monopolistic work privileges and enhanced the carters' abilities to share in the political process.

Family ties augmented the cartmen's identification with New York and their expectations of municipal patronage. John Baldrick, William Smith, Daniel Baldwin, Jacob Blanck, James Cowenhoven and Peter Demarest were the sons of prewar carters. In his petition Daniel Demorary noted that he had driven a cart before the war and "his eldest son is now able to assist him a great deal in that business." The Banta family were perhaps most numerous among the cartmen of this generation. In addition to Paulus Banta, John Banta, a veteran, drove a cart in 1780s and 1790s and owned a home at Spring and Orange Streets in the Seventh Ward. He was related to Paulus, Jacob, Peter and Henry, all cartmen in the 1780s. By marriage, John was related to Dirck Brinckerhoff and Jacob Bogert. The Bantas produced a number of carters in the early nineteenth century.[23]

Besides Daniel Demorary, other father and son cartmen who returned to the city to work were the James Sargeants, Robert and Newman Archer, the Abraham Martlings, the Cornelius Myers, the Peter Snyders, the Robert Thomases and the Benjamin Westervelts. Alexander Lamb and Rynier Skaats, Jr., were the sons of petty city officials in the prewar city.[24]

Cartmen endowed with the freemanship prospered. The warrants presented by the street commissioners and cartmen to the Common Council during the rebuilding days of 1784 reveal the lucrative nature of a license. Several cartmen received £135 for "digging a road through Mrs. Rutgers' land to the slaughterhouse." Alexander Lamb, Jr., who was fast becoming a leader among cartmen, supervised a team of carters who delivered wood to the impoverished. They received £44 for this work. John Bish headed a crew paid £32 for "filling a street at the Old Slip." These and the numerous other warrants demonstrate the continued mutuality of the cartmen and local government.[25] The allocation of supervisory posts to favored cartmen indicates the continuity of wealth differentials and status among cartmen. It also indicates that cartmen were able to continue direction of their labors themselves. Although the city hired them, the carters worked as they saw fit without great outside supervision.

A cartmen's license, combined with the freemanship, opened other doors to positions in city government. As Staughton Lynd has pointed out, many mechanics had their economic irons in several fires. The carters behaved similarly. Abraham Day, for example, held a license for 40 years. He also served as a watchman, a grain measurer, coal measurer and charcoal inspector.[26] His son, Abraham Day, Jr., held similar posts.[27] His brother, William Day, served as a wood and lime inspector during a career of carting which lasted from 1784 to 1826. His life reflects another aspect of many freemanship carters. At various times he attempted other work, including tailoring, bookbinding, masonry and brassfounding. During these ventures, he kept a cartman's license. Whenever these other positions failed, he returned to carting. Such experience is characteristic of the mobility of freemanship carters. Many tried other fields, yet eventually returned to driving. Holding a license and freemanship had additional advantages. John Ackerman, George Brown, Alexander Buchanan, John Harriot and Francis Passman were among those who were able to obtain other city licenses while maintaining a cartman's.[28]

City offices were sought by cartmen for many reasons. Some posts, like that of watchman, could be done on a part-time basis and provided a useful income supplement. By 1789, Alexander Lamb's contingent of cartmen/ watchmen received about 50 cents per night or nearly half a day's pay.[29] Judging by the complaints of the citizenry, watchmen did little real work. Inspectorships offered retirement sinecures for aged or infirm carters. The temptation to garner extra money through improper measurement brought out several warnings by city officials in the postwar years.[30]

Cartmen were also willing to serve in elective posts no one else wanted. Robert Berwick, for example, served as constable in the Sixth Ward from 1787 through 1799.[31] Although historians have viewed the constable's post as one which New Yorkers were unwilling to hold, 17 other carters besides Berwick were elected constables at one time or another.[32] Such posts not only added necessary income supplements, but also exempted them from jury or militia duty. There was very little supervision of these posts and, despite the complaints about performance, they were generally self-regulated. Moreover, such service was often the prerequisite for more lucrative appointments in public office. For politicians, providing a carter with a sinecure instilled loyalty.

Nearly all the appointive posts were obtained by petition. After a few years, a cartman petitioned to become, for example, an inspector of hay. His petition was endorsed by other hay cartmen, by the foreman of the carter's class and hopefully by prominent citizens. It was then presented to the Common Council. The entire process suggests a highly personalized, somewhat insular political situation. Without the close relations of city officials and carters, such methods would have been impractical. Even the elective posts, assessor, collector and constable, were seldom heavily contested in the 1780s. Nomination, a reward for long service, usually insured election. Overall, freemanship carters held 220 elective or appointive posts by 1800; nearly two out of every three of the 325 freemanship carters held some post.[33]

In addition, another 110 or about one-third of these carters were firemen. The advantages of being a fireman were several. It provided exemption from militia and jury duty, yet demonstrated the loyalty and civic service useful when applying for an appointive post. It also produced close fraternity. Familiarity, important to a trade like carting, led to employment, to advantageous relationships and to public recognition. Being a fireman had more enjoyable aspects, too, as they were known for their picnics, parades and outings.

The cartmen's culture still centered around the Trinity Church Farm, which comprised the old West Ward. Trinity Church announced early in 1784 that it would respect prewar leases. At least twelve, but certainly more, prewar cartmen can be identified on the rent rolls of Trinity in the 1780s.[34] These veteran carters were joined by younger cartmen who paid five pounds per annum, a three-pound increase from the 1760s.[35] Poorer carters moved into the area around the Collect Pond in the swampy Seventh Ward, formerly the Out Ward. There, on streets named after wealthy landlords including Rutgers, Roosevelt, Oliver, Catharine and Bancker, cartmen reestablished traditional living patterns. Carters also lived in the North and Bowery Wards where 155 of them constituted ten percent of the electorate. Cartmen were also numerous in the East and Dock Wards.[36]

The sizable concentration of cartmen in certain wards of the city, combined with their power to vote, increased their desire for greater political clout. Yet they found the postwar political situation still resistant to their demands. The debate over the status of Tories still living in the city dominated local politics in 1784. Conservative Whigs desired admitting Tories to the new government. Property rights would be respected. Popular Whigs on the other hand, demanded confiscation of Tory property and sought to deny by law Tory participation in public offices and employment. Such, for example, was the law passed by the Common Council barring from carting anyone who had received a freemanship during the British occupation.[37]

Tories were not the only New Yorkers excluded from carting. The postwar New York government and the cartmen continued to bar black New Yorkers from driving carts in the city. New York State remained a slave state far longer than its New England counterparts and did not initiate gradual emancipation until 1799. As in the colonial era, postwar cartmen doubtless regarded enslaved labor as unfair competition. Unlike the earlier period, New York City now became home to growing numbers of free blacks, many of them long term local residents or recent migrants from rural areas with skills in the management of horses. For free blacks, carting could serve, as it did for white New Yorkers, a means of social and economic mobility. Neither the city government or the white carters themselves extended welcome to free black New Yorkers. Unlike southern cities where blacks often carted, New York's cartmen retained the "wages of whiteness."[38]

A second Common Council election was held in the Fall of 1784. Thomas Ivers, a ropemaker and frequent contractor of cartmen, was defeated in his bid for reelection as alderman from the Out Ward by Nicholas Bayard, a merchant. Ivers protested the ballot and charged that not only had unqualified (Tory) voters cast ballots for Bayard, but that the latter lived in the city throughout the war and was therefore ineligible for office. The Common Council disallowed his protest.[39]

The year 1785 was marred by a depression. Trade stagnated as American entrepreneurs were faced with a credit shortage, a sluggish market and an inability to either pay or collect obligations. The defeat of Ivers signaled the downfall of the popular Whigs. Some, including Isaac Sears, Alexander MacDougall and John Lamb, became aligned with conservative Whigs by virtue of new wealth or appointed position. More Tories came out of hiding to unite with the conservative Whigs.[40]

That year, skilled artisans received about 55 cents per day while cartmen made anywhere from 25 cents to 50 cents per day. The carters petitioned Mayor Duane that license lists of cartmen be closed "as there is not enough work to go around."[41]

The assembly election of 1785 was marked by two controversies. First, the mechanics of the city began banding together to form a General Society of Mechanics and Tradesman. "An Exiled Mechanic" suggested electing assemblymen who would vote to incorporate the Society. Though the Society was denied a charter that first year, it was clearly a growing political force.[42]

The second controversy concerned the nomination of candidates who supported the interests of mechanics and other tradesmen. A writer in the New York Packett asked why lawyers and merchants were the only ones elected to the assembly. Men of other occupations were equally reputable and useful and deserved political preferment. "The pedantic lawyer and the wealthy merchant have their interest attended . . . the respectable mechanics and cartmen have not" was the complaint.[43] The following week, a second article agreed that cartmen and mechanics needed attention to their interests. This second writer then suggested a nominating slate including cartmen, shoemakers, blacksmiths, tavernkeepers, hatters, printers and blockmasters. The three cartmen suggested, "Messrs Dumree, Richie and Myers" were not among the cartmen given freemanships by Duane. Nor were the other laboring men listed among the political elite.[44] A week later, the Committee of Tradesmen and Mechanics nominated such local mechanic politicians as John Stagg, William Goforth and William Denning, as well as merchants Evert Bancker, Brockholst Livingston, William Duer and former Liberty Boy turned merchant, Isaac Sears.[45] No cartmen, tavern-keepers, hatters or blacksmiths made this second list. This split between the more middle-class Committee of Tradesmen and Mechanics and the "inferior mechanics" may have had something to do with the political reality of winning elections; it also demonstrated that mechanics were not as unified as once thought. When the General Society of Tradesmen and Mechanics opened its doors a short while later, no cartmen were among the original members, nor would they be for at least a decade.

Rebuffed in elective politics, the carters turned to older forms of political expression. Petitions were widely used in the 1780s. The trade showed its unity in the "iron-wheels" controversy. The debate over the use of iron-shod wheels had continued, literally, for centuries. While iron-shod wheels were obviously more economical than wooden ones, they created such a racket that the city government of New York banned their use. Shortly after the British evacuation in 1783, Alexander Lamb, Jr., and over 100 cartmen petitioned the Common Council to permit the use of iron-shod wheels. The practice apparently started during the war and was no doubt commonly used by both armies.[46]

The committee of the council appointed to review the petition rejected it and ordered a return to wooden wheels. The carters responded by complaining that there was not a sufficient supply of wooden wheels available and requested an extension of the ordinance by three months. Shortly before this deadline was up, the carters petitioned that they could not find wheels conformable to law. They were granted a six-week extension.[47] Two years later, a new petition signed by over 200 carters asked the council to consider their "great expense accruing by reason of their being obliged to have new wheels very often." The cartmen suggested iron-shod wheels of no greater width than three-and-a-half inches "and the nails even to the tire so that the Pavements cannot receive such damage."[48] Among the signers were former assemblyman William Goforth, Innkeeper John Simmons, Benjamin Blagge, Abraham Martling, Jr., Uzziah Coddington and Alexander Lamb, all of whom would play their roles in the cartmen's struggles in the 1790s.

Unfortunately, the Common Council was not impressed by this petition. The issue remained dormant until 1791 when, as a means of placating irate carters during an election, the council abruptly revived the petition and passed an ordinance permitting the use of iron-shod wheels. The steady and constant pressure exerted by the cartmen in this issue finally paid off.[49] As with the Oswego Market incident of 1771, the cartmen had shown unity over a trade issue.

The carters showed solidarity in other petitions. Farmers from New Jersey earned extra money by carting in the city during the Summer, then returning to their farms in the Fall, "by which means they evade the Payment of their taxes," complained 100 carters in a petition in early 1785. Boldly signed first by Alexander Lamb, followed by cartmen Andrew Lossye, John Davenport, Marmaduke Earle, Teunis Tiebout, John Day, Abraham DelaMeter and many others, the petition noted that the abuses of the city laws by the farmers "operate to the Prejudice of your petitioners, who are old inhabitants of the City and desirous of remaining in a place dear to them, and where the remains of their fathers are Deposited." The petition continued by saying that the "wisdom and justice of our honorable Board is what, alone, rescues us from Despair."[50] The cartmen were reaffirming important traditions in this memorial. Because of their historic relations with the city, the cartmen expected to be protected by the council. While the cartmen's tone was deferential, the number of endorsers reinforced the power of the message.

In 1788 Mayor James Duane and a commission of the Common Council ordered a reorganization of the cartmen. They formed eight "classes" of 50 cartmen, each headed by a foreman.[51] Duane's use of "classes" meant a division within a group, not a level within society, as we understand it.[52] While this reorganization no doubt reduced the day-to-day contact between Duane and the cartmen, the appointment of foremen placed responsibility for discipline and hiring with the trade itself. Foremen were required to report all problems and vacancies to the mayor. As the petitions for employment attest, the procedure for hiring, though not exclusively, would be for the foreman and a number of other carters to endorse the plea. It then went to the mayor for approval. For example, the petition of Nicholas Naugell noted that "he was well acquainted with the occupation before the war . . . and turned out for the defense of his country." Because Naugell was "always used to horses and carriages," several foremen including Alexander Lamb, John Day, Andrew Lossye, Isaac Blauveldt, and William Campbell endorsed his successful application for employment.[53]

During Duane's term of office, two other notable decisions were made. The Common Council and mayor announced in 1787 that they would not attempt to regulate either "tea-water men," who sold fresh water from barrels placed on carts or "dirt" carters who picked up garbage and manure on the streets.[54] Both of these decisions turned out to be important. By failing to regulate the tea-water men, the city lost for many years the opportunity to regulate the expanding number of street vendors. Soon many different types of street vendors sold hot corn, watermelons, clams, oysters, fruits, tomatoes, fish, meat, cattails for mattresses, milk and many other commodities. The cries of these vendors filled the air of the city.[55] The most common appear to have been clam and oyster sellers whose fresh food was the staple of fast eaters of the time. The street vendors proved more noxious to grocers and other merchandisers than to the cartmen whose monopoly was not directly affected by their activities.

The ruling: concerning "dirt" carters is more curious. This task had historically been one of the primary responsibilities of the cartman. Observed more in the breach than in practice, laws were still on the books requiring that carters pick up local garbage once a week. Fees were set and fines were established for negligence. Lack of enforcement and problems of compliance forced local government to seek alternatives. At various times in the colonial era, the city hired teams of scavengers to clean specific sections. By the 1780s the Common Council began to contract with private companies to remove dirt and manure. It declared that despite doubt "whether or not persons not licensed as carters should be permitted to collect and cart away filth from the streets of the city . . . it was determined that they should be allowed." At the same time, the Common Council, careful not to infringe upon the carters' monopoly, declared the right of carters to perform the same duty. It also continued to appoint scavengers.[56] Eventually, these varying methods caused great conflict between licensed and unlicensed carters.

Another area of controversy was the rowdy behavior of the cartmen. "A Citizen" complained in the *Journal* of September 22, 1785 about the "promiscuous behavior of carts." He declared that "a woman dressed as neat as a Quaker . . . is exposed to the mercy of every driver and the disposition to insults is too prevailing." Not only pedestrians, but businessmen were aggrieved by the cartman's surly attitudes. Cartmen regularly used downtown streets as waiting areas and left their carts and "vicious" horses untended before shop doors. Elkanah Watson and other businessmen petitioned the council to create permanent cart-stands to guarantee the peace and safety of downtown streets.[57] In the downtown and wealthier wards, few citizens were willing to tolerate the milling carters and their horses. Although their presence was necessary, they needed to be controlled. The cartmen, who lived in the poorer wards where horses and crowded streets were commonplace, could hardly be expected to sympathize with the grievances of the bourgeoisie. The council, more concerned about peace with the cartmen, chose to do nothing for the time being.

Traditional relations thus continued during the postwar period between city government and carters. Colonial regulations and the freemanship remained intact after the Revolutionary War. Older historical views of labor regulation in the postrevolutionary city, first expounded by Samuel B. McKee, and accepted by succeeding historians, have argued that the freemanship and regulations were dead issues by the end of the war.[58] The cartmen's experience reverses this assumption. Similar developments for bakers, porters, tavernkeepers, grocers, and other licensed trades, support the present conclusion. When government saw labor in the public and corporate interest of the city, it maintained control as long as necessary.

By the late 1780s consensus politics arose in the city. Merchants, mechanics and cartmen appear to have agreed upon the need for a stronger national government, on the continuance of government regulation and in favor of economic policies which would enhance the growth of the city. By 1788, the city was prepared to embrace the developing concepts of Federalism.[59]

This city's merchants, mechanics and cartmen demonstrated this civic consensus in the celebration in 1788 marking the ratification of the new Constitution of the United States. Divisions among the voters of New York dissolved in support of the new government and its popular leader, George

Washington. In the parade itself, numerous trades marched in formation, proclaiming their allegiance to the new government. One of the largest contingents marched in the eighth division. Three hundred cartmen, nearly the entire force, marched in their work uniforms of white frocks and trousers. A red cart with the words "Federal Cart" emblazoned in white on the side and adorned with green boughs headed the procession. Pulling the cart was a magnificent white and bay horse; the driver was Edward Fowler who wore a frock crossed by a blue silk sash. The entire process was led by four veteran cartmen, Thomas Ammerman, Abraham Martling, Jr., James Demorary and Walter Furman. They carried a banner upon which was enscribed the expectations and hopes of the cartmen for the new government:

> Behold the Federal ship of fame
> The Hamilton we call her name
> To every Craft she gives employ
> Sure cartmen have their share of Joy.[60]

The display of support and loyalty to the new government by the cartmen was matched by similar demonstrations by other trades.[61] The carters, like other trades, expected continued prosperity from the actions of the new government. However, in the next thirteen years numerous conflicts occurred between the carters and their putative masters in the local government. While portions of the trade continued to benefit from the corporate paternalism of city government, many other cartmen found the rule of mayor and council meddlesome and oppressive. This conflict was a key element in the political battles between the dominant Federalist party and the insurgent Republicans.

CHAPTER SEVEN

The Cartmen Organize, 1789–1795

As the 1780s drew to a close, the economy and society of New York City prospered. Led by a resurgent shipping industry, the city was fast overtaking Philadelphia as the leading port along the Atlantic Coast. The population grew to over 30,000 inhabitants by 1790 and then doubled to 60,000 by 1800. At the same time daily wages for laborers increased from 55 cents per day in 1785 to one dollar in 1790.[1]

As the economy grew, the need for more cartmen caused the mayor and Common Council to remove the cap on licenses. The number of licensed carters jumped from around 400 in 1789 to over 1000 by 1795. A second major change in the trade took place in 1790 when the newly appointed mayor, Richard Varick, determined not to award the freemanship to new carters when they were granted licenses.[2] This decision created a split among the carters. Not only did the freemanship provide monopoly rights and the vote, but it often led to lucrative public employment and to lower-level political appointments. Loss of the freemanship also made newer carters vulnerable to impressment as the British navy resumed its raids on New York streets in the 1790s. New cartmen without the freemanship found job security and suffrage to be at the mercy of the mayor. The cartmen reacted to the loss of the freemanship by intensified political organization to rectify their grievances.

For the freemanship carters, the late 1780s meant life as usual. Carters appointed between 1783 and 1788 were reaping the benefits of their close ties to city government. Mayors Duane and Varick and the Common

Council continued to award lucrative city contracts. Walter Sloo had a regular contract to convey vagrants to the Bridewell.[3] David Demarest filed a bill of £40 for filling up the Murray Street slip.[4] David Walton, Richard Lewis and George Hitchcock worked on roads for the city.[5] Alexander Lamb, Jr., held one of the most lucrative positions as head of one of the two divisions of city watchmen. The warrants placed by Lamb indicate aggregate weekly wages of £47 for 30 watchmen. Lamb was already the foreman of the first class of carters and would soon have other leadership positions.[6]

In 1788 the trade gave its support to the Federalist party. The Federalists, linked to the national leadership of Washington and to the economic policies of Alexander Hamilton, who worked on the local level as well, became the city's dominant party.[7] Federalists believed in preservation of the old order, in the privileges of property and wealth and in the interdependence of the elite merchant class and the "lower orders." Federalists derived their ideology from older strains of conservativism, including moderate Whiggery, Loyalism, and Anti-Clintonians, and were composed largely of the merchant elite of the city. The Federalists desired deference from the laboring man, but also believed in the efficacy of corporate paternalism. Two important local Federalists, Mayor James Duane and future Governor, John Jay, were supporters of mechanics' and carters' rights because they expected those groups to adhere to the commercial interest and vote accordingly.[8]

James Duane, however, had ambitions beyond the mayorality. After the Federalist national victory in 1789 he desired to become Senator for New York State. President Washington instead made him a United States District Judge. The long-time city recorder, Richard Varick, succeeded Duane as mayor in September, 1789. Varick was a native of Hackensack, New Jersey, where he and his father were well acquainted with numerous future New York City cartmen. Like Duane, Varick was a revolutionary conservative. His biographer referred to him as "cold, aloof, thoroughly Federalist." Political opponents would use harsher phrases. Varick was to serve twelve years as mayor, a period which embraces the Federalist decade of power and which remains the longest tenure held by a New York City mayor.[9]

In spite of their electoral success, the Federalists were insecure in their position. Confident of the political loyalty of the cartmen and other trades in prosperous times, the Federalists knew that downswings in the economy produced opposition. Varick perceived the protection of the Federalist party as a duty of his office and worked to disenfranchise unfriendly voters while continuing to award patronage to loyal carters. For example, he pushed through a law in 1790 requiring that all future appointments of firewood inspectors come from the ranks of superannuated or invalid cartmen.[10] Despite this favor, he created major dissension by ending the freemanship for carters.

In the last two years of his tenure, Duane granted freemanships to carters, but listed them as "laborers."[11] After he took office Varick named a number of freemen, but not a single cartman.[12] By early 1791 he increased the number of licensed carters to 600.[13] Thus, 200 new cartmen were potentially without the suffrage.

Furthermore, the economy was suffering. An indication of this was the suggestion of "A Poor Man's Friend" writing in the *Daily Advertiser,* urging a revival of the colonial practice of purchasing firewood by the city corporation and hiring cartmen to distribute it. The writer explained that 40–50 carters would gain 30 days' employment as a result. Carters would be hired on the basis of sobriety, industry, age and "narrowness of expectation," in that order.[14] Whereas Duane used this method to gain the cartmen's confidence in 1784, Varick chose to ignore the idea, thus offending the poor who expected wealth to be shared in time of hardship.

It was in this context of uncertain employment that a great controversy erupted that Fall of 1791 over Varick's attempts to channel the cartmen's political choices. These council elections were much like the previous polls in which the Federalists won overwhelming victories. In 1790, however, the Livingston family, one of the most powerful forces in the state and city, had broken with the Federalists and was seeking support from the mechanics and cartmen.

At some point during the summer of 1791 Varick called together the cartmen and informed the entire force that anyone who voted against the Federalist ticket could expect to have his license revoked. In the past, such bullying at the polls had frequently been applied to individuals. Now the entire force was subject to coercion.

Varick's actions produced an adversary and a champion of the cartmen in William S. Livingston. The assemblyman criticized Varick's behavior in the *Weekly Museum* and the *Daily Advertiser.* He accused Varick of using "an iron rod of power . . . in dreadful suspense over the head of . . . cartmen, butchers, tavern-keepers and all work men . . . under the sanction of a license." Livingston, using the pseudonym "Lucious," encouraged all citizens to remember that they were freemen and not to allow the freedom of elections "to be in any way retrenched."[15] This letter was followed a day later by one from "Cato" in the *Daily Advertiser* who assured the freemen and freeholders of the city that if the "chief magistrate—[the mayor] had been guilty of any improper conduct, you will soon have the opportunity to impeach him before the highest tribunal . . . He as well as other officers are within the reach of the law."[16] These letters cultivated the cartmen's desires: protection under the law, legal equity and rights as freemen. Political views were expressed alluding to their reduced circumstances and promising action. The cartmen were encouraged by thoughts that Varick might be impeached for intimidating them.

These letters were followed by a correspondence between Varick and Livingston. A year earlier, the two had a financial disagreement and Livingston now printed two letters which added fuel to the fire. Livingston referred to the mayor as a "coward" and suggested a duel. The mayor responded that his lawyers were "competent to manage such, business . . . the appelation of coward from such a desperado . . . claims contempt only."[17] This exchange must have produced great merriments in Simmons', Mrs. Amory's or Martling's, where cartmen enjoyed rum and cider while reading the newspapers. Livingston included new attacks on Varick. In the previous exchange, Varick concluded his reply by informing Livingston that all correspondence between them would now cease. Livingston retorted that all personal relations might be over, but he would respond to Varick in the newspapers. He satirized Varick's background and noted that while "I shall out of respect to the family to which you undeservedly belong . . . be more delicate . . . I shall talk first of your loss of teeth." Just under this letter was an insulting satire in which Livingston made great fun of Varick's agitation over the controversy. Varick was portrayed sitting in his office complaining that he should have known better than to pick on the cartmen because grocers and tavernkeepers were easier to manage. "Power," Livingston noted sourly, "was not annexed to office, where character does not add dignity."[18]

In the same article Rynier Skaats, Sr., long-time chief marshal, chimneysweep and doorkeeper of the Common Council, was quoted, "I warned you, Mr. Mayor, never to make freemen . . . the rich can buy a lot, but the poor have no other means of obtaining a vote."[19] Skaats' speech is revealing in several ways. It is replete with local allusions; for example, Livingston is referred to as the "little doctor with the chariot" and as a "barber." Using a tone of sly contempt, Skaats reviled Varick for endangering both their jobs although Skaats "shall loose a trifle compared to your worship." The implication was that the laboring-class official had a better understanding of political reality than Varick. Moreover, Skaats suggested that withholding freemanships from cartmen was his own idea. As chief marshal, Skaats was responsible for checking cartmen's licenses, reporting violations and collection fines. Although his son, Rynier, Jr., was a cartman, Skaats could not have been too popular among the carters. Here was an example of a split between the city official, linked to the Federalists, and his laboring-class counterparts, who were oppressed by his actions.[20]

The satirical use of Varick's and Skaats' speeches became standard practice for the Republicans who portrayed the licensed laborers of the city as more democratic and independent than their Federalist masters and their laboring-class flunkeys. Rather than the elevated tone of political rhetoric, the Republicans used broad satire to influence elections. Their offices made the satires of Varick and Skaats immediately recognizable to any cartman in the city. Finally, Livingston's attack suggested equation of the freemanship with the rights of the trade and citizenship.

Varick, clearly on the defensive, published a series of letters of recommendation regarding his character and military service. Culled from over the years, the letters included testimonials to Varick from such revolutionary figures as George Washington, Philip Schuyler, and John Morin Scott.[21] Trotting out such recommendations over a local issue demonstrated Varick's insecurity; perhaps he realized that his political position and power lasted only as long as party opinion of him remained favorable. Unable to refute the charges, Varick attempted to impugn Livingston's character while defending his own.

City wards were redrawn before this election. The old West Ward, home of many cartmen, became the Fourth and Sixth Wards. The Fourth Ward centered around Trinity Church and was wealthier than the Sixth, which was comprised of the newer and poorer portions of the Church's Farm on the outskirts of the city. Another cartman-inhabited ward, the North, became the Seventh.[22] In this election, the Sixth Ward remained Federalist while the Seventh split between a Federalist alderman and a Republican assistant alderman. The Seventh Ward, where newer and presumably poorer cartmen lived, seemed more amenable to Republican appeals.[23]

Livingston resumed the attacks the following spring when he introduced a motion in the assembly to make the mayoralty of New York City an elective office. The proposal had been controversial when it was first introduced in the early 1780s and it remained so now. The assembly debated the measure, but eventually voted it down. One opponent noted that opinion was overwhelmingly opposed to it. Support for the proposal came in a letter to the *New York Journal* on April 7, 1792. The writers, who identified themselves as both Federalists and Republicans, commented that the opposition was using rhetoric only and that the "prevailing sentiment seemed to be in favor of some sort of rotation."[24] The next day Livingston published "at the request of a great number of freemen," a speech he made before the assembly in favor of the measure. The proposal contained many reasons for the rotation of the mayor's office each year. Prominent among them were charges of improper conduct by Varick against the cartmen. Livingston noted that the powers of the mayor included that "no man can drive a cart without his permission." Livingston charged that Varick was misusing this power to deny the rights of freemen to work as carters. He argued that no one would deny that any worker who had served his apprenticeship, fought against "foreign powers," resided continually in the city and "filled the most respectable of offices" should be given a freemanship. Nor, argued Livingston, should the heirs of any freeman be denied the right. Yet these things were happening in the New York of Richard Varick, the "tyrant." Varick was quoted as threatening the carters that as "long as I shall continue in this office, you shall never be made a freeman."[25]

Each of these appeals struck directly at the cartman's dilemma. As long-term, loyal citizens, as veterans and proud of their trade's history, the cartmen expected protection for their rights and privileges. Instead, a tyrannical mayor denied them rights assumed by generations of cartmen and fought for in the War for Independence. Livingston's words struck deeply at their grievances.

Before the assembly election of Spring 1792, the cartmen met at taverns in the Sixth and Seventh Wards to endorse candidates favorable to the trade. The first meeting was held at William Day's tavern and attracted over one hundred carters who unanimously agreed to favor Republican candidates including William S. Livingston.[26]

Livingston's encouragement of the carters was repaid by massive support in the wards where cartmen were numerous. Thirty-five percent of the electorate for his successful candidacy came from the Sixth and Seventh Wards and helped produce for him the second-highest citywide total. Yet, the greatest vote catcher was Federalist merchant John Watts, who received support from every single voter in the two wards.[27] While the wards were willing to support candidates like Livingston, who attempted to defend the cartmen, voters were still unwilling to leave the Federalists entirely.

Federalists, although they won the overall election and retained the majority of assembly seats from the city, found their once-solid laboring class vote slipping away. Varick's abuse of the cartmen cost a portion of their support. To remedy this, the Federalists spent the remainder of the decade giving patronage to those cartmen who continued to support them and trying to deny the vote to those who opposed them. Republicans found that tailoring their political demands to particular laboring groups such as the carters produced political capital.

The cartmen found strength in numbers. One week after the election, some carters formed a Society of Cartmen.[28] Fourteen counsellors, including two freeman as treasurers and two freemen as secretaries, became the officers of the new organization devoted to "assisting the indigent and impoverished cartmen." Among the officers Samuel Arnet, Christian Smack, Moses Ely, Benjamin Westervelt, William Anderson, and Nathaniel Guion were among the first freemen registered as cartmen after the war, linking the revolutionary consciousness with the present turmoil.

Several of the officers of the Cartmen's Society also held political office. Samuel Arnet, for example, became first a grain and then a charcoal measurer. Matthias Nach became a city measurer of lumber.[29] But, whether freemen or not, the officers, the only members listed, reflect the strong traditions of the cartmen. Moses Ely came from a family of cartmen. His brothers, Abraham and Jacob, were cartmen as was his father, Abraham, Sr. Of the 19 Society officers, 12 were freemen with more than a decade of experience each.[30]

Two months after the election, Livingston again attempted to repay his cartman supporters. On August 21, 1792, a letter from "A Number of Citizens" in the *Daily Advertiser* reminded readers that the time was approaching when the Council of Appointment would nominate the mayor of the city for the next year.[31] Although the petition to change the procedure to direct election had not passed the assembly, the letter proposed "that the wishes of many of our fellow citizens . . . be made in a petition for several candidates and pray that one might be appointed." Livingston planned a meeting for "Saturday night at Mrs. Montanje's near the Fields." The use of the prewar name of this famous tavern, long since changed to Mrs. Amory's, is striking. The four candidates suggested in the letter were Henry Cruger, son of John, John Broome, John Watts and Gulian Ver Planck, all wealthy aristocrats.[32] "The citizens" apparently were not giving up on merchants, just on Varick, as his name was not mentioned. This unsubtle attempt to remove Varick was hardly lost on the cartmen. The following day, "A Citizen" suggested that the proposal be treated "with the contempt it deserves." The proposal was only an attempt to remove Varick, argued this "citizen," not a "demonstration of love for the cartmen."[33]

The meeting was a failure. Held in the pouring rain, it drew a disappointing crowd, one with few of the distinguished citizens whose presence had been promised in the original letter. Few cartmen attended and the host, William S. Livingston, left abruptly without making any plans for the future and without consulting any who did attend. The following day Richard Varick was reappointed.[34]

The Federalists used patronage to bolster their support among the carters. Varick's use of the city watch was particularly skillful. He appointed Alexander Lamb, Jr., first as acting head of the watch, then as permanent head after a heroic incident brought the cartman acclaim in 1791. Each night Lamb and about 30 watchmen, including 20 carters, patrolled the city streets. Each watchman earned 50 cents per night while Lamb received one dollar. The Common Council paid the watchmen every week. Service on the watch was a useful and timely income supplement for a few lucky carters and established Lamb as a leader of the carters. A year later, he was named captain of a new troop within the New York State militia.[35]

Varick also made use of the scavenger list as a payoff for loyal laborers. Although little work seems to have been done by the scavengers, their selection was a means by which the mayor could secure favor with the laboring men. Of the 30 scavengers employed by Varick between 1789 and 1793,

21 were promoted to cartmen.[36] After a scavenger proved himself useful and loyal to the city government he then gained a cartman's license.

By 1793, the split was widening among the cartmen. While many cartmen deeply resented the arrogance of the Federalists, others profited from the party's patronage. Some sided with the French Revolution by joining Democratic Clubs; others sided with pro-British merchants. There were reports of fistfights between cartmen over the meaning of the French Revolution.[37]

Some carters lived in poverty. Others had enough to invest in the speculative empire of William Duer, only to lose all in the panic of 1792.[38] Alexander Lamb, Jr., and other carters working for the city basked in the glow of city patronage. By 1793 Lamb became Superintendent of Streets for the Sixth Ward which, like his other posts, allowed him to allocate contracts and increase his power.[39]

Few carters built up large estates. Most left small amounts handled by letters of administration. Of the 36 cartman wills of the period from 1790 to 1795, 33, or 92 percent, were small enough to be so executed.[40] Even Lamb had little money. Although he sublet two lots in the Church's Farm in 1794, the income could not have been more than £30 per year, given the other rents paid in the area.[41] He surely earned more than most cartmen, but little in comparison with Varick who earned £500 annually from fees collected from cartmen, tavernkeepers, grocers and other licensed tradesmen.[42]

The political and social divisions among the cartmen were more apparent in the assembly election of 1793. In this election, William S. Livingston came under bitter attack from the Society of Tradesmen and Mechanics which refused to endorse him, declaring him "improper." The *New York Journal* called him "a pickpocket, a defender of a bawdy house and void of virtue and void of talents." The same paper referred to Federalist John Watts, so popular eight months before, as "insidious, crafty, selfish, mean, self-sufficient and forward." Despite these unsettling characterizations, a "numerous and respectable meeting of the general body of cartmen, attached to the National Constitution," met at Mrs. Amory's tavern and endorsed the Federalist ticket.[43]

The results of the elections in the Sixth and Seventh Wards showed a sharp drop in support for the Federalists. Though the party carried its slate in the city, support in these two wards was down as much as 50 percent from the previous year. John DeLancey, for example, polled 371 votes in the two wards in 1793, but only 284 a year later. The biggest losers were not Federalists, however. William S. Livingston lost his seat, as his support in the Sixth Ward dropped from 242 votes in 1792 to 39 in 1793. Although the two wards did give him a sizable portion of his total vote, he clearly was not the candidate he had been in 1792,[44] despite Republican victories in these wards. At the same time, the Federalists were able to elect two cartmen, Abraham Martling and John Ackerman, as constables in the Second and Third Wards.

The following year, the split widened. The Society of Cartmen met at Mrs. Amory's tavern, ratified the Federalist ticket, and published an announcement in local newspapers.[45] The *Daily Advertiser* gave editorial approval to the action. The unity shown by the trade, said the *Advertiser*, "must afford real consolation to real republicans." It dismissed the clamors of pretended Patriots "who must do something more than pronounce People, Liberty and Equality," in order to gain the confidence of the cartmen. The Society of Tammany also congratulated the carters for "doing honor to the good sense of patriotism."[46] In the election itself, the Sixth and Seventh Wards strongly favored Federalists. Richard Furman, butcher Jotham Post, John Watson and Nicholas Cruger, all Federalist victors, received more than 20 percent of their votes from the cartmen's wards. Despite these returns for favored Federalists, the largest votes in the wards went to Philip Livingston. Although Livingston failed to gain a seat, 28 percent of his votes came from the Sixth and Seventh Wards. The cartmen's loyalty to the Federalists did not deter them from rewarding the Livingstons for their support in the fight against the mayor.[47]

That Fall, the Republicans scored their biggest victory to date. Edward Livingston, Republican candidate for Congress, achieved a stunning upset of John Watts.[48] Federalists warned the carters that a vote for Livingston meant war and that instead of counting their gains, they would be reduced to starvation or "betake themselves to the precious trades of soldiers and privateers." Despite this grave threat, the "cartmen's wards" went strongly for Livingston, who outpolled Watts in the Sixth Ward by 358 to 96, and 158 to 133 in the Seventh, providing Livingston with his overall margin of victory.[49]

In April, 1795, the Republicans attempted to reap the full measure of their gains among the carters. The Society of Cartmen held a meeting at a Seventh Ward tavern to switch allegiance to the Republican assembly ticket. This appears to be the first time the Republicans were able to secure the confidence of the trade. The carters responded to the Republican slate by suggesting that the aged Thomas Ivers be replaced on the ballot by Alexander Lamb, Jr.; Republicans, sensing an advantage, quickly agreed.[50]

Subsequent meetings with other cartmen produced general approval. By giving the carters a single spot on the ballot, Republicans hoped to gain support for the entire ticket. They held up Lamb as proof that the party did not discriminate against any trade.[51] To insure success, they distributed an inflammatory handbill in the Sixth and Seventh Wards, which was reprinted in the *Daily Advertiser* just before the election. Addressed to the merchants of the city, it beseeched them to turn out in large numbers to vote against the cartmen on the Republican ballot. It accused the Republicans of trying to monopolize all power and asked "if it would not be a reflection on all of us, if a cartman and his associates were in the Assembly." It concluded with urgent pleas to all merchants to "outvote the lower class." This was followed in the newspaper by an indignant disclaimer by the Federalists. The handbill was described as a "base and infamous artifice . . . the rich and poor are still dependent upon each other." The Federalists sought to defuse the effect of the letter by emphasizing the traditional interdependence of cartmen and merchants.[52]

Lamb aided his candidacy by presenting a petition to the Common Council asking for an increase in the maximum rates for cartage. The petition noted that "the prices of house, rent, fuel, provisions and everything necessary to the support of a family have been rising" and were now "double the money formerly sold for." Also, the wages of "mechanics, laborers, and workmen of every description have risen accordingly, while the price of the petitioner's labor has been limited by law." The Common Council, now split between Federalists in the wealthier wards, and Republicans in the poorer wards, accepted the plea just before the election.[53]

In the election itself, Lamb swept to victory, gaining an amazing total of 408 votes in the Sixth Ward and 220 in the Seventh. These large votes helped overcome limited support in the wealthier downtown wards and gave Lamb the fourth-highest total in the city. He was the only Republican candidate elected.[54]

With a fellow cartman in the assembly, the trade now had the representation sorely needed to combat the abuses by Varick and other Federalists. Political power had been a glaring need since the onset of the freemanship crisis four years before. Although friendly politicians such as the Livingstons were helpful, there was nothing better than to have the most politically successful cartman in the assembly. In just a few years the cartmen learned to wield their votes effectively to elect their own candidate. The ascension of Lamb to the assembly, the first successful candidate from the laboring classes since 1784, demonstrated the political clout of the cartmen.

CHAPTER EIGHT

Problems with Politics, 1795–1801

Alexander Lamb's election to the assembly was a political coup for the Republican party and indicated the success of its appeals to the laboring men of New York City. Yet, as the Republicans were congratulating themselves for political acuity and planning future victories, some reflection was in order. The party had done little more than allow the cartmen to fill a spot on their ticket. Alexander Lamb had been for many years a functionary in the Federalist city government and was only recently "converted" to the Republican cause. Lamb had served under the Federalists as foreman of the first class of carters, head of the watch, commissioner of streets in the Sixth Ward and captain of a new militia unit, all patronage positions awarded to him by the Federalists. His father, Alexander Lamb, Sr., had been doorkeeper and librarian for the Common Council and the assembly from 1737 until 1775. His son no doubt spent some boyhood days playing in the back of assembly meetings. From childhood Alexander Lamb was quite familiar with the benefits of elite party politics.

Alexander Lamb's career was typical of cartmen blessed with the freemanship. A Revolutionary War veteran, Lamb was among the first cartmen to renew his license in 1784. He quickly began to receive patronage contracts for street cleaning, delivery of wood to the poor and hay delivery for the city, all of which happened during the Federalist years of power. Lamb owned several lots on the Trinity Church Farm and sublet them for a modest profit, which certainly did not place him on a level with Federalist merchants but did give him a standard of income well above rank and file cartmen.[1]

Over the next two years Alexander Lamb's performance in the assembly would greatly disappoint both the Republicans and those cartmen who desired reinstatement of the freemanship. The unhappy carters would take out their grievances on citizens in the streets.

During Lamb's election, another canvass was underway in which the carters had little to say. The gubernatorial election, restricted to those with at least a £100 freehold, went to a Federalist for the first time. The retirement of the long-time governor, George Clinton, and the tepid support given by the Republican party to his chosen candidate, Robert Yates, allowed the Federalist John Jay to win rather easily.[2] Jay was elected in absentia as he was then negotiating with the British in London the treaty which bears his name. When reports filtered back to the United States about the provisions of Jay's Treaty, many, including artisans and cartmen, were deeply upset. For many Americans, the treaty constituted a surrender to the British and an acceptance of their depredation of American shipping on the high seas. In the previous years the British had regularly stopped American vessels and confiscated materials believed to be headed for French ports. Not only was this system quite arbitrary and insulting, but the British also impressed seamen they believed to be Crown subjects. The losses stemming from the British actions and the arrogance with which the impressments were performed angered many New Yorkers. The general support among the artisanry and cartmen for the French Revolution and the widespread hatred of the British made the treaty seem even less tolerable.[3]

Jay's Treaty required that the United States give up its policy that "free ships make free goods" for at least 12 years. This concession to the British concerns evidenced in the treaty offended many Americans and caused fears of a trade recession. Moreover, the British made no overt guarantees that impressment would stop. American ships were still susceptible to inspection and even confiscation if deemed necessary. The British agreed to reopen reciprocal trade with the Americans, but restricted the lucrative West Indies trade to vessels of less than 70 tons. This cut deeply into the profits New Yorkers might derive from the treaty. The British also agreed to remove troops from several forts along the western frontier which would allow for freer trade with the Indians and for land expansion by American farmers.[4]

New York's citizens perceived the treaty as a Federalist document. The chief benefactors were to be merchants trading with the British and land speculators holding large tracts of land upstate and in the West. Many such individuals were among the elite members of the Federalist party. Even with these apparent gains, many others saw the treaty as unacceptable. Some Federalists, including President Washington, were dismayed that Jay had obtained less than had been anticipated before his departure. For the common man, the treaty was an act of submission to the imperious British and an act of betrayal of the French who were seen as loyal allies in the War for Independence and as co-revolutionaries in the 1790s. It offended their sense of patriotism and citizenship. Jay returned to his new post as Governor of New York State amidst the greatest controversy since the Revolution.

Opposing Federalist positions, New York City's working people, including the cartmen, strongly supported the French Revolution. The Democratic Society, formed in 1794, toasted the French Revolution with six cheers and proclaimed "Liberty, Justice and Humanity," in praise of the French. A general meeting held before City Hall on July 19, 1795, attracted from 5000 to 7000 New Yorkers. The working people turned out in droves. One caustic Federalist described the meeting as composed of "mechanics, laborers, cartmen with their horses, the hod men, the clam men. . . ." Attempts by the silver-tongued tongued Alexander Hamilton to turn the meeting into a pro-treaty rally were angrily dismissed by the citizenry. Later that day, Hamilton was reportedly stoned while attempting to address a group of cartmen on the virtues of the treaty. A third meeting held two days later saw a crowd of 5000 roar its approval at 28 proposed objections to the treaty. Petitions began circulating in the poorer wards intended for presentation to Washington in hopes of convincing him to change his judgment of the treaty and not sign it.[5]

The cartmen's anger stemmed from the view that the treaty had been drawn up without any consultation with the citizenry. This offended their ritualized sense of patriotism and political involvement. Worse, it did not lessen the danger of impressment. Just two months after their stirring victory in the assembly, the carters were faced with an edict coming directly from the hated British and proposed by the arrogant Federalists. For the Federalists, the Jay Treaty accentuated the growing split between them and the ever increasing political consciousness of the cartmen. The Federalists' one-time solid block of votes was rapidly slipping away. Yet they found they could depend upon one cartman. In his first important vote as an assembly-man, Alexander Lamb voted for the Federalist candidate for senator and against a Republican sponsored bill to end slavery in New York.[6]

Federalist concerns about the cartmen were rooted in more than elec-toral politics. The party still believed strongly in "habits of subordina-tion." Both the older guard, represented by Richard Varick, and the newer, younger leaders now emerging, saw deference as a cornerstone of political and social relationships. It was in this context that the Federalists formed their strategy for dealing with the insurgent demands of the cartmen. Pa-tronage was reserved for freemen who could vote in both municipal and assembly elections. Their number was declining, however, and by 1795, a dozen years after the Revolution, the freemen in the city totaled only 170, not all of whom were cartmen.[7]

Younger carters lacked the freemanship and close ties with Varick and were unable to gain patronage. For younger carters, the mayor had little to offer except trouble. After 1795 the Federalists revived the heavy-handed techniques initiated by Varick in 1791 to impose political deference and em-barked upon what the Republican press referred to as a "Reign of Terror."

The policy of enforced deference came to public attention later in 1795. Two incidents, the *Thetis* incident and the two ferrymen affair, caused the Federalist mayor, Richard Varick, openly to confront members of the labor-ing class. In the first place, Varick was accused of ordering ten convicts to be led in chains down from the Bridewell to the waiting British ship, the *Thetis,* where they were inducted into the British navy. This impressment elevated anti-British feeling to a high pitch. To the local laborers, the *Thetis* incident was cruel and unusual punishment and rivaled British actions on the high seas, except that in this case, the impressment was performed by a local official, the mayor. Varick's haughty response to outcry was to insist that the convicts had asked to be taken down to the ships rather than re-main in jail. Scarcely had this issue hit the press than Varick was involved in another incident, again involving the civil liberties of laborers.[8]

Two Irish ferrymen had been involved in an altercation with a Federalist alderman who, feeling insulted, ordered their arrest. The presiding judge, ex officio, was Varick. He ordered the two ferrymen held without bail for 12 days despite the questionable legal basis of the complaint and the willingness of several citizens to stand the pair's bonds. In the ensuing trial Varick punished the ferrymen with two more months in jail for "insulting an officer of the city." One, deemed more guilty than the other, was given an additional punishment of 25 lashes. A young lawyer, William Keteltas, witnessed the trial and accused Varick of denying the two ferrymen bail, denial of proper defense and other injustices. For the next two months, Keteltas kept up a steady barrage of letters in the Republican newspapers in which Varick was consistently portrayed as a tyrant. A petition was circulated calling for Varick's impeachment.[9]

These two incidents reinforced the cartmen's hostility toward the mayor. Many of them signed the petition, instigated by Keteltas, demanding Varick's removal. They soon found that a vengeful mayor refused to renew the licenses of signers of the petition. A doggerel poem circulated in the poorer wards lampooning the meaning of Varick's name.

The poem was an ethnic slur which unsubtly referred to the Dutch meaning of the mayor's name, "hog," and demonstrated the discontent of licensed tradesmen toward him.[10] Not only was he taking their license fees for his own enrichment, but he was hostile to their basic rights. Cartmen, porters, ferrymen, grocers, bakers, butchers, and tavernkeepers were all under the authority of the mayor and deeply resented his imperious attitudes and abuse of power. These groups, particularly the cartmen, formed the basis of laboring class alignment against the mayor and, by extension, against the Federalist party. Their sentiments found sympathy with the Republicans.

The battle lines were now clearly drawn. Varick expected subordinate behavior from licensed workers; they, in turn, openly confronted him, devoting their energies to his removal. As William Keteltas kept up the attack on Varick into the Spring, the two ferrymen affair became a major issue in the assembly elections. From the comments of a "Citizen" in the March 20, 1796 issue of the *Argus,* it appeared that the Council of Appointment was close to accepting the petitions seeking the impeachment of Varick.[11] The writer claimed that the "honor of the law would be vindicated" if Varick were removed. Keteltas became so insistent in his demand for action by the assembly against Varick that the legislators eventually cited the young lawyer for contempt. Keteltas was ordered jailed by the assembly in a divided vote. Alexander Lamb joined the Federalists who voted to have Keteltas

THE

Strange and Wonderful

ACCOUNT

OF A

DUTCH HOG.

WHO RESIDES IN NEW-YORK.

COME Nathan, give a Penny Bill,
 To Nab or Bryan Kitchell,
We'll send for Laffer half a jill,
 And make a mug of Switchell;

II.

For business now is at a stand,
 And cash,—there's no such thing Sir,
So take your comrade by the hand,
 We'll drink about and sing Sir.

III.

There is a man lives in our town,
 Whose tricks are now in vogue Sir,
And though his name I can't set down,
 It sounds somewhat like Hog Sir,

IV.

And all the Dutch Men great and small,
 Who live beyond New-York Sir,
Or Pig, or Shoat, or Hog, do call
 A Coochey or a V-rck Sir,

V.

He is a Man of courage true,
 A Quixotonian Knight Sir,
But as his teeth are rather few,
 He'll neither bite nor fight Sir,

VI.

For once a certain Colonel White,
 With fierce intent to flog Sir,
Did chace around a Waggon quite
 This formidable Hog Sir,

VII.

He often sits upon a bench,
 Much like unto a Judge Sir,

[. . .]
 To wilful [. . .]

[. . .]
He [. . .]
And [. . .]

IX.

We all are friends together,
 And he among the rest Sir,
But then he would that every one,
 Should do as he thinks best Sir,

X.

He acts as tho' he fancies now a
 Were made but for his life Sir,
And when it is—in luckless hour,
 He'd turn it to abuse Sir.

XI.

For once two vulgar Ferrymen
 Some thought let freely slip Sir,
But oh! he sent them to a Den,
 And made them feel the whip Sir.

XII.

This Hog, I vow, it is not fit
 That folks so well should feed him,
It would be right that they should let
 A CERTAIN Doctor bleed him.

XIII.

Or send him to his Pen so close,
 'Twould be a funny joke Sir,
An iron ring upon his nose,
 And on his neck a yoke Sir.

Tavern song satirizing Varick, New York, 1796, New York State Library. The cartmen joined ferrymen, butchers and other licensed works in singing their contempt of the mayor.

98

imprisoned, thus offending his cartmen supporters. Lamb's popularity dropped so precipitously that the Republicans declined to renominate him and he accepted instead the support of the Federalist party, who now styled themselves "Federal Republicans."[12]

In the *Argus* of April 26, "A Citizen" accused Lamb of deserting his followers over the Keteltas affair when the question of Varick's guilt came up. Lamb was linked with other Federalists who "willfully or ignorantly betrayed [the cartmen]." "Citizen" asked the cartmen readers if "you think they can impose Lamb upon you and tie you up and disgrace you forever?"[13]

As a Federalist candidate in 1796, Lamb was not as popular as in the previous year. Although he won re-election, it was largely on the coattails of Federalists from other wards. The Sixth Ward, where he garnered 408 votes in 1795, gave him only 189 votes in 1796, the lowest number among the Federalist winners. By contrast, Philip Livingston, an overall loser, received 473, or 28 percent, of his votes in the Sixth Ward. The Sixth and Seventh Wards continued to shift toward Republicanism.[14]

The following year Lamb received the patronage post of superintendent of the new State Prison on Greenwich Road.[15] He held this post for about a year and then returned to carting. He reclaimed his foreman's post in the first class of carters, but for unknown reasons left again after a year. He died in 1802 at the age of 54.[16]

After Lamb's appointment to the State Prison, no other carter stepped forward to take his place on the electoral circuit. In the elections of 1797, the cartmen failed to publish their preferences for the first time since 1797. The carters' ostensible neutrality in this instance worked to the advantage of the Republicans, given the trade's historic alignment with the Federalists. In the assembly elections of 1797, the Republicans swept to their first city-wide majority of the decade. Despite the Federalists' attempts to confuse the electorate by referring to themselves as Federal Republicans and by nominating candidates in common with the Republicans, the insurgent party outpolled the Federalists in the Sixth Ward by more than three to two.[17]

Despite their new power, the Republicans did little to act upon the long-awaited removal of Varick. Moreover, when a major test of the cartmen's interests occurred, Republican support was openly lacking. On November 14, 1797, Richard Varick, responding to the complaints of many citizens, called in the cartmen's licenses for inspection, a power allowed him by city charter. Varick was ostensibly responding to public outcry over price-gouging, improper use of the license, fake cart numbers, and rude behavior. The mayor issued a notice in all of the local newspapers that all carting licenses had to be turned in for inspection within two weeks and proper ownership and bonding papers be produced in order to obtain renewals by December 15.[18]

No cry of impeachment came from the Republican press. The only comment came from a caustic "A.B.C." writing in the *Daily Advertiser.* He chastised the mayor for wasting money by reprinting the announcement. One notice might have allowed the mayor to escape notice by the public of just how badly the cartmen abused the law. "A.B.C." cited injunctions against riding on the cart and refusing to work for set fees for any citizen as laws particularly abused by the carters. He felt the prohibition against riding on the cart was most ignored. "The deviation from [this one] is the most injurious . . . the lives of children, deaf and infirm are frequently at hazard and several fatal accidents have occured which demand the close observance of the law by the mayor."[19]

This acute statement of the city's difficulties with the cartmen demonstrated the failure of Varick and other Federalist citizens to bring the trade into line. They remained obstreperous in a politically heated environment. Varick's repression of the freemanship, combined with the uncertain economic times, rendered the cartmen not deferential, but more antisocial than ever. The mayor's bullying of the carters was met by open misconduct.

The lack of support offered by the Republicans for the carters was not surprising. Despite their strong rhetoric at election time, little was done by the party the rest of the year. Moreover, the Republican leadership, composed of merchants and leading mechanics, could often be as desirous of deference as were the Federalists.[20] When deference was lacking, as in 1797, the Republicans withdrew support from the carters. The general public saw the trade as underregulated bullies. The mood of the people was not for tolerance of individual initiative and relaxation of government controls, but for tighter enforcement of existing laws. Popular attitudes remained as traditional and custom-oriented as ever toward the city's vital transportation workers. This mood set the tone for further expanded regulation of the cartmen in the so-called age of laissez-faire.

A further Republican response to the problems of regulation came a few months later. The *New York Journal* published a long story by a "citizen and friend of justice," who lamented "seeing every law for the regulation of this city trampled on ... does this not have the tendency to render them and the corporation into disrespect?" The problem, argued the "friend of justice" was not in the laws but in the mayor. Varick was simply not doing the job. The cartmen were abusing the poor. Citizens who demanded the carters charge the regulated fees were "sure to be brow beaten and shamefully abused." Ironically, given their problems with Varick, the carters were seen by the "friend of justice" as above the law because of their powerful influence as voters.[21] This letter illustrates the crucial problem between citizens and the cartmen. While the citizenry may have been willing to accept less regulation in other trades, it clearly was not so in the case of the cartmen.

The Republicans enlivened the April 1799 elections by accusations that the Federalists, guided by an artisan identified as an "old taylor," had decided to withhold licenses to disloyal carters. Federalist merchants, it was also alleged, agreed not to employ any carters who voted Republican. The Republican press gleefully reported that the Federal Republicans, their threats notwithstanding, were unable to get their ticket approved by the Society of Cartmen.[22]

The attempts by the mayor and merchants to bully the trade gave the Republican press all the ammunition it would need. It accused "some of our aristocrats of threatening our cartmen with loss of employment should they vote Republican." Republican propaganda urged "that we know too much of that independent and honest class of men [the carters] ... that they will be intimidated. ..." Other letters were addressed directly to the trade and beseeched the carters to "evince to the world that you are free born sons of American Independence and exhibit to all mankind the unfettered spirit of an honest soul." One letter made frequent mention of Federalist propaganda which allegedly claimed the cartmen "will soon be in rags unless they show themselves to be anti-Republican." By appealing to the spirit of the freemanship and the memory of the glorious revolution, Republican attacks on the privileged and tyrannical tied in with the cartmen's self-perceptions as "freemen and independent."[23]

The Republicans kept up a barrage of humor at the expense of cartmen supporters of the Federalists. Great fun was had over the half-built home of

Uzziah Coddington, a cartman who worked for the Federalists in the Sixth Ward. Uzziah was urged to leave other cartmen alone and work on putting a roof over his head. As evidence of Federalist brutality, a rumor was also spread that a cousin of Uzziah's, cartman Abraham Coddington, had been kicked and fired by a Federalist merchant named Neilson for refusing to vote for Federalists.[24]

The Republicans also published reports from Baltimore of actions by cartmen to resist merchant demands of political deference. The *Argus* of April 30 cited the intimidation of cartmen in Baltimore by the merchants. Carters there "irritated by such a diabolical attempt to deprive them of all Freedom and choice voted for the Republican ticket in defiance of the junta." The *Argus* urged that such action be taken by New York cartmen.[25]

In all the appeals to the carters the Republicans emphasized the alternatives of slavery or freedom for the cartmen. The cartmen's drive to reinstate the freemanship became identified with economic rights and political liberty. The Republicans clearly tailored their political campaign to the carters in a story carried in the *Argus* of May 2. The writer told of overhearing two recent Irish immigrants who spoke of how "it was improper to allow cartmen and other laborers the suffrage in any election." In their country no such people enjoyed the vote. This early appeal to the nativism of the cartmen suggested that their places might be taken by newly arrived Irish immigrants who possessed little of the political ideals cherished by the trade.[26]

The Republicans pulled no punches in trying to secure the cartman vote. "Seventy-six" urged that all old Whigs, Republicans and fellow citizens should come to the aid of the cartmen who were harassed by the enemies of the revolution. "Master Mosey," the tailor who suggested the merchant boycott of Republican cartmen, was accused of looking with "sheep's eyes" at the cartmen and telling them to vote Federalist. "Mosey" was accused of forcing Federalist ballots into the hands of cartmen, telling them that "if you are a good citizen, you will vote with these."[27] At the polls, the Republicans accused the Federalists of such gross violations as bullying and improper voting by visiting British soldiers, negroes, prisoners and residents of the alms house. Throughout this the Federalist press remained silent.

In the election Federalist candidates won in all wards except the Sixth. There, the Republicans gained 69.7 percent of the 1059 votes cast. The Seventh Ward, however, went Federalist by a sizable margin as their candidates won 549 or 55 percent of the 994 votes.[28] The *Argus* complained that the Federalist chicanery meant deprivation of legal rights and asserted that the party's lawyers were totally ignorant of "sound and liberal legal principles." It mocked the Federalists for being unable to "smooth down the rough plaits of the cartmen." A few days after the election, "Plain Truth" lamented that the Federalist electioneering tactics were not just rhetoric but truth: "We are now two societies and the election has made vassals of the cartmen."[29]

In the next year the Republicans initiated year-round preparations for the elections of 1800. The *Argus* became the *American Citizen,* edited by the often-vitriolic James Cheetham. Cheetham also founded a second paper called the *Republican Watchtower.* Through these papers the Republicans kept up a steady appeal to the carters. At the same time Cheetham published his highly influential "Dissertation Concerning Political Equality and the Corporation of the City of New York."[30] Cheetham affirmed that the principle of equality was the measure of liberty in the United States. He argued for universal male suffrage, and in a message sure to please the cartmen, demanded that the mayor be elected by the people. During the assembly elections of April 1800 Cheetham published three letters directed to the cartmen. One reminded the carters of Federalist persecutions of past years. It referred directly to the trade when it noted that "no class of freemen has been so grossly insulted or subjected to tyranny than the cartman of this city." It recalled the fraudulent voting of the past year, the humiliations attended upon the trade by merchants and the mayor and asked "if the cartmen have not as good a right to political independence as the lawyer of his client, the doctor of his patients and the merchants of this customer." The writer asked the carters to be firm, "be unanimous . . . defy your enemies."[31]

To insure that no carter forgot Varick's impositions on them, the Republicans circulated a broadside. On it appeared a caricature of a hog holding a card in its snout, and the inscription, "Varick, the worst card in the Federal pack." Under this were similar attacks on Federalist ward leaders.[32]

The Republicans once again set themselves up as the saviors of the cartmen. A second letter reminded the cartmen to remember the "Spirit of '76." A third described the carters as the "middling class of citizens" and urged them not to resort to fashion in voting. These appeals presented the Republicans as the natural vehicle for achieving the independence and equality of the carters. A vote for Federalism was a vote for despotism and imposed deference; a vote for Republicanism was a vote for Liberty.[33] During this period, mythologized as the "Reign of Terror" by Republican propagandists, Federalist recalcitrance and rigidity enabled the Republicans to gain the vote of the carters.

Several days before the assembly election, the Federalist Common Council irritated the cartmen further by publishing a special broadside issue of the city laws governing carts and cartmen. Not only did the broadside spell out in detail each of the city ordinances governing carts, but it gave special attention to the penalties which cartmen incurred for violations. In order to facilitate citizen complaints, the council listed the names and addresses of the 20 foremen of the carters. Citizens with complaints against a certain carter could get his name and address from the foreman by supplying the license number. Of the 20 foremen, 15 were freemen of the 1780s and all lived in either the Sixth or Seventh Ward.[34]

In the election of 1800, the Republicans enjoyed the fruits of their efforts. The Sixth Ward gave the Republicans 813, or 69.7 percent of the votes and the Seventh went Republican for the first time in three years by giving 782, or 61.7 percent of its votes to Republican candidates. These high percentages helped the Republicans squeak through with a 52.7 percent of the 5869 city-wide votes.[35] "An Independent Cartman," writing in the *American Citizen,* rejoiced that "our enemies have been defeated . . . no longer do we have to be disgraced into submission."[36]

The Republicans, now running strong in both city and county elections, captured control of the assembly in 1801.[37] The Council of Appointment, now sufficiently Republican, used a broad scythe and ousted thousands of Federalist appointees across the state. Among the victims was Mayor Richard Varick, who was replaced by Edward Livingston, whose record was more acceptable to the carters.[38] Livingston had been elected as Republican congressman in 1794, was a foe of Jay's Treaty, and a cousin of one-time cartman favorite, William S. Livingston. The *American Citizen* commemorated the passing of Varick's tenure by noting that he was "a pestilence more destructive than the yellow fever . . . to the administration of justice, he was a stranger." For over a week, Cheetham reviewed in article after article the transgressions of the ex-mayor.[39]

VARICK

The Worst Card
IN THE FEDERAL PACK
Black at Heart
As the Ace of Spades;
INFAMOUS AS

RUFF HIM THE KING.

And as Notorious as the Tory Knave,

JONES.

Add the remainder of the Tory Ticket
Pack, it will make up a precious hand

In National cribbage.

Broadside displaying the cartmen's hostility to Mayor Richard Varick, New York, 1800, New-York Historical Society

With the removal of this hated foe, the political fortunes of the cartmen moved into a new era. The previous 12 years had seen the bonds between city and trade sink to an all-time low. Although the basic contract remained and although city offices were still available to the politically faithful, the vast majority of the trade were so antagonized by the Federalists and Varick that they organized their society as a political unit. Creative politicians within the Republican party realized that votes could be obtained by appealing to the grievances of the cartmen. Although some remained tied by patronage, personal and official ties to the Federalist city government, Republican propaganda attracted cartmen who saw their positions threatened by Varick's policies. The Republicans' emphasis on egalitarian voting was also able to attract the ever-growing numbers of cartmen without the freemanship, enabling the party to overcome the trade's ties with the Federalists. The Federalists not only lost the political support of most of the cartmen, but Varick's irritation of the cartmen produced antisocial behavior. The mayor and carters were often so alienated that little communication was possible.

Shortly before the November 1801 Common Council elections, the cartmen demonstrated how seriously they wanted the freemanship reinstated. Three hundred cartmen gave a petition to the new mayor, Edward P. Livingston, demanding a return of the freemanship. He expressed his "constant willingness to cooperate in a measure which might tend to the welfare and happiness of his fellow citizens."

A Committee of Cartmen visited aldermen to secure their approval for the measure. The Republican aldermen, Joshua Barker and Mangle Minthorne, expressed their support. The petition now only needed two more endorsements to become law. Committeemen Henry Reynolds and Thomas Green next visited Jotham Post, the former butcher and candidate for the assembly who had received cartmen support in the 1790s. Post, a Federalist, refused to sign the petition and explained that if the petitioners were made "free" there would be 3000 other inhabitants who possessed an equal claim. When asked whether it was not their right to become freemen, Post responded that "undoubtedly it was . . . but that it would be attended with consequences very dangerous if so large a body were made free." Reynolds countered with a compromise proposal by which only the cartmen would receive the freemanship, not the general public; did Post "not suppose that they would elect a proper character to the council?" Post admitted this, but argued that the cartmen might well "choose a man not possessed of a freehold . . . who might do damage to those who had." When alderman John Bogart refused to endorse the petition for the same reasons, the proposal died.[40]

As this incident makes clear, the freemanship was by no means a dead article. While the petition was initially for all citizens, the cartmen were willing to restrict the privileged to their trade. Moreover, the incident indicates the political equality felt by the trade. Rather than listen deferentially to promises from officeholders, the cartmen formed a committee which actively canvassed the Common Council and the mayor.

The failure of the petition demonstrated to the cartmen that they needed not only to change the mayor, but the Common Council as well. The *Republican Watchtower* of December 8, 1801, reminded the cartmen shortly after the failure of the petition that "the council takes the law into its own hands and refuses to make men free, while it is their duty to punish these citizens for not having the freedom." Rather than being content with securing a major victory by banishing Varick, the cartmen learned that further political change was necessary to protect their interests.

The principal focus of the cartmen in the last decade of the eighteenth century was the restoration of the freemanship. Because he was considered the greatest obstacle to this, Richard Varick had to be removed. By supporting Republican suggestions for changes in the selection process, cartmen showed their desire not only to oust him but to gain control over his office. Since the mayor was their putative boss, control over his office effectively meant self-control.

As Varick had grossly offended the trade by denying them their fundamental rights, won and affirmed by the Revolution, reinstatement of that privilege would be the initial goal after his departure. That search would force the cartmen to take an even greater role in the reform of local institutions of government.

CHAPTER NINE

Creating Security within
the Municipal Government, 1801–1818

At the beginning of the nineteenth century the cartmen faced imposing dilemmas. While they had succeeded in ousting their long-time nemesis, Mayor Richard Varick, they still lacked the political power to reinstate the freemanship. Very few carters had sufficient property easily to pass election qualifications. Although the trade had shaken off the demands of deference to the Federalists, the carters were now bound to the Republicans who also could insist upon obedience.

Further, the government was no longer protecting the trade as it had in the past. Blacks using unlicensed carts freely sold fruits and vegetables on the streets. Farmers from Long Island and New Jersey, unconcerned about licenses, worked in the outer regions of the city. In addition, the Republican city government was under constant pressure from wealthier citizens living in the downtown commercial wards to correct the reckless driving and careless habits of the carters. The Republicans were not as adept as the Federalists in doling out patronage to the cartmen. One major problem was that each position now had 20 or more applicants.

In addition, greater divisions were occurring in the trade. Specialization developed as some cartmen now worked exclusively "riding" wood, hay, manure, dirt or sand. This was a marked change from the generalized nature of the occupation in the eighteenth century. Certain types of carting, particularly wood and manure, developed strong characteristics of capitalism and were frequently criticized (in the opening years of the century) by citizens and other carters for engrossing and forestalling.

The cartmen's problems with the government epitomized their dilemmas. Although the Republicans promised in their campaign rhetoric to continue the cartmen's monopoly, the changing nature of the city and the party's often slippery political tactics made the cartmen's bond with the city government uncertain. Other trades, most notably the bakers, were moving away from the web of regulation which characterized eighteenth-century New York's political economy.[1]

The cartmen faced dangers from deregulation from which other, more skilled occupations were immune. Driving a cart was a common skill for early Americans; deregulation could quickly cause an overabundance of cartmen. Clear threats to the cartmen's monopoly over intracity transportation came from the city's many blacks, from the increasing number of Irish, and from the crowds of unemployed whose numbers swelled with each economic recession.

The political power of the white carters bolstered the power of their racial exclusivity. Free blacks now numbered over three thousand in New York City. In 1799, the state passed a gradual emancipation law, which began a slow process ending slavery in New York. By 1800, more than 3300 free blacks lived in New York City. That local laws and customs barred them from carting, an entry level occupation, sharply restricted their economic chances. True, the law protected white carters from falling into poverty level jobs, such as Seth Rockman has uncovered in Baltimore. New York City's labor market could easily have matched Baltimore's situation. Free laborers, white and black, and enslaved men were abundantly available in early nineteenth-century New York, yet the white carters held a stranglehold on a generic occupation. They did so only because the municipal government respected the historic bond of attachment. That bond restricted blacks and indicates the underside of government patronage.[2]

The solution for the cartmen lay not in movement toward a freer form of labor, but rather in a tighter continued relationship within the city government. More than any other occupation in the city, the cartmen needed to assert their political strengths quickly in order to protect their economic existence. To insure such protection, the cartmen sought to capture important seats on the Common Council or at least fill them with sympathizers and, failing that, to expand their place within the ever-growing municipal bureaucracy. Whether these were conscious choices, we do not know, but the cartmen moved inevitably toward both of these goals in the first two decades of the nineteenth century.

Their success was in no small part due to the public attitudes. As was evident in the previous, tumultuous decade, New Yorkers evinced little desire to free the cartmen of city laws. Richard Varick's failure successfully to control the carters was certainly part of his downfall. During the early years of the nineteenth century, regulations were enhanced as new ones were added and older ones strengthened. Price gouging, reckless driving and refusal of service by the cartmen, for example, were all met with stiff resistance and outcry by the citizenry.

Although the cartmen were seen as urban problems by the middle-class, they perceived themselves as respectable, industrious citizens who deserved protection and relief from the depredations of Varick and from the insistent complaints of the bourgeoisie. Mayor Varick's manipulation of his power over their licenses was a key grievance. As veterans or sons of veterans of the Revolutionary War, the cartmen felt entitled to their place in the political economy of the city. Exclusion of the Irish and blacks was, in the minds of the cartmen, still accepted wisdom.

Ethnic stability in the trade continued. The trade survived the "Reign of Terror" of the 1790s, as the Republicans liked to call it, in firm shape. Cultural solidarity remained strong. Anglo-Americans and Dutch continued to dominate the occupation. Of 1050 carters in 1801, 610 or 57 percent had English surnames; another 358 or 34 percent can be identified as Dutch. Sixty-eight carters were Irish and only 14 had French names. Nine hundred thirty-five, an overwhelming majority of the carters, lived in the crowded Sixth and Seventh Wards. The Sixth Ward, the old Trinity Church Farm, remained the most popular neighborhood for cartmen, as 645 or 61 percent of the city's licensed cartmen lived there. The Seventh Ward contained the next largest number of cartmen with 290 or 27 percent, while the remainder was scattered throughout the lower wards or on the outskirts of the city. Both the Sixth and Seventh Wards were racially segregated. Only 173 or one percent of the Sixth Ward's residents were black; the Seventh which included poorer areas further uptown had but 322 or two percent of the city's black residents. The Irish were more strongly represented in these two wards as nearly 2100 of New York's Hibernians lived in them.[3]

Despite the troubles of the 1790s, carting remained the occupation of generations of New Yorkers. Timothy Jarvis' two sons, John and Jacob, were carters. Cornelius Ryan's son worked the streets as a carter as did his younger brother, Peter. James Caldwell, a freemanship carter, had three sons, all of whom were carters. The same was true for David Demarest whose sons, Joseph, David, Jr., and Jacob, held licenses in 1802. John Blauveldt's son, Garret, joined his uncle Garret Westervelt as a cartman. A cousin, Stephen Westervelt, worked the streets. Jacobus Bogert's grandson was a cartman. Peter Bogert was the grandson of Servaes Vlierboom, who carted in the early eighteenth century. Peter was related to cartmen Abraham Ackerman and John Ackerman; Peter Post married Jannette Haring, another descendent of Servaes Vlierboom. These familial relationships between New York City cartmen kept alive eighteenth-century social patterns emphasizing inheritance of occupation.[4]

Carters controlled certain patronage positions. Though nomination was increasingly difficult, many carters still monopolized inspectorships for hay, wood, lime, sand and manure. New laws creating positions as inspectors of mahogany, bricks, charcoal and stone required appointment of a cartman. The carters remained the largest group within the nightly watch.

One major change was the decided break with the Federalist party. This became clear in early 1802 when Alexander Hamilton complained that the "cartmen were absorbed in jacobinsim." He observed that, although merchants had resolved not to hire any cartmen who voted against the opinions of an employer, their "stubborness" made the merchants "give up all hope of restoring the cartmen to order and good government."[5] Another story circulating at the time involved a chance meeting between the General and a cartman after Hamilton attended a cartman's meeting.

"Well, General, since you have come to be a cartman, you ought to put on your frock and trowsers and mount your cart—I wish you would lend me a hand, I have a job riding timber, and if you'll help we'll go snack on the profit." The General treated the offer with contempt. The value that will be set upon the conduct and character of such a brother cartman, the fraternity are best to judge.[6]

Hamilton's success with the cartmen was far more limited than in the 1790s. A cartman complained that some in attendance at the same meeting were "new made cartmen . . . They will cart you to the polls and dump you down." Soon after these words were printed in the newspaper, the Society of Cartmen met at Martling's tavern to endorse the Republican ticket. In the ensuing election, the Republicans swept all nine local assembly seats.[7]

The one major hurdle obstructing the cartmen's goal of a restored freemanship was the Common Council. Voting in charter elections still required a £20 freehold which angry cartmen found was just beyond the assessed value of their property according to Federalist election inspectors. The Republican press urged all citizens in 1803 to "take into consideration measures to be adopted to insure the right of suffrage in charter elections." As a means of getting out the cartmen vote, the papers printed reminders of Varick's "Reign of Terror," of the Coddington incident and of the dangers of a penitentiary workhouse to their interest. That year the Common Council urged the employment of local convicts on city work projects as a means of saving money. The idea, which was a direct threat to the employment of many carters, no doubt stimulated their support of the Republicans who won the council seats in the Sixth and Seventh Wards. In what was now a ritual, a post-election satire poked fun at Varick who was pictured harassing cartmen at the polls. The former mayor, caustically derided for pro-British attitudes, was described as a "mad bull" who "whisked his tail at the cartmen." They were advised to give him room as "he'll break his neck."

Despite this merriment, there was cause for concern about Republican attitudes. Some carters, beset by demands for loyalty from merchants of both parties, declared "that it was too much trouble to vote." Republican merchants, sounding much like their Federalist counterparts, retorted that it was "not too much trouble to search all over the city to give the carters their business." The threat was clear.[8]

The freemanship remained the big issue. The *Watchtower* reported in early 1804 that "the Federalists opposed the extension of the suffrage because the city would be ruled by a mob." James Cheetham commented in the *Watchtower* that such a belief showed "contempt of the cartmen, the butchers and the tavern-keepers, who legally cannot work without a freemanship." In a broadside circulated in the streets, the Republicans noted that from November 1, 1783, to March 12, 1792, 676 citizens were made free; from 1792 to 1804 only 70 became freemen. In the last charter election only 108 freemen could be found. A vote for Morgan Lewis for governor, argued the broadside, would insure the return of this "fundamental right" of "all tradesmen, mechanics and cartmen who are now held to be unworthy of the freedom of the city." The *Republican Watchtower* was also filled with attacks on the character, structure and performance of the Common Council.[9]

The election of Lewis insured reform and on April 21, 1804, the *Watchtower* were filled with reports of major changes by the assembly. It had voted to extend the suffrage in New York City charter elections to anyone renting property for over $25 per year and who had six months' residency. Such a person "shall be entitled to all the rights and privileges of a freeman of the city."[10]

This reform recreated the political substance of the freemanship but did little to reinstate the exclusive clauses previously enjoyed by cartmen and other licensed tradesmen. While the reform gave the carters the vote, it did not make their monopoly more secure. Indeed, it appeared to open the door for further reform which could threaten their positions, if any new citizen might be considered a candidate for a license. It was up to the cartmen themselves to enforce their monopoly through power at the ballot box.

Actually, some of the exclusive requirements did remain. Applicants for positions had to swear loyalty oaths to the city and federal governments and to uphold the laws, particularly the market laws, of those governments. Forestalling and engrossing were specifically renounced in the oaths sworn by cartmen, butchers, inspectors, gaugers and other measurers. In addition, applicants had to demonstrate six months' residence in the city. A clause was added to the laws governing cartmen which required that licensees demonstrate residence to their foremen every two months. Failure to do so meant suspension.[11]

To insure maximum political benefit from this victory, the *Republican Watchtower* printed all the greatly liberalized charter election changes alongside reminders of Federalist impositions upon the cartmen. Thus spurred to vote, the cartmen helped the Republicans to a seven to two majority in the first open charter election.[12]

Signing oaths of allegiance was not in the least irritating to the highly patriotic cartmen. It was a time of reverence for the glories of the Revolutionary War, of egalitarian attitudes, and also of incipient nativism. Parades celebrating the Fourth of July and Evacuation Day were chances for the cartmen to ride through the streets atop their horses and dress in ribbon-covered frocks. Patriotism was now an important part of their ideology. Just as the freemanship had created pride in citizenship of New York City in the eighteenth century, so now the glories of Washington and the American Revolution gave a glow to the national government, no matter who was in power. The cartmen, like other tradesmen, took great pride in their contribution to American government. On July 4, 1804, the carters, along with thousands of other New Yorkers, flocked to the newly expanded Vauxhall Gardens on upper Bowery Road to view the oil paintings celebrating the Constitutional Procession of 1788. There in living color was the procession of over 300 cartmen led by Daniel Demoray and Abraham Martling, Jr. Behind these leaders rode the cartmen, covered with ribbons and flowers.[13]

Martling was getting a reputation in political circles. His tavern, nick-named the "pig pen," had become the headquarters of the Tammany Society, by now the most important wing of the Republican party. Martling and his cohorts acted as ward leaders, doling out patronage at "wigwam meetings," and insuring the laboring class vote for the Republicans. Martling himself was a good example of how the system worked. A veteran, Martling came to New York in 1783 from his home in Rockland County. His father and uncle before him had been New York City cartmen. He worked as a scavenger under Richard Varick before opening his tavern in 1787. Later he served as constable in the Fourth Ward and then as a tax assessor. All the while he remained a cartman. He held two city licenses while serving in two electoral offices. Such multiple office-holding was as much the key for success in the lower echelon of society as at the top.[14]

During these years the relationship between the cartmen and the Republican party prospered. The cartmen gained back their revered freemanship and received patronage through Martling's tavern. The Republicans used the images of Varick, Hamilton and the Coddington incident to spark cartman anger against the Federalists every year. As long as the economy prospered and jobs were plentiful, the relationship worked.

But problems loomed. First, the Republicans were squabbling among themselves. Followers of Aaron Burr quarreled with those of the Livingston family. Not everyone supported Morgan Lewis for governor in 1804. James

Cheetham's *American Citizen* and *Watchtower* inevitably offended nearly everyone in the party. More importantly, the party had to bow to national decisions made by the President, Thomas Jefferson. The most unpopular of these was, of course, the Embargo of 1807. What seemed quite plausible for Virginian Jefferson as a means of combatting the British was a terrible blow to New York's economy and to the cartmen. John Lambert, a British traveller, described how the wharves of the city, once bustling with cartmen, were, by the Spring of 1808, attended by "less than a dozen, and they were unemployed." The Embargo, argued the Federalists, was a "visionary and pernicious method" of fighting the British; a return by cartmen to the party would mean employment. The Federalists attempted to show their own patriotism by proposing to employ many cartmen to work on a fortifications project on the tip of the island. The only answers the Republicans could muster to this solid proposal were more reminders of Varick and Coddington.[15]

The Republicans suffered a second embarrassment in the Spring of 1807 when their candidate for mayor, Judge Thompson of Albany, was found ineligible "because he was not a freeman or freeholder" of New York. The mayoralty had by then become a political football. His Honor had been stripped of the lucrative right to all license fees and instead was given a fixed salary. Although the salary was a healthy $5000 per year, that was little compared to the $12,000–$15,000 a year which DeWitt Clinton had earned two years before. Friends of Governor Morgan Lewis conspired with Federalists to place Thompson as mayor; in response the *Watchtower*, indicating the split among the Republicans, referred to the candidate as a "shuffling, cringing, time-serving pol." Not only was the Republican party unable to decide who should be mayor, but it was openly squabbling.[16]

Just before the Spring 1807 elections, 74-year-old Marinus Willett was named mayor. Willett was a famous Revolutionary War officer who commanded many cartmen. Despite this, his reign was to prove a costly one in the relationship between the cartmen and the Republicans. To insure the victory in the 1807 election, however, the Republicans produced several affidavits demonstrating Federalist impositions upon the cartmen. In one instance a Federalist loyalist assured voters that he had been requested by party contractors to fire Republican cartmen. When he refused, he lost lucrative contracts.[17]

Although the Republicans once again swept to victory, they were to face further problems. As the party in power, they now had to face the re-

"Family Electioneering: Or, Candidate Bob in all His Glory," William Charles, 1807. Courtesy of The Henry Francis du Pont Winterthur Museum. Charles portrayed young politicians trying to sway the cartman's vote shortly after Mayor Marinus Willett recalled all their licenses. Few of the independent cartmen would sell their liberty for so cheap a price.

sponsibility of controlling the cartmen amidst mounting criticism of their behavior. Mayor Marinus Willett found himself faced with a local crisis in the fall of 1807.

On October 24, 1807, a Mr. Prall was taking an afternoon ride with his two little boys in the family carriage. At one point Prall and his family passed through Anthony Street "which was always nearly blocked up with carts collected between a blacksmith's shop and a wheelwright's." As Prall attempted to negotiate the "dangerous place, he first struck a cart on one side. The jostle of the carts dumped Prall and his sons out of their carriage; at first the gentleman appeared to be unharmed but soon after, he complained of headaches, then collapsed, and died.[18]

The furor over Prall's death led to the publication of other incidents. The *Evening Post* editorialized that "the manner in which cartmen drive through our streets ... has become a public nuisance." According to the *Post,* "It is a prime ambition to possess the fastest pacers and the public streets are the race tracks." The cartman "who can drive at the fastest speed, and especially can turn a corner without slackening speed, is the subject of universal envy among his brethren of the whip." Though some carters have lost limbs as a result, "that is nothing to them; and with their trotting horses who can catch them?"[19]

The *Post* then went on to describe a current cartmen sport of terrorizing women. As a pretty woman attempted to cross a street, speeding carters would bear down on her as fast as possible. Just before running her down, they "bring the cart to an ell. . . . The closer to the woman the greater the skill." Two women were terrorized on Greenwich and Barclay Streets while many cartmen sat by the side of the road, "splitting their sides with laughter." Although the number of the cart was 55, examination of the licenses with the mayor showed that several men held that number.[20]

Washington Irving immortalized another contemporary cartman practice in *Salamagundi.* Irving caustically described a scene in the city streets: "Saw a cartman run down a small boy on Broadway today. What of it? Served him well. Shouldn't have been there in the first place." Irving used the incident to satirize city officials who passed laws "against pigs, goats, dogs and cartmen" by comparing the aldermen unfavorably with tinkers: "whether it takes greater ability to mend a law than a kettle," especially "laws that are broken a hundred times a day with impunity."[21]

The Republicans were now in the same position as the Federalists ten years before. As party policies made the cartmen suffer, the trade responded by intimidating citizens. Just as Richard Varick did in 1797, so Marinus Willett asked the entire force of 1200 cartmen to turn in their licenses for inspection, further souring relations between the occupation and the Republicans.[22] The death of Prall and the terrorizing of the women also pointed out the widening split between the cartmen and the bourgeoisie of the city, a split which would later have political ramifications.

Even though the cartmen were increasingly unpopular with middle-class New Yorkers, they still held the respect of politicians. The measures enacted to reduce suffering from the trade recession caused by the Embargo indicate how true this was. During the hard winter of 1807-1808, "Philanthropist" made a suggestion very similar to ones proposed in previous hard times. "Philanthropist" suggested that the Common Council purchase all extra firewood and hire cartmen to distribute the fuel to the poor. Addressing the council directly, the writer noted "on you, gentlemen, devolves the important duty to provide for the approaching distress and to see that no person in this city suffers from hunger or cold."[23]

The council was too preoccupied with other affairs, however, to take action on this well-meaning proposal. Unemployed mariners were threatening direct action to obtain food and money. Blaming the city government for inaction on the economic crisis, the mariners were meeting in public demonstrations which shook the Republican council. After the second such meeting nearly turned into a riot, the council enacted immediate relief by creating work on the fortifications for Castle Island. Significantly, the greatest number of jobs created were not for mariners, but for cartmen. A city audit revealed that while mariners, ships' carpenters and laborers were actually working at reduced wages during the crisis, the 135 cartmen so employed were earning $1.75 per day which was well above the standard wages for skilled labor. Political clout could pay off in times of need. This incident also indicates the further extension of corporate paternalism in this era. Rather than move toward laissez-faire, the city government showed that it preferred to use the resources of past examples.[24]

Despite these remedies, the trade was experiencing difficulties. For the first time in many years, there were openings in the various "classes" of cartmen. In 1808 Mayor DeWitt Clinton published a roster of all 26 classes of cartmen; of 1300 available licenses, 292 or 22 percent went unclaimed. Three classes, the sixth, twenty-fifth and twenty-sixth, had more than 40 percent of their licenses vacant. Years of political bullying combined with economic disaster had made the trade far less attractive than before.[25]

Further ruptures in trade solidarity were evident in the controversies over firewood. It appeared that a few carters were purchasing all the firewood at the docks and then raising the prices to unconscionable levels. Engrossing, as such a practice was known, was a heinous crime to the popular mentality. The reaction of the Common Council to a petition by 144 cartmen protesting such engrossing by a few of their brethren is a good litmus test of the limited growth of a capitalist ethos among the common people in the early nineteenth century. The petition complained that a few carters in collusion with some corrupt inspectors were monopolizing all the firewood; one inspector was even accused of purchasing all the fuel available at Peck Slip. The petitioners requested that the city enforce its own laws, replace any corrupt inspectors and if necessary the city corporation should purchase all the firewood and sell it at a rate determined by the buyer's income. The cartmen accused of engrossing were derided by their fellows as "making a market of the poor man's miseries . . . all for dirty gain." The council was unable to mount much of a response to these accusations, but did move shortly to issue reminders to all cartmen that there was a maximum fee per load of firewood. Neither side, neither the aggrieved cartmen nor the council appeared to have the slightest interest in deregulation. Rather, the laws were considered just and only the corrupt at fault.[26]

At the same time the revived Federalist party battled with the Republicans, now torn between factions, for the votes of the cartmen. In 1808, for the first time in years, the Federalists amounted an effective campaign against the ruling party. "Cartman," writing in the *Commercial Advertiser,* blasted the Republicans for constantly crying "tory, tory, Coddington, Varick and the like while never helping a cartman get a job." "Cartman" accused the Republicans of "being office-holders only who make many times what any cartman makes." While the Federalists admitted past wrongs against the cartmen, they commented that the "oppression of those young pretended patriots [the Republicans] is nearly equal to that of the British."[27]

The day before the Spring 1808 election, the Federalists cited the dismal results of the Embargo. Among them was the "cartman, who was growing rich by his labor, now finds himself scarcely sufficient to purchase straw and provender for the horse he drives. . . . He goes to his customary stand, looks in vain for employment; returns empty to his family and beholds wretchedness and despair, staring them in the face." The Federalists were reminding the cartmen of the interdependence of merchants and cartmen.[28] To this melodramatic spectacle the Republicans could only mount a weak response, reminding the trade of the "Reign of Terror" and suggesting that the cartmen are a "shrewd and discerning body of man and can readily distinguish their friends from their foes."[29]

On the day of the election, the Federalists put out an extra edition claiming that "a band of Irishmen, paid by the Republicans, marched through the Sixth Ward, shouting Jefferson and the Embargo, they then attacked a number of inoffensive cartmen and beat them unmercifully." While the modern reader will marvel at how the cartmen have changed from bullies and tyrants to "inoffensive" victims in the space of a few months, a more important current can be observed in this incident. The Federalist were using the growing nativism of the cartmen to portray the Republicans as the party of the Irish and thus betrayers of the cartmen. Nevertheless the Republicans, with general aid from the cartmen, once again swept to a victory, prompting the Federalist press derisively to observe that the carters needed "the taste of a three-year embargo . . . go along, supplicant fellows . . . kiss the rod and worship the hand that smites you." Despite these contentious words the Federalists had gained two important themes in this election, the interdependence of cartmen and merchants, and nativism, which would be effectively used in the future.[30]

The continued unpopularity of the embargo, coupled with the growing strains of nativism within the city, helped the resurgent Federalists in 1809. Even though the Embargo was ended just before the April 1809 elections for the assembly, the Federalists scored points with the cartmen by reminding them that "they would be back where they started" because of the Republican programs. Even though the Republicans won all 11 seats in the city, the Federalists captured a statewide assembly majority. As important as this election was, there were greater tensions for the Republicans within the streets of New York. The Republicans were splitting wide-open in a confrontation between James Cheetham and Tammany, sequestered at the tavern of Abraham Martling. The *Watchtower* accused Tammany of collusion with the Federalists and kept up attacks on it all spring.[31]

While this was occurring, citizens from Coffee House Slip, Front Street, Beekman Street, Coenties Slip, Pearl and Water Streets presented petitions to the Common Council asking that the cartmen be restricted from driving along their roads. The complaints were that the carters were leaving their "vicious horses untended, that carts were blocking entrances to houses and shops, that cartmen were rude and disorderly and that there had been several accidents.[32] The *Watchtower* noted these complaints with a scathing attack on the cartmen. After deriding the mayor and Common Council for being afraid to enforce corporation laws, the newspaper referred to the cartmen as the "greatest enemy in the world of equality. . . . The devil of a bit of road they will give you. . . . They know they can ride you down and down you must go. . . . If these lords (they are worse if possible than the English at sea) . . . will only permit you to pass without running you down . . . you feel all the gratitude of a very subject." As the cartmen support for the Republican ticket began to slip, the party grew less tolerant of the trade's misconduct in the streets.[33]

Eventually, the Common Council was forced to act in the face of repeated complaints. The council created cart-stands to be assigned to individual cartmen by their foremen. Place and order would be earned by seniority and type of work. In itself this reform instituted a sort of hierarchy within the cartmen and greatly increased the foremen's powers.[34]

The council was hardly innovative in its solution of the problems created by roving cartmen. Stands were first created in London in the sixteenth century and the New York City Common Council was actually reaching backwards into history for example. Again, the attitudes of New Yorkers simply would not permit deregulation to free the cartmen from government control. In fact, greater control was added.

The Common Council did make an unprecedented move in 1810 to solve the problem of insufficient drivers. Since 1677 minors under 21 years of age had been banned from carting. This was done for safety and to avoid undercutting the pay of the cartmen with cheap, juvenile labor. By mid-1810 the number of active cartmen dropped so far that the council reluctantly issued licenses to minors. Minors were required to make a deposit for bonding and security unless their fathers were cartmen. For example, one week after the council issued the first licenses to minors, Henry Thorpe appeared at the council meeting to request a license for his son. Thorpe explained that he was too ill to drive and asked that his son be allowed to take his place. This request was accepted without any requirements of bond. Within a short time other fathers sought licenses for their sons, and, because of the shortage of drivers, were usually successful. As the shortage decreased, however, the council allowed licenses for minors only to sons of cartmen.[35]

There are three important elements in this decision. First, the council clearly favored sons of carters. Their method of licensing was easier and less expensive. Tradition and continuity within the trade was encouraged. Secondly, the council was the agency acting upon these requests, not the mayor. Symptomatic of the declining stature of his power in recent years, the mayor was not even consulted about changes in one of his most important functions. As the Common Council now appointed the mayor, tenures were quite short and even the dynamic DeWitt Clinton had difficulty with the council. Moreover, the council's actions on licenses for minors were part of a trend, encouraged by the cartmen, to place more and more responsibility for their relationship with the city on the Common Council. As aldermen had by now learned the power of the cartman vote and were more likely to be acquainted with the local needs of the trade than the mayor, the carters turned to the council to resolve problems.

A third point about granting licenses to minors has to do with the nature of the occupation itself. As a general skill, carting could potentially be rapidly casualized. In London, employment of minors was the first step in the breaking of self-control by the cartmen. As small boys took up the trade under loosened regulations and worked at far cheaper rates than the older cartmen, wages fell and regular employment became a distant memory.[36] Unlike the older cartmen who stayed on the job for decades, the lads were often in and out of carting within five years. In New York, a burgeoning population and the relaxation of regulations in other trades made carting vulnerable to a surplus labor pool. The carters were able to prevent this only because of their power within the city government.

By 1811, the cartmen increased their numbers and regained some of the stability lost during the Embargo years. The mayor's license book for 1811–1812 records licenses for 1381 cartmen. In the following year there was only a nine percent turnover within all of the classes. Stability reigned. Richard Robertson continued as the foreman of the first class of cartmen, a position he had held since Alexander Lamb's departure in 1798. Three carters in the first class died in 1811; one moved out of town. The remainder of the fifty cartmen in the first class included some very familiar names. Elias Ward and Jacob Crum were among seven who received their first licenses in 1784. Abraham Coddington was famous for having been "kicked" by his employer back in 1798. Abraham Day celebrated his fiftieth year in a career stretching back to 1761. John S. Johnson, a name to be heard more frequently in future years, received his first license in 1797.[37]

Overall, Anglo-Americans still dominated the trade. At least 743 or 68 percent of the carters appear to have been Anglo-Americans. The second

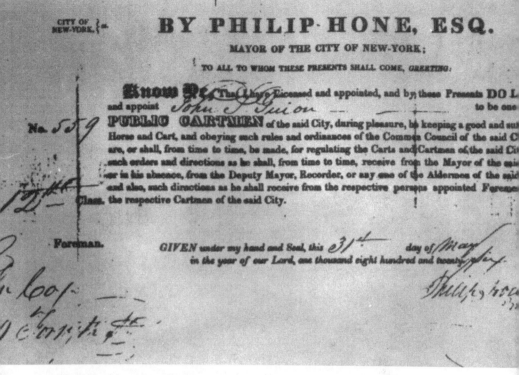

Standard form of the cartman's license, 1826. City Municipal Archives, Department of Records and Information Services, City of New York.

largest group, however, was no longer the Dutch, but the Irish. The numbers of Irish in the city had been growing rapidly and by 1811, 275 or 20 percent of the cartmen were of Irish extraction. Dutch cartmen accounted for the remaining 163.[38]

Geographically, the cartmen were beginning to move out of the old Sixth and Seventh Wards. The newly developed Eighth and Tenth Wards attracted many cartmen. The Sixth and Seventh Wards were now heavily Irish which may have had something to do with the rush for new lands by Anglo-American carters.[39]

The growing tensions between the Anglo-Americans and the Irish were postponed briefly by the War of 1812. Available records do not permit a true compilation of the number of cartmen who went off to war, but the numbers were sufficient for a Federalist Common Council to award licenses to Irish aliens in the absence of veteran cartmen.

Those native-born carters who did remain behind enjoyed lucrative contracts with the federal government. The deputy quartermaster hired 600 cartmen at $1.65 a day to work on navy projects in Williamsburg. Such carters were exempt from all other military duty. The Common Council offered employment by hiring 50 cartmen to move 20 pieces of heavy military weapons from hiding places around the city down to the Battery and back again twice a week. This seemingly meaningless exercise was to insure that the cartmen were capable of moving the artillery in case of attack. Practice runs occurred on Tuesdays and Thursdays every week in 1813 and 1814 and paid $1.50 per day.[40]

The end of the war brought many veteran cartmen back to the city to reclaim their places. They found that frequently the Common Council had issued licenses to Irish aliens. This was bad enough but was made worse by the Irish practice of undercutting the general fixed fee for a common load. Moreover, the Common Council had sharply reduced the number of licenses from 1400 down to 1000, thus increasing competition for any opening.[41]

Angrily, the cartmen petitioned the mayor to cancel licenses held by aliens. Mayor Cadwallader Colden agreed to cease offering licenses to aliens but would not revoke those already earned. Such a measure, he argued, would deprive the aliens of income and would create hardship.[42]

The problem lay dormant for two years. In the meantime, commerce increased and fewer hardships were felt. The cartmen turned their attention to other matters. Back in 1810 the carters first proposed to the city government that the position of Superintendent of Carts be created. The person chosen would work directly for the mayor and would insure that the corporation laws were observed. One individual was proposed but was rejected by the cartmen; the post was then dropped for unknown reasons until it was revived just before the election of 1816.[43]

Arguing that the cartmen's expenses had gone up during the many years since the last increase in their wages, a committee from the Society of Cartmen petitioned the Federalist Common Council for a raise. Delaying action until just a week before the April 1816 election, the Common Council gave the trade its biggest political victory since the election of Alexander

Lamb in 1795. The agreement between the council and the Committee of Cartmen indicates their continued strength. The document proclaimed:

The committee to whom was referred the petitions of John N. Johnson, John Delzemere and others, cartmen of this city, praying for an advance on the present rates of cartage and certain other regulations for their general benefit and interest—Report that they have given the petition the attention due to so numerous a portion of the community and have also had an interview with a Committee appointed by the cartmen and after full deliberation, they are convinced that an advance on the present rates which were established many years since when House, Rent, Horse feed and indeed many of the necessary articles required for the support of a family were far cheaper than they are now, is not only a justifiable but a necessary measure and in conformity with that opinion they herewith present a new rate which while it tends to relieve the cartmen does not bear oppressively on the community at large.

The committee further respectfully suggest to the Common Council the propriety of limiting the number of cartmen and that no person receive a license except that he is at the time a resident of the City and County and that in all cases a preference be given to men of families and those who have had the longest residence in the city.

That a person, nominated by the cartmen in such manners as they themselves prescribe shall be appointed from time to time and during the pleasure of the Common Council, to be called the "Superintendent of Carts," whose special duty it shall be to prevent the forestalling of firewood—the driving of carts without a license and without being numbered—to report to the clerk of the Common Council the names of all cartmen who may die, remove or become disqualified and to keep a Register of the same to gather with a general register of all the cartmen, their numbers and to generally enforce the various ordinances of the Corporation relative to Carts and Cartmen.

Then each cartman on receiving his license and in the course of the month of May each year thereafter, shall pay to the Receiver of the Mayoralty fees, one dollar each, which sums after deduction therefrom $750 per annum for the salary of the Superintendent of

Carts and the expenses incidental to the printing and delivery of the Licenses shall constitute a fund for the relief of poor, infirm and disabled cartmen—shall be placed at the disposal of a Committee of Trustees appointed by the cartmen for that purpose and by them appointed in such manner and under such regulations as the cartmen may direct. That is shall be the duty of the Cartmen to make a selection of the Said Committee of Trustees in the month of May of each year and file the names of those chosen with the Clerk of the Common Council on or before the first day of June next ensuing.[44]

"An electioneering trick," cried the Republican *Advocate*. "Nonsense," retorted the Federalist *Post,* "the cartmen's petition was under negotiation for some time and the timing was purely coincidental." True or not, the sizable cartman vote helped the Federalists sweep to a big victory.[45]

As much as their vote helped the Federalists, so the council's decision aided the cartmen. They now had a protector within the city government, paid for by their license fees, and whose responsibilities included insuring that none but qualified citizens could gain a license. Moreover, the Society of Cartmen now had a source of cash for its benevolent fund. Wending its way through legislative channels in Albany was a bill which would incorporate the society. The steady infusion of money from license fees would protect the cartmen against economic loss, and could also be used as a source of political clout if their monopoly was ever threatened. Moreover, the cartmen controlled the entire process.[46]

Equally remarkable was the unimpeded success that the Committee of Cartmen had in negotiations with the Common Council. Contrast their accomplishments with those of the journeymen cord wainers, who were convicted of criminal conspiracy in 1809 for petitioning for higher wages. In this instance and in others at this time, courts held that workers making grievances for better wages or conditions were engaging in unlawful combinations against the public interest. The cartmen gained rights and better wages, even when dealing with the conservative Federalist party.[47]

The importance of access to city contracts is indicated in the high wages paid for construction work on Broadway and Love Lane. Merchant John McComb, Sr., served as overseer of the roads between 1817 and 1821 and hired favored cartmen for "riding" stone, lime, bricks and mortar to work sites. Cartmen Richard Burke, Oliver Waldron, John Fisk and Jonas Black earned over two dollars per day for numerous jobs throughout these years. McComb also benefited from private trade with these cartmen. He supplied them with building materials which they then carted to customers. After collecting money for the materials, the cartmen repaid their sponsor. In effect, they were middlemen in transactions which required enormous trust. Customary relations between merchants and cartmen affected both public and private employment.[48]

Having established autonomy within the municipal government, the cartmen next moved to exclude the Irish permanently. This goal became more critical as the economy dipped downwards. The cartmen sent a fiery, anguished petition to Colden in 1818 demanding that the aliens be excluded from carting. Proclaiming that the "Rights, Liberties and Privileges of Freemen," were being abused, the cartmen cited themselves as veterans or sons of men who "had relinquished individual interest and substance by spilling their Blood and Laying down their Lives to obtain the rights and privileges of freemen and bequeath their inheritance to their offspring."[49] Having paid the price for the nation's freedom, the cartmen clearly believed they had the right to receive not only respect but also the protection of community and government. Throughout their appeal the cartmen enunciated their rights as "New Yorkers and as freeman," suggesting that the memory of the freemanship was still strong.

Colden, a crusty aristocrat, responded without too much sympathy. He acknowledged the concerns of the cartmen and pointed out that he had not licensed an alien in two years. Depriving those aliens of licenses, however, was inimical to the rights of free Americans. Colden suggested that the problem would take care of itself "within a few years." This did not placate the cartmen. They responded that it would take fifty years before Colden's solution would take effect and it could not be foreseen what future mayors would do. The cartmen then took the problem to the Common Council, but that body declared, after years of awarding licenses, that the power to give the right to drive a cart in New York City, as in English law, resided solely with the mayor.[50]

By this point relations between the cartmen and Colden were becoming quite strained. They were hardly helped by reports in the newspapers that the cartmen were using an outlying road, Love Lane, as a race track.

Every morning and on Saturday afternoons the carters gathered on this path to race their "swiftest pacers" with little regard for the presence of pedestrians. Indeed, one cartman even told a complaining citizen that the speed limits were not being abused, as he drove two miles per hour in the lower wards and ten near Love Lane, thus averaging out within the five mile per hour speed limit.[51]

The cartmen were becoming so rude and surly in their behavior that Colden finally called in their licenses for inspection, the third such action in only twenty years.[52] His drastic remedy put a temporary stop to the issue of alien exclusion, but only for a short while. Significantly, the cartmen sought not less protection in this incident but more. Their actions were not predicated on individual advantage, but rather on collective interests.

Colden paid for his lack of concern for the cartmen's privileges. In the next election, the cartmen voted "the Martling-way" for Tammany candidates and deserted the Federalists for the first time since 1809.[53] While the cartmen could establish patterns of loyalty, they did not cleave to a particular party or individual, but rather what that party or man could do to protect them in a changing world.

Stung by the defection of the cartmen, Mayor Colden agreed a few months later to restrict aliens to the less palatable and less lucrative business of dirt carting. This compromise gave temporary satisfaction to the cartmen, but, as we shall see, they continued their drive toward complete exclusion of the Irish.

In the first two decades of the nineteenth century the cartmen were successful in fulfilling goals of political equality and muscle. Both political parties, as well as Irish aliens and frightened ladies trying to cross Broadway, learned to respect if not admire the cartmen, "because they are a powerful group of voters." Within twenty years the cartmen moved from client status under the Federalists to a relatively autonomous position within the municipal government. They were able to retain their traditions intact and challenge the changing nature of New York's political economy. That they were able to do so is a testament not to the fairness of their principles but to the force of their actions. Those principles and actions would again be tested in coming years, but by 1818 the cartmen had become a political and social power in New York City.

CHAPTER TEN

Political Consolidation
and Challenge, 1818–1835

In the decade and a half after the alien controversy of 1818, the cartmen maintained their monopolistic grip upon intra-city transportation. Even though more carriages and hackney-coaches appeared than ever before, the cartmen still dominated city streets. The cartmen protected their secure position by vigilance toward forestallers, even if they were fellow cartmen, and toward other violators of the city regulations. Through petitions and informants the cartmen brought transgressors of city laws to the attention of the Common Council and demanded they be punished.

The cartmen's political powers continued through the 1820s. Political parties, particularly Tammany, took a lesson from the hard experiences of Federalists and Republicans. Further, the cartmen's social and political unity intersected with the economic needs of the city merchants and with the methods of control exerted by Tammany. In the election of 1824, for example, the key issue was opposition by merchants and members of the "commercial trades" to a tariff. Cartmen joined with ships' carpenters, ropemakers, blacksmiths, masons and blockmakers, "those whose interests are connected with coastal and foreign trade," to resolve in favor of the extension of unfettered commerce. Such meetings were replete with ample nativist appeals against the Irish "who were seen to be undermining trade and prices." Despite these concerns, however, the city's shipping industry boomed with an era of peace and with the completion of the Erie Canal in 1825, the cartmen's essential position within the economy was only enhanced. The number of cartmen jumped to 3000 by 1830.[1]

Tammany, which arose out of the ashes of the old Republican and Federalist parties, combined the egalitarian goals of the former with the expert patronage of the latter. Tammany was also successful in part because it did not attempt to disturb the customs and traditions of laboring groups such as the cartmen; rather the Hall tried to gain leverage with them by nativist and protectionist rhetoric. The cartmen continued to demand protective regulation and patronage from the city government. Tammany proved expert in fulfilling these needs. The maintenance of a century and a half of tradition easily kept the cartmen from having any interest in opposition platforms such as those proposed by the Workingman's party in 1829.[2]

As their relationship with city government and merchants strengthened, the cartmen's culture survived in the midst of rapid and massive changes in the society. This culture continued to be centered around the home, tavern, and blacksmith's shop. The close living patterns of previous eras were repeated in this era of enormous population growth. Cartmen began to shift away from the Sixth and Seventh Wards toward newer neighborhoods in the Eighth and Eleventh Wards. Irish dirt carters, amidst their many kinsmen, began to replace native-born cartmen in the older wards. Irish groups and carters fought in the streets on election days.[3]

The cartmen's culture still held forth at the tavern where a plethora of activities included drinking, politicking, gambling, and sports. After leaving the tavern, the cartmen felt free to race through the city streets, secure in the knowledge that neither the government, fearful of offending "so powerful a group of voters," or the watch, often composed of superannuated carters, would do much about it. City residents fumed as drunken carters turned avenues and streets into race tracks. City streets with blacksmiths' and wheelwrights' shops were clogged by carts.[4]

The 1820s was the last decade before New York City began to shift into a manufacturing and service economy. Mercantilism still reigned as the dominant philosophy. Accordingly, the presence of cartmen indicated the prosperity of an area. A contemporary poem made this point succinctly:

Next the thousand streets appear
Some filled with carts and some clear
Bespeaking where is best for trade
And where all business is dead.[5]

New Yorkers paid for this prosperity with deafened ears. The cartmen competed with the many unlicensed fruit and vegetable dealers for the citizen's ear. Street cries from chimney sweeps, hot corn girls, oyster sellers and clam men shattered the peace of urban dwellers. But such voices sang sweet songs compared with the sound of the "war of carts." The cartmen drove fiercely down city streets causing one visitor to comment on the "crashing sound of carts." Along with other reasons, the racket caused by the iron-bound cartwheels compelled many upper-class citizens quickly to leave Broadway behind for quieter locales north of Canal Street. Even there, however, they might be rudely awakened by the sound of "hundreds of cartmen, racing their vehicles at dawn."[6]

The rise of an impoverished class in New York in this era caused the carters discomfort and anxiety about the maintenance of their monopoly. The need to find employment caused many poorer New Yorkers to evade the restrictive regulations for driving a cart. A growing sentiment viewed regulation and licensing as left-over tyranny from the era of British control. Unlicensed drivers and entrepreneurs who wished to use their own carts also threatened the sanctity of the cartmen's privileges.

The cartmen were able to protect their monopoly at this time because the Common Council both agreed with their sentiments and found it politically expedient to respond to their demands. Although the Common Council had abdicated its powers in the alien dispute, it demonstrated its willingness to defend its protective laws in various judicial decisions involving carts and cartmen.

One such council decision in 1818 occurred around the time Mayor Colden was attempting to solve the alien crisis. In May of that year cartman Robert Ferguson gained a city contract for rubbish removal. Subsequently Ferguson was accused by other cartmen of using unlicensed carts and drivers on the project, thus placing him in violation of city laws and creating a dangerous precedent. Ferguson protested that he was using the unlicensed drivers on a single site off the streets and had no intention of ever using them on a city road. The council decided in favor of the complainants and ordered Ferguson to use only licensed drivers and carts and to cease using any unlicensed carts immediately.[7]

Later in 1818 came another test of the cartmen's regulations. Cartman Alexander Carlow was accused of driving two carts under one license in

"The Wood Carter," Nicolino Calyo, 1840. Courtesy of Leonard Milberg. For over two centuries the wood carter delivered measured cords to your doorstep. Credit was freely given for this essential service.

violation of regulations dating back to 1691 which forbade cartmen from owning more than one cart and horse. Such a law protected the cartmen from formation of companies which could quickly control fees and debase the value of a license. Carlow admitted driving two carts, but argued that the late mayor, Jacob Radcliffe, had given him permission to drive both carts under one license. While the council could hardly argue the veracity of his claim, it still ordered him to sell one cart immediately. Significantly, the complainants in both cases were other carters; self-enforcement remained the best insurance of regulation.[8]

Cartmen fought bitterly against forestallers even when they were trade leaders. John N. Johnson, Jr., the primary endorser of the highly successful petition of 1816, was not immune to criticism from his fellows. Johnson began carting in 1797 and worked alongside his father who began his career as a carter in 1783. Johnson, Jr., entered politics soon after getting a license

"The Dirt Carter," Nicolino Calyo, 1840. Courtesy of Leonard Milberg. Dirt removal was a constant problem in early New York. By the 1820s "dirt carters" became a separate breed of worker.

and was elected constable in 1798 and won reelection the following year. After being defeated in the Republican sweep of 1800, Johnson's political career languished until 1809 when a Federalist victory returned him to his post as constable. Reelected seven times by 1816 he became a leader among cartmen. A month after the election of 1816 he was rewarded for his help to the Federalists by the lucrative post of firewood inspector for the West Side dock area.[9]

Johnson held this post for the next three years during which he acquired a stranglehold on the best firewood coming in from New Jersey. Because Johnson controlled the flow of fuel and charged exorbitant fees for his required services, 65 wood carters filed a petition with the Common Council asking for his dismissal. Although the council agreed that Johnson should not, by law, be purchasing firewood while an inspector, it essentially ignored the complaints of cartmen and boatmen who joined in the protest.

When Johnson's Federalist patrons were defeated in 1819, he was forced out of office. He and his son, John Johnson, III, were, however, fortunate enough to obtain a contract hauling wood for the poor house. He yearned to return to his inspectorship and petitioned for his old office.[10]

Johnson may be seen as self-interested and entrepreneurial and as representative of the rise of the capitalist spirit within the laboring class. Yet his sins were ancient ones, problems for local government centuries before the birth of Adam Smith. Nevertheless, Johnson was an aberration from the traditional behavior of the cartmen. By abusing his position within the structure of government regulation and using political leverage to gain an insider's advantage, he violated the ethics of his fellows. The response was a collective petition against him; ultimately it was successful. Significantly, Johnson did not then move into the arena of private business, but spent his remaining years attempting to return to the bosom of local government patronage.

A case with large ramifications was the dispute over manure collection. This had long been one of the cartmen's most neglected duties. Over the years, the Common Council, in its desperation to clear city streets of the ubiquitous filth, awarded scavengers' contracts. An erstwhile cartman named William Hitchcock left the trade in the late 1780s to form a company and secure contracts with the city as a manure collector. Hitchcock cleared the streets of manure and used dumping sites north of the city near the Tenth Ward. In time he was named Commissioner of Streets and Scavengers. For a long time, this arrangement worked well. Hitchcock's main competitors were the hogs and goats who roamed the streets; his dumping grounds were far enough north not to bother any residents. In time, however, manure collecting became more lucrative, particularly for the Irish of the city.

Hitchcock's dumping ground attracted flies and mosquitoes, and as the city developed northwards inhabitants of the Tenth Ward, where many cartmen lived, complained that their drinking water was polluted and the air filled with an intolerable stench. The city ordered Hitchcock and the alien carters to use piers north of the city for dumping. A short time later, the council reversed an earlier decision and declared that any person wishing to pick up manure in the city, was required to take out a "dirt carter's" license. Contracts such as the one awarded to Hitchcock ceased.[11]

"Clio, the Hot Corn Girl," Nicolino Calyo, 1840. Collection of the author. Clio, the muse of history, descended to early New York City in the form of a hot corn girl. Clio's lovely, lilting voice charmed New Yorkers from 1830 until 1870. She was one of many black entrepreneurs who sold food in the city streets.

The council's apparent decision to bring "dirt carting" under city rule was evident in two test cases. A number of unlicensed carters were accused of stealing dirt from Corlear's Point, near the outskirts of the city. They were fined ten dollars each and ordered to obtain licenses before performing any further work. While this initially appeared to be a pro forma decision with little enforcement power, the city seemed determined to bring these unlicensed carters under the sanction of the law. Meanwhile, several dirt carters petitioned the city to be allowed to cart stone as well as garbage and manure. The Common Council denied the petition and ordered that dirt carters restrict themselves to substances described in the regulations: manure and dirt. In both of these cases the city moved to protect the sanctity of the cartman's licenses by restricting and punishing violators.[12]

"Dirt carting" became the solution of the alien controversy. In late 1818 the cartmen and Mayor Colden agreed to a compromise. The two sides agreed that aliens henceforth would only be allowed to hold "dirt carters' " licenses; aliens were thus forbidden to engage in the more palatable and lucrative forms of carting. By the end of the year this method was put into practice.[13]

Two years later, the cartmen. complained of "summer cartmen" working the city streets. The carters successfully petitioned for a one-year residency requirement. By 1824 the carters' drive toward exclusion culminated in a Common Council resolution regarding licenses. To drive a cart, decided the council, an applicant needed to be a citizen over the age of 21 with at least one-year residency in New York City. Local address had to be verified by the fireman every two months. Carters were required to swear that they owned their carts and were free and clear of all debts.[14]

In 1826 the council finalized its policy toward Irish aliens. The law committee recommended that a prohibition on licenses to aliens "ought to have a salutory effect. . . . To be a citizen of the United States ought to be considered a high privilege and as aliens are exempt from many duties to which citizens are liable, duties and privileges ought to go together." This clause became law.[15]

The importance of this nativist law may be seen in the rapid change in the ethnic composition of the cartmen between 1824 and 1828. In general, turnover in the trade was slight, averaging only 11 percent of the 2500 carters from 1824–1825. After the council ruling that only citizens could hold a cartmen's license, changes in the classes of cartmen mounted to nearly 20 percent between 1827 and 1828. Of 1150 Irishmen within the trade in 1824, only 640 or 55 percent were still working by 1828.[16] This massive exclusion of Irish carters set the stage for political attacks upon the cartmen's monopoly in the 1830s.

The council also moved in 1826 to restrict licenses to minors. It noted that the "practice of granting licenses to minors and to the indigent was pregnant with mischief and danger. . . . The office of cartmen has some

"The Watchman," Nicolino Calyo, 1840. Courtesy of the Old Print Shop Inc., New York City, Kenneth M. Newman. The watchman unsuccessfully tried to keep order in the city. Although many cartmen worked in the watch, they referred derisively to such officers as "dogberrys."

value except in these cases." The council ruled that there were far too many cartmen and ordered the mayor to cease providing any licenses to minors unless their father was a carter and to deny a license to any without a bond. The bond was set at $250, a prohibitive sum.[17] Clearly the council intended these regulations to give protection to the cartmen. Within a few years it moved by key decisions and resolutions to protect the trade from encroachment by the Irish, farmers and minors. By cutting down the potential number of applicants it protected resident carters from competition.

Each of the resolutions derived directly from the right of the freemanship. Although the freemanship was virtually in disuse except as an honorarium, the powers inherent in it which protected citizens were very much in force. Moreover, the council protected the rights of individual carters by preventing and curtailing the rights of private companies to hire unlicensed carters for any related work in the city. The vigilance of the cartmen was necessary to insure compliance; their dominance over the streets helped to insure it.

Petitions for licenses demonstrate the difficulty of obtaining the right to work as a carter. Robert Slater petitioned for a license noting in 1825 that, while he was not yet a citizen, he had served one year in the regiment of artillery. He was denied a license.[18] John S. Vander Pool, an indigent carter, requested a waiver of the ownership regulation. His friends were willing to loan him a horse and cart if the regulation could be relaxed. The mayor granted a license only with great reluctance and later his application was cited as an example of the kind of petition which should be denied.[19] In 1825 Samuel Edgar requested a license after his move to New York from Albany. Edgar had been a carter in Albany, where similar regulations were used. His application was accompanied by recommendations from the mayor and alderman and from His Excellency, DeWitt Clinton, Governor of New York State, "under the privy seal" of the State. Edgar received his license but the need for such distinguished referrals indicate the high degree of exclusion.[20]

An important development in the increased power of the carters was the establishment of a bureaucracy. By 1825 specific offices and functions were installed in the mayor's office to handle the cartmen's affairs. The mayor remained the official head. Immediately under him was the superintendent of carts who not only oversaw all cartman activities, but also acted

"Fulton and Market," William Bennett, 1828. Print Collection, The New York Public Library, Astor, Lenox and Tilden Foundation. Cartmen working around the principal food market of New York City. Note the fine example of a cartman in his frock on the lower left side.

as their representative. This officer, under the agreement of 1816, was nominated by the general body of cartmen. He and the inspector of carts were paid $500 and $250 annually from money taken from the license fees of the carters. The inspector's responsibility was to see that all carts were in good working order and complied with city regulations. He, for example, checked wheelbase sizes, inspected license numbers and compared them with assigned numbers. A common trick of unlicensed carters was simply to adopt a number. Licensed carters also disfigured numbers to avoid identification. The inspector handed out summonses answerable before the Common Council for reckless driving, forestalling and other violations. Eventually the inspector's position was taken over by the superintendent.[21] Underneath these two offices were the foremen of each class. They acted as street-level leaders of the carters, received additional compensation and reported to the Superintendent about day-to-day activities, vacancies and disciplinary actions. When a new class of 50 was formed, a foreman was

"Maiden Lane at South Street," William Bennett, 1834, Print Collection, The New York Public Library, Astor, Lenox and Tilden Foundations. Much of the cartmen's labor centered around the "fish-smelling wharves." Note the ease and informality with which cartmen and merchants treated each other. Even in the 1830s, the cartmen maintained their distinctive gowns, which symbolized their work tradition.

chosen from senior carters. This practice provided a limited form of mobility within the trade and gave recognition to senior carters.

Beyond the foremen lay other areas of appointment. Each year, for example, the cartmen's licenses were renewed. Cartmen appeared at City Hall to refresh their licenses and paid nominal fees which ranged from 25 cents in prosperous times to 12½ cents in times of economic distress. While the mayor was required to "lay his hands on each application" the number of applications involved made this very unlikely. During the 1820s the mayor hired part-time clerks of carts, paid about $1.40 each day, to collect license fees. A controller of carts prepared financial statements for the mayor and Common Council. His reports appeared in the *Minutes of the Common Council* and demonstrate that by the mid-1820s the city was collecting significant amounts from licenses. This money was then distributed to the incorporated Cartmen's Fund.[22]

Beyond these appointments were the armies of inspectors, weighmasters and petty officials who served the cartmen. The traditional pattern of appointing these officials from the ranks of aged and infirm carters continued in the 1820s. The petition of Erastus Smith is indicative. Smith petitioned to become a coal inspector, using his cartman experience as a qualification. He asserted that the number of coal inspectors was insufficient and that more were needed. His petition was endorsed by numerous members of the trade. The Common Council created a new position for him.[23]

Gideon Manwaring's petition for weighmaster cited his 15 years as a cartman. He, too, was approved. Soon after his appointment Manwaring became involved in a dispute. He arrived at a grocer's shop around five p.m. on a Friday to check the weights and measures. The grocer asked Manwaring to return at a less busy time. After a few hostile words, the grocer demanded to see proof of the inspector's authority. Manwaring pointed to his horse and cart and asserted, "There is authority enough. Show me your weights." However pompous, Manwaring's behavior is evidence of the high self-regard of the cartmen.[24]

Many carters enhanced their position with the city government through membership in the firemen's associations of the city. These volunteer clubs were appointed by the Common Council and were loosely organized by neighborhoods. Membership was considered highly prestigious and an ornate certificate was awarded to volunteers. Although firemen were not paid, city government assisted them in the purchase of engines and other equipment and built firehouses for them throughout the city where the "fire laddies" could await the next disaster in comfort.[25]

When the keen-eyed watchmen perched on top of fire towers did proclaim a fire, the fire companies roared out of their houses, pulling the massive engines behind them. Those with horses were at an advantage of course and their careless driving became cause for much civic rebuke. Either way, "riding the tongue" of the wagon, cartman-style, was reserved for the bravest. When two clubs arrived at the fire at the same time, fist fights broke out over the honor of battling the blaze. Such brawls alarmed New Yorkers who initiated the call for a professional force.

Once the fire was extinguished the firemen paraded their achievements through the city streets. Actually no prerequisite was necessary and firemen were known to parade at the drop of a hat. They appeared regularly at the Fourth of July celebrations, on Evacuation Day, in honor of Washington's birthday, at funerals or any other celebration. After marching up Broadway, the firemen repaired to the Bull's Head tavern on the Bowery to roast and eat fresh-killed oxen. The firemen were often joined by politicians eager to curry favor with laboring-class groups.[26]

Pageantry and glory were not the only good reasons for desiring appointment to a fireman's association. Membership was the first step up the patronage ladder in city government. Two hundred seventy-eight cartmen started their ascent as firemen between 1800 and 1831.[27] For nearly all, membership was followed by other appointments to paid positions. It assisted them in making lateral movements into other licensed occupations, including those of butchers, tavernkeepers and grocers. Seventy-seven cartmen joined the firemen, then shifted into the watch.[28] Although this post was hardly prestigious and often open to ridicule, it paid a dollar a night by the 1820s. Such income supplements were common for cartmen who used them to help make ends meet. Other cartmen used their firefighting experience as leverage to obtain appointments as hay weighers, as charcoal, wood, mahogany, manure, coal and timber inspectors or any of the many lower-echelon posts in the burgeoning city bureaucracy.[29] For cartmen on the rise in the city bureaucracy, service as a fireman made good sense.

Cartmen were also prominent in other processions. One event which tells us much about their sentiments was the commemoration of the French Revolution of 1830. The carters prepared for this parade in a mass meeting at the Fifteenth Ward hotel. There, they were urged to "honor the debt owed the French" from the American Revolution. Jonathan Knapp, secretary of the Society of Cartmen, exhorted the membership to "conduct themselves to gain the respect of all the classes of the American community . . . so that the character of cartmen may rank as high as any class."[30]

In the parade itself, Richard Robertson, foreman of the first class of cartmen since 1800, was joined by seven other carters each with over 50 years' experience. Behind them rode 300 cartmen on horseback all wearing the white frock of the trade, emblazoned with a badge representing a horse and cart, harnessed by the inscription, "cartmen" over it and a tricolored cockade hat. Underneath the badge was a commemoration of the "Evacuation Day, November 25, 1783." Central to the procession was a panorama entitled "Lafayette, disciplus, Washington, Galliae Insignia Liberator." The panorama was described as "the triumph of liberal principles, and the disenthrallment of a nation from the shackles of tyranny and oppression. In the background was the sun of science rising in splendor and dispelling the dark clouds of ignorance and superstition which have obscured the vision of the oppressed in the foreground....A branch of laurel and lilly, held together spread out on either side of the design and on the top are the arms of the United States and France, surmounted by the eagle of America whose protecting wings are extended over both. Underneath the whole is written 27, 28, 29th July, 1830."[31]

This striking panorama indicates the cartmen's adherence to the mythology of the American Revolution, their reverence for its heroes and their belief that the Revolution had rid them of the tyranny of the British. The presence of the aged cartmen affirmed their continued commitment toward the traditions of the occupation. Unlike the Constitutional Procession, which pledged an allegiance to a particular political ideology, the strengths of the cartmen in 1830 came not only from the Revolution but from within themselves.

The cartmen's protection within the city government remained strong. The Common Council also favored the past methods of labor relations. This is apparent in a ruling concerning licenses in 1826. For many years applicants for licenses petitioned the council as well as the mayor. The chief magistrate's exclusive right to award licenses was becoming blurred by the council. To avoid contact with hordes of office-seekers, the council ruled that all future petitions for licenses be directed to the mayor. The aldermen noted that the right to appoint and decline applications had been given to the mayor by charter. He had "unqualified right to license ... this power existed in English law and has long been the custom here." In an occupation so vital to society and economy as carting, the Common Council was unwilling to disturb custom.[32]

The council also reasserted its determination to establish a fair load. Since the early eighteenth century the size and shape of carts had been regulated in order to insure standard loads. Each cart was to be at least two feet four inches wide in the back and to have rungs at least four feet

Running under Carts or Coaches.

Careless children, in spite of warning, often run across the streets, and sometimes are in great danger, if not knocked down and run over, and killed. Here we see a wretched child under the wheels of a loaded cart, where it is in danger of being crushed to death, in spite of the efforts of the man to stop the horse. There are a multitude of carts constantly passing along the streets of New-York, and we advise children, before they cross, to look up and down the street.

"Running Under Carts," from Mahlon Day, *A Book of Caution for Children*, New York, 1828. Collection of the author. Cartmen and children often played a deadly game of "chicken" in the streets. Small boys were usually the losers.

above the floor. When the council routinely printed the regulations for carts in 1823, it received a petition signed by numerous cartmen asking that the standard size be repealed. The petition claimed that enforcement of the "rungs" regulation would be injurious to the cartmen. In fact, the petition claimed, calculation of the costs revealed a loss of $56,300 annually. The council was no more able than the modern reader to determine what arithmetic was used to arrive at such a figure, so it denied the petition. It asserted that "laws should be so framed as to measure out with equal justice both to buyer and seller." In so denying the petition the council reasserted the doctrine of a just price. It may, as portraits of city life of the time reveal, have been overly conservative in its ruling. Larger trucks and wagons were beginning to appear on the city streets and cartmen were forced to battle again with farmers and other teamsters who sought to break into their monopoly.[33]

The council's attempts to work equitably with both the cartmen and the public are evident in the controversy over hay carting in the early 1820s. Hay carting had long been the province of elite carters and many foremen came from its ranks. By 1820, however, petitions of numerous downtown residents indicated an inadequate number of hay carters. This problem was exacerbated during the panic of 1820 when the council agreed to set a decrease in the fixed fee for hay carting. At the council meeting, hay carters presented a petition protesting the cut in wages. The unity of the cartmen's appeal convinced the council to reinstate the old rates. Hay rates were raised along with general carting rates to keep wages apace with inflation. The council also allowed the hay carters to tack a 12½ cent fee for inspection charges on to the cartage fee.[34] Several years later the council again heard from the hay carters who complained that their present rates were less than general carting rates. Again, the council was sympathetic and the rate for a standard load of hay, measured by weighmaster, was raised to 87½ cents, establishing hay carting as a lucrative form of work.

These decisions demonstrate the council's favorable treatment of the carters. Routine renewal of most regulations, additional restrictions of licenses to nonresidents and aliens, adherence to custom in price and standard load, all testify to a determination by the council to continue its regulatory function and to preserve the transportation monopoly of the cartmen.

"View of the Parade of the New York Fire Department, *Gleason's Pictorial Drawing Room Companion,* July 5, 1851. Collection of the author. Cartmen and other citizens observe a procession of "fire Laddies." Many of the firemen came from the ranks of the carters.

Yet there were signs of change as well. Cartmen did not enjoy universal popularity or power. Many New Yorkers were outraged by their behavior. The citizens' appeals to the council reveal a desire for greater, not lesser, regulation. Public attitudes often revealed their frustration at the usual regulation of carters. In an incident in 1818 a cartman was accused of willfully running down a small boy. This came at the heels of several other incidents of reckless and dangerous driving. Although the council did little to investigate, the incidents were caustically described in the *Evening Post.* The paper noted that the carters driving at "full filt through the thronged streets has become a great and alarming nuisance." It commented that "laws we have in abundance," but those whose duty it was to enforce them were simply not doing the job. It urged that stronger laws be enacted to prevent more "serious evils." It then reported three separate incidents in which cartmen had either run down or seriously endangered pedestrians. The cartmen's attitudes were summed up in one driver's retort that the "Citizens may get out of the way."[35]

Despite the anguished and often furious comments of the citizenry about the behavior of the cartmen, little was done. Despite reports of races down Love Lane and of "hundreds of cartmen racing down the Bowary," there was general despair of the city's doing anything.[36]

The political agreements of the 1820s and the protection they gave the cartmen began to fracture with the appearance of the workingman's movement in 1829. This movement, composed largely of mechanics, journeymen and opportunistic politicians, sought the abolition of the system of city licensing. Centering their appeals upon the licensing of butchers, the workingmen demanded an end to the system of awarding market stalls through auction and license. This system, argued the workingmen, was injurious to the spirit of free trade, was a denial of the right of free Americans to enter the trade of their choice and kept the occupation in perpetual bondage to unscrupulous politicians.[37] The workingmen's petition cited numerous abuses by politicians who awarded licenses on the basis of patronage and corruption without the slightest notice of merit. It also cited the numerous instances of political coercion of the licensed trades and argued that if the system of licenses were abolished, the rights of the general citizenry would be greatly enhanced. It further argued that the licensing system was a remnant of the repressive laws of the English era.[38] The issue of licensing put the carters squarely at odds with the reform-minded "Workies." Unimpressed by the workingmen's argument that every man should have the free right to use his skills and property unhindered, the cartmen sought to keep the lid on licenses to avoid competition.

A similar threat came from a petition of city merchants requesting that the council grant them licenses so that they might employ carters who did not own horses or carts.[39] The merchants complained that the growth of the city meant that not all areas were properly serviced by the cartmen and that private carts, if licensed, would offer much needed service to outlying areas of the city.

The Society of Cartmen rose to the defense of the trade and presented a petition signed by hundreds of cartmen to the Common Council. It beseeched the city government to reaffirm their "ancient privileges." The Common Council considered the petitions in committee and, after some delay, strongly supported the position of the carters. A new code of laws on "Carts and Cartmen" stated flatly that the occupation should at all times be reserved for residents of the city, for citizens and for adults.[40] At the same time Chancellor James Kent published his influential volume, *Charter and Notes*, which reflected the consensus of legal opinion in the city. Kent commented on the duty of the mayor and Common Council to regulate the carters "because the business and trade of the city and the comfort and safety of the persons and property of all classes of citizens" was dependent upon regulation of the trade. According to Kent, "all classes of the city are concerned with the regulation of the cartmen."[41] The destiny of the cartmen remained intertwined with public conceptions of fair practices. New Yorkers were not about to permit such an essential occupation to go uncontrolled.

Although the cartmen escaped with their privileges intact, the Workingmen's Petition was a harbinger of things to come. The Tammany Society began to adopt the ideology of the "Workies" as a method to deter discontent.[42]

Tammany had other problems as well. As the local representative of Andrew Jackson's Democratic party, it had to defend his banking policies which were receiving mixed responses in New York. The political campaign of 1834, the first in which New Yorkers were able to elect a mayor, indicates the great inroads the Whig party was able to make into the cartmen's loyalty to Tammany.[43]

The Whigs, composed of disaffected Democrats and many merchants, aimed much of their strategy at the "commercial trades," particularly the cartmen. "The cartmen should have a meeting," exhorted the *New York Evening Post*. "They must be sensible to the change in their condition . . . they do not earn half as much as they used to," declared a *New York Star* editorial which insisted upon the mutual suffering of merchants and cartmen from the "tyrannical" banking policies of Andrew Jackson.[44]

The Society of Cartmen posted an invitation signed by over 400 carters to a meeting held at the Fifteenth Ward Hotel. At the meeting Jackson was blamed for "deranging the currency and striking a death blow to the laboring part of the community." A Committee of Five, led by a new cartman leader, Robert Milliken, sponsored resolutions supporting the Whigs, condemning Jackson for being surrounded by "irresponsible men," and affirming that the election was not a contest between rich and poor, but for "tyranny or the Constitution." A second meeting days later urged that other "commercial trades," such as sailors, blacksmiths, stevedores, porters and ships' carpenters, join in the cartmen's protest.[45]

Subsequent meetings chaired by Milliken passed resolutions stating that Jackson was "not worth the drayage . . . that it is time to dump him into the dock of disgrace and load up something better." Much like the election slogans of the 1790s which used trade language and images to make political capital, the Whig campaign cut into the cartmen's support for Tammany.[46]

Milliken and his cohorts were very well organized. On the day of the election a 26-member finance committee, one member for each 50 man "class" of cartmen, collected dues from each carter for the Old Man's General Committee and urged support for Gulian Ver Planck, the Whig mayoral candidate. To avoid coercion at the polls, cartmen were advised to vote in groups.[47]

The election itself was a stunning victory for the Whigs. Despite the Democrats' razor-thin victory in the mayoralty, abetted by a riot in the Sixth Ward in which "inoffensive cartmen were attacked," the Whigs captured the majority in the Common Council. A victory celebration was planned for Castle Garden a few days after the election. Among the featured luminaries was Robert Milliken. He offered numerous toasts couched in the language of carting. The first declared that the "cart of state has broken its haims and unless taken to the Constitutional Blacksmith, the cart will go to pieces and the load will be lost." The mayor-elect, Jacob Lawrence, was like a "cart without a horse." Over a thousand carters in attendance roared their approval as Milliken declared that the "Albany Regency has broken down, baulked the old horse and thrown its cunning driver (Van Buren)."[48]

The election demonstrated the trade solidarity of the cartmen and their concern over economic issues mixed with the ideology of the Constitution and the American Revolution. The carters organized themselves, developed their own leadership and voted according to their own interests. The Whigs were able to tap traditional interdependencies between merchants and cartmen by directly addressing the trade's grievances.

The election of 1834 broke the 15-year partnership of Tammany and the cartmen. The insurgent Whigs, composed of disaffected bankers and merchants, were able to secure political favor with the cartmen by appealing to the economic interdependencies. As the consensus of the revolutionary era faltered in the face of a changing society and economy, the cartmen returned to their old allegiance with the merchants. Threatened by "newly-minted citizens," most notably the Irish, and by the widening influence of the Workingman's party, Tammany attempted to absorb those pressures. This meant, however, that Tammany had to loosen its cozy relationship with the cartmen. As the city's population grew even larger and the Irish vote more important, the cartmen's vote lost some of the allure of previous years. When the Irish tried to batter down the cartmen's monopoly through politics and fistfights in the streets, the carters faced their greatest crisis in decades.

Tradition saved them in 1834. Chancellor Kent's affirmation of the positive value of regulating the cartmen still rang true to pedestrians trying to cross Broadway, but was less convincing to Irish and black wagoners who wished to work freely in New York City. As the crusade against licensing grew louder in the 1830s, the cartmen's battle for survival was just beginning.

Their new relationship with the Whigs was perhaps natural and stemmed from historic ties with the Federalist Party, but it had serious drawbacks. After nearly twenty years of equality in negotiations with city officials, the cartmen were now part of the minority party again. Continuation of their monopoly required being part of the majority.

CHAPTER ELEVEN

The World of Isaac Lyon:
Continuity and Change, 1835–1845

Great fires swept New York City in 1835 and 1836, destroying acres of homes and businesses. In the midst of these disasters citizens complained bitterly of cartmen who charged exorbitant rates for moving possessions away from the flames or who refused to serve any but the wealthy. Similar criticism had been heard during the cholera epidemic of 1832.[1] Such predatory behavior by the cartmen was familiar throughout their history, but now their actions and the angry reactions of the city and residents signaled the emergence of new philosophies toward municipal control over the occupation. This development, translated into the political realm and into the streets, greatly hampered the cartmen's ability to retain a grip on local transportation.

The citizens' displeasure at the cartmen had long been a fact of urban life. In the eighteenth century, New Yorkers could count on the Common Council to slap heavy fines or suspensions upon the carters. By the early nineteenth century, however, the carters' political clout made effective action against their depredations rather difficult. In fact, the Common Council seemed to shield the trade against the complaints of irate citizens.

By 1836 there was a political alternative. Although the Workingman's party had achieved little electoral success, it did affect the political habits of the Democratic party and its local organization, Tammany. Combined with the desires of newly made Irish citizens for greater political power, easier access to occupations such as the carter's and to party patronage, the ideas espoused by the Workingman's Petition of 1829 were fast becoming political wisdom.[2] Sensing a change in New York's political climate, Tammany was quick to embrace such attitudes and bring the disenchanted "workies" and the Irish into the fold. As Tammany welcomed the Irish into the party, more were able to attain patronage posts within the government. One rapidly expanding municipal department was street cleaning and sanitation.[3]

The cartmen largely went over to the Whig party. Seduced by Whig assertions of patriotism, nativism and the natural alliance of merchants and "commercial trades," the cartmen gave heavy support to Whig candidates in annual elections. Unfortunately, the Whigs were seldom able to dislodge the Tammany coalition which meant the carters supported a minority party, further endangering their corporate protection.

The rate-gouging by the cartmen demonstrated a change in their attitudes toward city governance. True, few cartmen in the past ever resisted an opportunity to make the best of someone else's misfortune, but previously such opportunism was more the exception than the rule. By 1835 the cartmen were regularly violating public conceptions of fair and just prices. In so doing the carters further alienated public attitudes, damaging their chances to maintain their monopoly.[4] The doors of opportunity in government patronage were still closed in the late 1830s to Irish aliens and black New Yorkers. Even as Irish immigrants were making initial gains into the patronage of local governments, particularly as "dirt carters," Whig opponents of this assimilation mirrored the attitudes of many native-born Americans by condemning and ridiculing the Irish. Similarly, that group long oppressed and excluded by American society, the free black American, found little access to public office or trade in this period. The cartmen in particular practiced segregation. They were joined in this by virtually every other licensed trade with the exception of hackney coach drivers and chimney sweeps whose ranks were filled by "free" black New Yorkers. Petty public offices such as clerks, inspectors, gaugers, measurers and overseers were closed to African Americans. One looks in vain in the civil lists for black New Yorkers benefiting from the patronage which provided an income for their white counterparts.[5] Nor were attempts to improve blacks' conditions acceptable. Abolitionists were met by riots, destruction of printing presses and savage violence.[6]

Cartman Isaac Lyon's memoirs illustrate these continuities and changes. Isaac Lyon was born in Parsippany, New Jersey, in 1807, the son and grandson of rural cartmen. He spent much of his early life in Boonton, New Jersey, a town near his birthplace. There he worked as a store clerk, apprentice carpenter and schoolteacher. This latter position came from his association with the local elite in the Boonton Literary Club where Lyon formed his lifelong love for books. In 1834 he married Jane Davenport of New York City and in the Spring of 1835 Lyon and his wife, pregnant with their first child, moved to New York City.[7] Their first home was at 159 West 13th Street in the Fifteenth Ward which by this time had found the reputation of the "Home of America's truckmen," because of the many cartmen living there.[8] Lyon at first tried to earn a living as a carpenter, but after the birth of his daughter, Mary, in April, 1835, he acquired a horse and cart and became a licensed cartman. After painting license number 2489 on the side of his cart, Lyon was ready for business.[9]

Jane Davenport Lyon gave birth to seven children of which three survived to adulthood. The Lyon family was highly traditional and close-knit. Lyon's children stayed in the household to late in adulthood until they were able to find homes of their own. May, their first daughter, never did leave the home and took care of her parents.[10]

Although from New Jersey, Lyon identified strongly with New York City. He praised the cartmen as the most knowledgeable New Yorkers. The cartman, he argued, had to "know everybody and everything . . . the exact locations . . . what time a ship sails and whether there were any runaways on board." Lyon's reference to self-emancipated slaves is a rare but telling reference indicating that white workers aided slave catchers hunting down self-emancipated enslaved people. By the time of his first annual license renewal, a cartman "should know all the churches, schoolhouses, preachers and professors." "If he don't know these things and a good deal more," claimed Lyon, "then he is set down as a know-nothing." Lyon pointed out that the cartman was the most ubiquitous of New Yorkers. His tasks took him to the "damp and loathsome vaults of the dead . . . to the stately marble palaces of the rich, into the attics of six-story hotels and down to the fish-smelling wharves . . . into the vaults of banks and into a lady's dressing room." Lyon claimed that "no one questioned why he is there . . . everyone supposes that it's all right." Moreover, the cartman, according to Lyon, was among the most virtuous of New Yorkers. He was "true as steel and could be trusted by everyone." The cartman of 1835 was an "honest, intelligent and upright man," who was "known by his cartman's frock and open, hon-est countenance." Secrets were confided to the cartman "by ladies of the very highest standing." Businessmen valued a cartman of good character as "a person of more than ordinary intelligence and importance and treated him accordingly." For Lyon, "New York is the greatest and the fastest town," and "none can surpass the cartman's knowledge of it."[11]

Like other cartmen, Lyon was a strong patriot. He revered the memory of the American Revolution and its greatest hero, George Washington. Ly-on's first published work was a homage to Washington in which he argued for a monument to the first president. Lyon argued that because New York-ers had "more benefited and enriched from the labors of Washington than the people of any other portion of the country," the city should be the site of a monument to him. Costs for construction, claimed Lyon, could eas-ily be borne by donations of one dollar per year from each of the city's 400,000 inhabitants. The citizens of New York "would willingly pledge themselves to contribute any amount desired," and in appreciation for their gifts, each donor's name would be chiseled into the inner walls of the mon-ument."[12]

Lyon was a nativist and racist. Unlike some of the harsher negrophobes of his day, Isaac Lyon was more condescending to blacks than openly hos-tile. He frequently employed them as helpers, but used contemptuous labels for their names. Later he wrote that the Civil War had been a mistake and the Fifteenth Amendment was "illegal and immoral." He was even more hostile to the Irish who were displacing native-born carters like Lyon. His memoirs include numerous anecdotes in which Irish characters are pick-pockets, prostitutes, charlatan beggars, counterfeiters and horse thieves. Each time "Paddy" is mentioned in Lyon's memoirs, it is with derision and distrust. Nor were Irish carters treated with any sense of equality. Rather they were to be scorned as "dirt carters" to whom one sells a horse when it is on its last legs, or as dangerous and reckless drivers to be avoided in the streets.[13]

Yet, Lyon was fiercely egalitarian. He had several altercations with mid-dle-class citizens who attempted to tell him how to run his business. In each instance, Lyon's knowledge of the city and of his rights won the day. He had a particular animosity toward ministers. His cart-stand was in front of St. Thomas's Church at the corner of Broadway and Houston Street and though he was a member of the church, Lyon showed great hostility toward clergymen who failed to live up to their principles. In one incident Lyon provided firewood to a pastor on credit and then called at the end of the month for his payment. The pastor put Lyon off by offering him food, card games with his daughters and finally outright evasion. When eventually Lyon learned that the pastor had pulled a similar trick on other carters, he threatened legal action. Only in the face of a suit and possible imprisonment did the minister come across with payment in Canadian money which Lyon found to be heavily discounted.

Lyon deeply disliked ostentatious behavior. He ridiculed "young gentlemen" as "unwilling to work" and noted with grim satisfaction that he had frequently "carted young gentlemen down to the Bridewell." He also related tales of outwitting "smart young fellows" and exposing "stock-jobbers" as little more than crooks. As in English working-class autobiographies, Lyon's memoirs are filled with many incidents of the hypocrisy of ministers and other "professionals," and the immorality of young gentlemen.[14]

As a sign of changing behavior, Isaac Lyon did not use the standard fees set by the Common Council. He charged customers according to the difficulty of his labors. Once Lyon was hired by several "young gentlemen" to rush their trunks over to the wharf for the Albany steamer. After lashing his horse through the streets in hot pursuit of the fast-approaching time of departure, Lyon demanded twice the fixed fee. When the men protested, Lyon argued that the standard rate was for driving at an average speed, "while this rate pays for almost killing my horse." Lyon won the argument. In other incidents Lyon charged not what the city rate was, but what seemed fair to him. He claimed never to have overcharged, but only to have gotten what he perceived his labors were worth.[15]

Lyon was different from other cartmen in one unusual respect. Whereas most cartmen still indulged themselves with bull baiting, cart-races or visits to the Vauxhall, Lyon found his greatest pleasure in a book. He would await work at his cart-stand, reclining on his cart-tail, reading *Paradise Lost, Tristam Shandy* or *Stow's Survey of London*. Lyon became a keen book collector while moonlighting as nightwatchman in a bookstore. He avidly accumulated history books and even owned copies of the first editions of Stow's *London* and Daniel Denton's *Survey of New York*. Lyon became an expert bidder at auctions and was able to acquire, for example, numerous imprints by Benjamin Franklin's press. Later he became an amateur historian who lectured and published a book on the history of Boonton.[16]

Isaac Lyon was fiercely independent, proud of his occupation and defiant toward those who would impose deference upon him. Although he gave respect to honest employers, he viewed the emerging professional classes such as professors and doctors with suspicion and perceived lawyers as "little better than thieves."[17] At the same time he had little sympathy for those below him in status. Lyon described blacks and the Irish with undisguised opprobrium. Beggars and other poor were viewed as fakers and thieves. Lyon proclaimed that if a man was willing to work, America "would give him an income." That, according to Lyon, "was as much as any man could ask."[18]

Lyon's views on his fellow citizens reveal an ill-concealed class resentment. He was aware of the many changes sweeping New York City and was clearly unhappy with its enormous population growth, the arrival of the Irish and the acceptance of "forestallers and engrossers." Lyon's cartman was a character who upheld values of honesty, hard work, patriotism, family and pride in his trade in the midst of swirling change. This change he found unfortunate because "New York may be a great deal larger and faster, but it's no better."[19]

Isaac Lyon was but one of 3400 cartmen in 1840, but his brethren were much like him, with the exception of his literary interests and talents. The men who signed the "Oath of the cartman" to uphold the laws of New York City were similar to trade ancestors. Anglo-Americans and Dutch continued to dominate the trade. The restrictive laws relegating Irish immigrants to "dirt carting" meant few Irish were among the numbers of "catch carters" on the mayor's list.[20] Sons of cartmen from past eras were common among the ranks of cartmen. Abraham Romaine was the son of Casparus Romaine. James Brower the son of Peter Brower. Abraham Banta, Jr., took over his father's license. William and Charles Vanderhoof first received their cartman's licenses as minors in 1810. James Demarest was the grandson of David Demarest, a freemanship carter and Revolutionary War veteran. The Blauveldt family was represented by William, Cornelius, Steven and Abraham, all sons or nephews of past cartmen. Abraham Ackerman's son, John, received a license in 1838. Mathew Ely was the son of Moses Ely; his cousin, William Coddington, was the son of Abraham Coddington who had so many troubles with merchants around the turn of the nineteenth century. Such family associations helped the cartmen to maintain traditional attitudes and to preserve cultural traits. One sign of modernity was literacy. Of the 2400 cartmen in 1836, 2100 or 87 percent could sign their own names.[21]

Although Isaac Lyon seldom mentioned the benefits of government protection and patronage, other cartmen of this time continued to seek help from the Common Council. During the panic and depression of 1836–1837, for example, the carters went to the Common Council for assistance on several occasions. Manure carters received an increase in pay from $2 to $2.50 per day from the Common Council in 1836.[22] At the same time a petition from over 1500 cartmen asked successfully that the price for renewal of a license be lowered to 12½ cents.[23] As the panic of 1836 continued the Common Council used past methods of relief by ordering the superintendent of streets to hire as "many cartmen to clean the streets as necessary."[24] The carters fortunate to gain these jobs were paid $2.50 per day which was far above the wages paid to skilled labor at the time. Yet even that proved not sufficient and the following Spring, 750 cartmen went to the Common Council to seek a second increase in pay to $3 per day; this time they were unsuccessful.[25]

The Common Council did move to protect the cartmen in other areas. In 1835 it declared that the superintendent of carts should be more vigilant in detecting unlicensed carts. The practice of "persons not licensed to transport to various parts of the city goods sold by them in their own carts and to charge cartage to the purchaser was unfair to the cartmen" argued the council. It ordered that a ten dollar fine be levied on any business or person who used "an unlicensed cart" or who hired unlicensed drivers.[26] Such intentions, however, were difficult to fulfill. Although Isaac Lyon referred to the 1830s as the "Golden Age of Carting" because there was so little competition from railroads, express wagons, farm wagons and omnibuses, there were far more vehicles on the streets than ever before. By the 1840s the streets were clogged by vehicles of all sizes and shapes, many of which were in direct competition with the cartmen. Further, New York was no longer a compact "walking city" but stretched far up the island. The multiplicity of streets was impossible to police and as cartmen preferred working downtown along Broadway or at the docks, the upper regions of the city were open to exploitation by unlicensed drivers.

A Common Council ruling in 1837 had a twofold effect upon the cart-man's monopoly. Many New Yorkers were ruined by debt in the depression of 1837. The laws governing carts and cartmen had perennially affirmed that each cartman should own his cart and horse "free and clear of debt." This law was on the book to prevent secret ownership of carts and horses by second parties or companies; it thus kept the cartmen independent. It also meant that in case of accident or loss, the cartman would be liable, not some invisible investor.[27]

But in 1837 this law was hindering many carters from working. Cart-ers beset by indebtedness could not therefore renew their licenses, thereby creating further misery. The council found it unjust that "a cartman of well-established character and business obtained by years of labor, should, by the thousand causes which are daily ruining honest and confiding men, be de-prived of the means of supporting his family." The council ruled that the section of the cartman's law be changed to allow cartmen in debt to renew their licenses. While this innovation clearly was needed to permit cartmen hurt by the economy to continue work, it also opened the door for capital-ist investment in the ownership of carts and horses.[28]

Reform measures did not effect racial exclusion in carting. The coun-cil and mayor continued to bar blacks from carting. In 1836 a "free" black named William S. Hewlett, who had been employed as a porter, petitioned the mayor for a cartmen's license, using forty firms as refer-ences. He was described as "a worthy man, honest, temperate, of ami-able disposition, muscular frame and good address being a member of the Society of Friends." Hewlett owned property on William Street but wished to work with his own hands. The mayor, despite these glowing recommendations, refused to grant Hewlett a license "on the grounds of public opinion."[29]

Three years later Anthony Provost, another black man, applied for a li-cense. He had "as good a horse and cart as was to be seen on any dock." Provost was described as "being of high moral character" in a petition signed by some of the "heaviest millionaire leather dealers in the swamp," and by "some of the oldest and most respectable cartmen." When Provost approached the mayor he was told that "it was not customary for colored men to drive carts in the city." Provost, however, drove without a license and fared well until a number of white cartmen complained. He was fined

"May Day," from Henry Peter Finn, *Comic-Annual of 1831*, (Boston, 1831). Print Collection, The New York Public Library, Astor, Lenox and Tilden Foundations. Americans were greatly amused by this image of an overloaded cart on New York's frantic moving day.

and ordered to sell his horse and cart. Provost was "forced to betake himself to more menial employment."[30]

Samuel Cornish, the editor of the *Colored American*, the leading black newspaper in New York, attacked the official excuses of Mayor Cornelius Lawrence. Lawrence reportedly said that he denied licenses to blacks to protect them from whites "who might dump their horses and cart into the river." Who are these cartmen?" demanded Cornish rhetorically. Were they, he wrote, "savage, illiterate barbarians?" Taking a different tack from the usual complaints about cartmen racism, Cornish appealed to the cartmen's sense of fairness and argued that ordinary carters had no objections to accepting blacks into their ranks. He stated that cartmen were men or moral worth and enterprise who did not discriminate. Rather the fault lay with the municipal government which retained the old discriminatory policies. Cornish noted how ironic were the cartmen's demands for equality in white society where "they are leaders in the cause of equal rights for themselves."[31] But was not the mayor bound to protect all citizens? A correspondent in the *New York Emancipator* replied that Mayor Lawrence was catering to southern slaveholders and plunderers by keeping the black man down: "We will keep them poor . . . lest they should arise and give your

Isaac S Lyon

"Isaac Lyon (1807–1882)." Collection of Boonton, New Jersey Historical Society. Isaac Lyon was a cartman, historian, poet, and citizen.

doctrine the lie."[32] Such well-placed criticism did not sway the mayor or Common Council, though, and no blacks were licensed as cartmen. Not until the mayoralty of Fernando Wood in the 1850s could blacks obtain a cartman's license. Even in the twentieth century, few blacks were permitted in the transportation industry of New York City.[33]

Racial restrictions were not the only source of criticism of the cartmen. Emerging animal rights advocates focused on carterly mistreatment of their horses. In the nineteenth century, horses were often regarded as "living machines," with limited utility and without the sympathy of past eras. Beginning in the 1840s, middle class urbanities criticized the cartmen's abuse of their horses and sought, though regulation, how the carters treated their animals.[34]

Such racial discrimination, combined with the other protections provided by the government, gave a continued framework to the white cartmen's culture. The cartman's way of life was much like before, despite the enormous growth in the city's ethnic population. The cartman's culture was still neighborhood-based and constructed around favorite taverns, blacksmiths' and wheelwrights' shops. Certain neighborhoods, the Fifteenth and the Eighth, were known as the "Cartmen's" wards. Within these wards, the trade dominated many streets. For example, 56 of Isaac Lyon's neighbors on West 13th Street were cartmen.[35]

The cartman was still largely the master of his own destiny. Isaac Lyon rode from his home down to his cart-stand at Broadway and Houston Street each morning. There he sat reading a book while waiting for work. Lyon printed a business card identifying himself as a "fine arts carter" who specialized in moving antiques and rarities. He also worked as a wood carter. Although city laws required him to work for any citizen who requested his services, Lyon often flouted the law and had "preferred customers."[36]

He demanded equality for his fares. Lyon expected that a customer would sit down with him for a drink sometime during the job and discuss life. If the customer proved convivial, Lyon would buy him a drink. Lunch was eaten on the street at any one of the hundreds of oyster and fruit stands. Usually Lyon finished the day by three o'clock, repaired to the tavern or headed home. There he would eat his supper with his family, spend a little time in the evening collecting bills from his steady customers or attend

FIRST OF MAY IN NEW YORK.

The good people of Gotham seem to possess an irresistible desire to change their residences on the first of May annually, and the ludicrous scenes produced by everybody, and everybody's furniture, being in the street at the same time, has been the subject of many a humorous poem and laughable prose sketch. Our artist has taken his cue from life, and the mad scene he has given us above is no exaggeration upon the actual truth. Porters, draymen, men, women and children, horses and carts, dogs and pigs, all seem licensed on this day to run [...] restrained, but to appreciate the picture one must have been in New York on the first of May, and run the risk of his life, by being run over and trampled upon by the motley crowd of men and animals. In New England now, the first of May is a sort of annual holiday, when people go into the country for a breath of fragrant and pure air, and to join each other in the festivities often of dancing about the May pole as they until no one in olden times, and as we in civilized in our last number. The first of May in New York is a very different occasion.

May Day chaos in the streets. Undated image. Collection of the author.

a book auction. Though it does not sound as if Lyon worked too hard, he earned enough to leave New York City in 1855 with $2000 for retirement at the age of 48. But other than improvement of his mind, Isaac Lyon was not interested in social mobility. He was a cartman and that was good enough for him, and to use one of his favorite phrases, "Why shouldn't it be?" He had enough income to support his family easily, was intellectually vigorous and healthy and was part of a great tradition of labor which prided itself on independence and worthiness. Lyon's knowledge of the city, common to any worthwhile cartman, was, in his opinion, the equivalent of the learning of any professional.[37]

The one day of the year on which the cartmen did strive to accumulate as much as possible was May Day. The First of May was moving day in New York City. A quirk of city law required that all tenants be out of their apartments or houses by nine o'clock in the morning and into their new lodgings by noon. Those three hours produced a mad rush for carts

THE FIRST OF MAY IN NEW YORK CITY.—[DRAWN BY THOMAS WORTH.]

Cartmen and middle-class New Yorkers negotiated terms on May Day. Source: *Harper's Weekly*, May 8, 1869. Collection of the author.

"City Enormities—Every Brute Can Beat His Beast," *Frank Leslie's Illustrated Newspaper,* October 28, 1865. Collection of the author. This graphic illustration of the cartmen's brutality toward their horses prompted the establishment of the American Society for Prevention of Cruelty toward Animals. This illustration was used by the society for many years as a call to arms.

to move family possessions. On May Day, noted Lyon, proudly, everybody referred to him as "Mr. Cartman."[38] All day long "streets were filled with loaded drays on which are pitched tables and carpets rolling to and fro." A visitor to New York City, Dr. Joel Ross, observed that "everyone is lucky who does not get a bumped head, a strained back or a torn coat from May-Day."[39] An anonymous poet's appreciation of this event described the "clouds of dust raised by a couple of thousand cartmen."[40]

Fuller description of the event is found in Seba Smith's novel, *May-Day in New York or House-Hunting and Moving.*[41] The novel's narrator, a suspicious, cunning Yankee named Major Jack Downing of Downingville, New England, attempted to find a flat in the northern section of Greenwich Village, not far from Isaac Lyon's home. Major Jack was astonished at the dirt in the street and the number of hogs. He noticed that "you see more hogs walking the streets down here in half an hour than you should see in

"Arrested for Cruelty," *Harper's Weekly,* January 13, 1872. Collection of the author. A second example of the ASPCA's campaign to reform the cartmen's treatment of their horses.

Downingville in a whole year." Particularly disturbing were the "shabby streets, chock fill with hogs and boys and you couldn't hardly tell which was which." After some hilarious encounters with landlords who were beginning to achieve their modern reputation, Downing rented a flat. The next step was to hire a cart to move his "housen-stuff."[42]

He noticed that "there wasn't no ox-teams sich as we have in Downingville, but there was no end to the one-horse teams hauling little carts and going like split atoms all over the city."[43] Despite the carts going "full chisel," Downing stood in the middle of the road trying to flag one down. After nearly being run down he was dismayed to see the carter thumb his nose at him and drive along. After several futile attempts and insults, Downing finally forced one driver to stop. When he offered two dollars to the carter, the reply was that nothing less than ten dollars would do on May Day. When Downing protested that two dollars was the standard rate, the cartman sneered, "You must be pretty green," thumbed his nose at Major

Jack and sped away. It took Major Jack a long time to move his goods that day.[44]

An actual rather than fictional incident on May Day suggests that the citizens might have had a little more recourse to the law than Smith's novel indicates. On May 1, 1835, a cartman was employed by a woman to move a load of furniture from Mulberry Street to Anthony Street. He loaded his cart and drove off unaccompanied by his customer. On arriving at the new house, he was informed that someone else lived there and that his customer had no right to send the goods to the house. The cartman then moved the goods back to Mulberry Street, but in the interim a new set of tenants occupied the old quarters and refused to let the furniture be moved back in again. The cartman could not find the woman who employed him and as he pondered his situation, a second woman came up to his cart and claimed possession. In order to show her determination, she mounted the top of the cart and sat on the pile of goods. Nothing the cartman could say would convince her to leave.

The cartman's problems were now doubled. If he dumped the load, then he must dump the lady as well. Then she could arrest him for assault and battery. He took the load and lady over to the police office where his situation was greeted by much merriment. Finding no assistance there, he decided against all hazards to cart the lady and load back to Mulberry Street and there dump them in the middle of the road.[45]

May Day problems were fleeting. More ominous political trends threatened the carters' monopoly. There were signs of change at hand. The drive toward deregulation increased amidst charges of corruption and mismanagement within the government. The merchants, who long had been the primary protectors of the cartmen's monopoly, now declined in influence on the Common Council. Moreover, their attitudes were changing as more retailers became wealthy merchants. Retailers had few of the loyalties to the cartmen felt by the older merchants. The city was also growing too large to permit effective enforcement of the cartmen's monopoly. The city government accepted this fact in 1837 when it declared that the laws governing carts did not apply north of 48th Street.[46]

In 1841 the Common Council struck a major blow against the licensed monopolies of the city when it repealed the market laws on the grounds that "they no longer are observed and do not serve the people's interests." A howl of protest arose from the licensed butchers who saw the value of their leases on market stalls vanish overnight. Despite their claims, the Common Council upheld the new law.[47]

The following year the Special Committee on the Contracts for Cleaning the Streets performed an audit on the hiring of cartmen to cleanse the streets. It found that the street department was spending over $35,000 annually to hire independent cartmen to work for the city. The committee recommended that the government hire cartmen on a permanent basis to avoid such costly contracting. Thus began the Department of Sanitation. For many carters it meant a permanent position, but it also continued the division within the trade between city employees and independent carters.[48]

On August 1, 1842, James McCabe presented a petition to the Common Council seeking licenses for his wagons "for the purpose of delivering small parcels through the city." Two days later the cartmen and porters presented a remonstrance against granting licenses to McCabe.[49] The stage was set for a battle over the cartmen's monopoly. After some debate the Committee on Ordinances stated that McCabe's petition sought a license to have "a number of horses and waggons and to employ persons to drive them and thus monopolize all the trade of carrying small parcels and consequently, none but heavy packages would fall to the share of the cartmen." This, in the opinion of the council, "would be an act of gross injustice to this highly respectable portion of the community and is contrary to the spirit of the constitution under which we live, that guarantees to all, both rich and poor, equal justice and equal rights." The council denied McCabe's petition.[50]

Even though these ringing affirmations of their rights must have heartened the cartmen, their licensed privileges still hung on the thread of a council decision. Uptown real estate interests and retailers continued to press for licensed companies. The following year, on September 5, 1842, McCabe was back again, this time with the assistance of a number of lawyers, headed by Edward Kent, a nephew of Chancellor William Kent.

Rather than press the issue of competition with the cartmen, the petitions of Kent and McCabe alluded to poor service in the northern areas of the city and the need to provide proper transportation in those areas. This worked well with the Common Council. On January 3, 1843, the Committee on Laws stated that it was "of the opinion that the great extent of the city and its constant increase seems to call loudly for additional facilities to our citizens in the transacting of their daily business." The committee recommended that McCabe and Company be given licenses.[51]

The cartmen protested that the committee's decision would "insure slavery for all of them." The council responded that the licenses in no way affected their privileges, that separate, licenses would be given to each vehicle and that supervision of McCabe's wagons would remain under the superintendent of carts. Furthermore, licenses for McCabe and other applicants like him would be ten dollars as opposed to the usual fee of twenty-five cents.[52]

Despite these assurances the cartmen's control over intra-city transportation was finished. The new laws not only allowed companies to hire carters at debased wages but they also permitted aliens to enter the lucrative commodity trade. The two principal pillars of the cartmen's protections were demolished.

In truth, time had run out on the carters. The city was now much too large to support their monopoly. Rapid changes in transportation technology rendered their two-wheeled carts obsolete. While the city government was quite willing to continue to accept fees for licensing their carts, its philosophy of government no longer afforded protection. The cartmen were no longer as important politically as in the past when their votes could swing an election. Now their powers were outstripped by retailers or by Irish citizens who wished the cartmen's privileges destroyed so they could have equal access to the city streets.

Perhaps the cartmen were their own worst enemies. By refusing to accommodate the demands of the Irish, they created an opposition which eventually overwhelmed them. Yet xenophobia had been a trait of cartmen for generations and they could hardly be asked to think reasonably in a time of rapid change.

Nor could they be expected to understand that the merchants, their traditional allies, were losing power in the city. Retailers and real estate speculators, who had little interest in the traditional rights of the cartmen, gained power in the 1840s.

"August in Town—Broadway, Opposite St. Paul's Church," *Harper's Weekly,* August 3, 1859. Collection of the author. By the 1850s the cartmen and their two-wheeled carts were but a small part of the sea of vehicles crowding New York's most important throughfare.

Within a few years a reform of the city charter stripped the laws on carts and cartmen of all the old protections with the exception of the feeble injunctions against aliens and nonresidents, laws observed more in the breach than in practice. The council declared that it was removing most of the cartmen's laws "because they were really unnecessary." The new philosophy of government favored a relaxation of older forms of regulation,[53] negating the exclusive privileges once held by the cartmen and forever destroying their once-tight bond with the city.

CHAPTER TWELVE

Epilogue

On July 23, 1850, over 1000 cartmen on horseback paraded down Broadway in a procession in memory of Whig President Zachary Taylor. The cartmen, who had been planning for the event since Taylor's death on July 9, were, according to the *New York Tribune,* one of the most impressive sights in the parade. The Society of Cartmen used the occasion to promote trade unity by beseeching all carters to attend whether they wore "frocks or citizen's clothing." After the parade carters joined other Whigs at dinners commemorating Taylor's career. Ritualized toasts saluted the political marriage of Whigs and cartmen. The massive turnout, the demonstrations of allegiance toward the Whigs and the fervent patriotism all evoked cartman unity of previous times. At the same time the sight of cartmen marching without their frocks indicated a more divided and troubled future.[1]

For over 200 years the cartmen dominated transportation in the city. The key to this control was government regulation. Until the 1840s the municipal government, run by mercantilist politicians, protected the cartmen against any attempts at reform. Believing that regulation of the carters was essential to a stable society and economy, politicians allowed the trade to develop a substantial and autonomous bureaucracy within the city government to defend its monopoly. After 1844, however, political power in New York shifted from merchants to manufacturers who were thoroughly imbued with newer philosophies of free labor and markets. For such men, the cartmen's privileges were vestiges of English rule and as such were undemocratic, hampered American initiative and fostered corruption. By 1849 charter reforms swept away all but the skeleton of the cartmen's regulations.

Although still required, the license lost much of its value when the numbers of cartmen increased to over 8000 by 1855; many cartmen worked for companies and could be discharged at will. This introduction of capitalist labor relations into carting produced another change as well. For generations carters had been general laborers required to perform any task for any citizen. Some specialization had occurred earlier in wood and hay delivery and in manure and garbage collection. But most cartmen worked on many different jobs. By the 1850s cartmen working for employers became much more dispersed throughout the economy and developed greater allegiances to businesses than to the collective efforts of the trade.

Carting was again changing along ethnic lines. Irish New Yorkers, benefiting by their association with Tammany, became the largest group within carting by 1855. Irish carters formed companies of 20 or more men working for daily wages. Anglo-American carters, now in the minority for the first time, stayed small entrepreneurs owning but one horse and cart. Black cartmen made their entrance into the streets through the tolerance of Mayor Fernando Wood; blacks tended to work as single entrepreneurs. Many Irish cartmen worked exclusively for the city government on sanitation, road work and land-fill projects. While the pay at around $1.75 per day was not spectacular, it was dependable and regular. During hard times, municipal carters often received raises.[2]

Isaac Lyon viewed many of these changes with dismay. He had little admiration for Irish carters and believed that by forming companies, the Irish were becoming "monopolists."[3] For Lyon, only the single, entrepreneurial cartman was dependable, honest, and "truly American." Lyon was fond of recalling times past and condemning the present; such nativist nostalgia was common among cartmen who looked into the past for inspiration. Indeed, the cartmen's history was often glorious.

In his recollections, Isaac Lyon emphasized the individual qualities of which cartmen had boasted for generations. Isaac Lyon and other cartmen perceived themselves to be honest, independent, reliable, quintessentially urbane and utterly essential to any business or family. Fiercely egalitarian, the cartmen proclaimed their equality with any white man and deeply resented any insinuation of superiority from rising professional groups. Dis-

"West Street," *Harper's Weekly*, September 4, 1869, Collection of the author. This bird's-eye view of West Street shortly after the Civil War shows a plethora of vehicles including carriages, express wagons, stagecoaches and, everywhere, carts.

rupters of the trade ethics such as forestallers and engrossers were considered "thieves" by the cartmen.[4] Their bigotry reflected the harsh racism of northern white laborers.

If Lyon neglected the collective efforts of the cartmen in his memoirs, it was no doubt because the trade's powers were fading in his era. Yet there was a rich tradition of trade unity and effort. From the earliest days of the city the cartmen united and became politically active and powerful. Aware that political power was necessary to maintain their monopoly, the cartmen formed an important block of voters in early New York. Although generally allied with the merchants in politics, the carters would quickly form new ties if dissatisfied with the patronage accorded them or if the politicians attempted, as in the 1790s, to impose deference upon them. The carters were a "shrewd and discerning group of voters," who knew well what their ballot meant and what they desired in return. They acted for generations from an ideology which emphasized maintenance of status, employment, patriotism and protection of their cherished monopoly. Politically, the cartmen were independent, resolute, proud and intelligent.

By the middle of the nineteenth century rapid population and urban growth, political reform, technological change and the rise of the capitalist ethos seemingly doomed the cartmen's traditions. The small one-horse cart was shouldered aside by larger express wagons and trains. As New York City became a major metropolis it could no longer sustain traditions of labor organization and culture which dated back to thirteenth-century England.

Yet customs and traditions die hard. New York's methods of regulation and control over its carters were copied by numerous cities across the country. The Teamsters Union, the largest single union in America, remains composed largely of small entrepreneurs driving their own trucks. Politically powerful, conservative, often biased and corrupt, the Teamsters' Union remains an uncharted area of labor studies.[5]

More recognized in historical studies are the lineages from the cartmen to municipal workers. Such lineages are clearest among sanitation workers and in the organization of the Transit Workers Union, but the cartmen's tough-minded political actions stand as examples to any of today's municipal workers, regardless of race.[6]

Perhaps the greatest example of cartmen's culture in our time are the New York City cabdrivers. These hackmen are organized by laws directly borrowed from the cartmen's regulations. Every day the cabdrivers cruise the city streets or wait at hack-stands for fares. Politically opinionated, wise in urban mores, the cabbies drive recklessly through the streets, terrorizing pedestrians, flaunting traffic laws and acting just like cartmen.[7]

APPENDIX 1

Chronology of Freemanships, 1657–1801

Source (Mayor unless otherwise indicated)	Years	Total Number	Number of Trades
Great Burgher Right	1657–1661	20	—
Small Burgher Right	1657–1661	239	21
John Lawrence	1675–1676	35	—
Cornelius Steenwyck	1683	28	—
Nicholas Bayard	1686–1688	1	1 (Merchant)
S. Van Cortlandt and Peter Delanoy	1688–1690	61	—
Abraham DePeyster	1692–1694	18	—
Charles Lodwick	1694–1695	63	16
William Merrett	1695–1698	365	28
Johannes DePeyster	1698–1699	82	27
David Provoost	1699–1700	14	11
Issac De Riemer	1700–1701	25	14
Thomas Noell	1701–1702	44	23
Officers and Soldiers of H. M. Garrison	1702	203	74
Lord Cornbury's Gentlemen and Servants	1702	19	10
Philip French	1702–1703	23	13
William Peartree	1703–1707	56	25
Ebenezar Wilson	1708–1710	63	32
Jacobus Van Corlandt	1710–1711	16	8
Caleb Heathcote	1711–1714	62	25
John Johnston	1714–1716	108	44
John Johnston	1716–1719	72	29
Jacobus Van Corlandt	1719–1720	36	17
Robert Walker	1720–1725	184	57
Johannes Jansen	1725–1726	41	19
Robert Lurting	1726–1735	446	84
Paul Richard	1735–1739	323	63
John Cruger, Sr.	1739–1744	286	55
Stephen Bayard	1744–1747	348	43
Edward Holland	1747–1756	554	77
John Cruger, Sr.	1756–1766	698	76
Whitehead Hicks	1766–1776	611	91
James Duane	1783–1789	524	47
Richard Varick	1789–1801	54	31

Occupations of Freemanship Recipients, 1695–1801

Occupation	1695–1735	%	1735–1776	%	1783–1801	%	Total
Government	93	.053	115	.04	6	.01	214
Colonial Officers	4		7		—		11
Local Officers	27		5		4		36
Unidentified "esquires and gentlemen"	62		103		2		167
Service							
Professionals	64	.036	65	.02	2	.003	131
Apothecary, Druggist	6		5		—		11
Doctor, Physician, Surgeon	21		18		1		40
Lawyer, Attorney	18		20		1		39
Organist, Dancing Master	—		2		—		2
Schoolmaster, Dr. of Science, Mathematician	19		20		—		39
Retailers	97	.055	42	.015	16	.027	155
Bookseller, Bookbinder	1		6		1		8
Chandler	17		18		1		36
Clotheseller, Haberdasher	5		5		—		10
Grocer	—		2		14		16
Pedlar	—		1		—		1
Trader	1		1		—		2
Victualler	73		9		—		82
Retail Crafts	210	.12	334	.12	21	.036	565
Baker	59		104		3		166
Butcher	62		47		2		111
Confectioner, Chocolatemaker	2		4		2		8
Shopkeeper, Storekeeper	24		73		2		99
Tailor, Breechesmaker	55		97		11		163
Seamstress	1		—		—		1
Tobacconist, Snuffmaker, Pipemaker	7		9		1		17
Building Crafts	184	.105	289	.107	19	.033	492
Bricklayer	34		42		2		78
Brickmaker	—		6		—		6
Carpenter	79		151		16		246
Glazier	3		2		—		5
Joiner, Shop Joiner	45		40		—		85
Mason, Stonecutter, Paver	16		26		1		43
Plasterer	—		1		—		1
Painter	7		21		—		28
Travel and Transport	161	.09	173	.064	350	61	684
Blacksmith, Farrier	54		87		15		156
Boatman	7		6		2		15
Carman, Cartman	93		40		328		461
Innkeeper, Holder, Tavernkeeper	3		40		4		47
Porter	4		—		1		5
Other Services	68	.04	502	.186	73	.126	643
Barber	23		8		1		32
Cook	3		—		—		3
Cutler	4		5		—		9

Laborer	13		403		72		488
Printer	3		2		—		5
Pumpmaker	1		—		—		1
Razorgrinder	—		1		—		1
Wigmaker, Perrukernaker	21		83		—		104
Industrial or Handicraft	62	.035	93	.01	6	.01	161
Textile Trades							
Buttonmaker	—		1		—		1
Draper	2		2		—		4
Dyer, Silkdyer	4		1		1		6
Feltmaker	28		29		—		57
Hatter	3		23		3		29
Hosier	—		2		—		2
Weaver, Stockingweaver	25		35		2		62
Leather Trades	167	.095	270	.10	21	.033	458
Glover	5		2		—		7
Sadler	13		18		1		32
Shoemaker, Cordwainer, Heelmaker	122		220		16		358
Tanner, Currier, Leather-dresser	24		28		4		56
Skinner	3		2		—		5
Food and Drink Processing	48	.027	21	.007	2	.003	71
Brewer, Maulster	15		2		1		18
Distiller	8		8		1		17
Miller, Bolter	15		10		—		25
Vintner	10		1		—		11
Shipbuilding Crafts	50	.028	109	.004	6	.01	165
Blockmaker	6		11		1		18
Mastmaker	—		1		—		1
Pullymaker	1		—		—		1
Ropemaker, Rigger	7		18		2		27
Sailmaker	7		15		—		22
Scalemaker	1		—		—		1
Shipwright, Ship Joiner	28		64		3		95
Metal Crafts	79	.045	109	.04	10	.017	198
Brassfounder, Brazier	10		15		1		26
Clockmaker, Instrumentmaker, Watchmaker, Compassmaker	11		10		2		23
Goldsmith, Jeweler	17		18		—		35
Gunsmith, Armorer	11		29		—		40
Ironmonger	—		—		2		2
Pewterer, Tinworker	6		7		2		15
Ivoryturner	—		1		—		1
Coppersmith	4		9		2		15
Silversmith	16		9		1		26
Wheelwright	4		11		—		15

Furniture Crafts	17	.009	41	.015	8	.013	66
Cabinetmaker, Chairmaker, Upholsterer, Coachmaker	3		20		8		31
Carver	2		2		—		4
Turner	12		19		—		31
Miscellaneous Trades	10	.005	20	.007	7	.012	37
Casemaker	—		1		—		1
Combmaker	3		2		—	5	
Potter, Potbaker	—		6		—	6	
Soapboyler	1		4		1		6
Staymaker	3		6		5		14
Whitesmith	3		1		1		5
Maritime Commerce	345	20	453	.168	22	.039	820
Mariners	142		164		3		309
Sea Captains	—		2		—		2
Merchants and Ancillary Trades							
Bookkeeper	—		1		—		1
Clerk, Scrivener	—		6		—		6
Cooper	35		125		10		170
Merchant	168		155		9		332
Unclassified	27	.05	59	.021	6	.010	153
Chimney Sweeps	1		—		1		2
Farmer, Gardener, Yeoman	28		39		4		71
Fisherman	2		—		—		2
Spinsters	2		—		—		2
Widows	9		—		—		9
Drummers, Cryers	2		—		1		3
Unknown (no listing)	43		20		1		64
Totals:	**1742**	**.34 of whole**	**2695**	**.53**	**575**	**.11**	**5072**

Sources: "Burghers and Freeman," *Collections of N-YHS for 1885;* "License Book of Mayor John Cruger, Jr., 1756–1765," N-YHS Manuscript Collection. The arrangement for occupations was adapted with a few changes from Jacob M. Price, "Economic Function and the Growth of American Port Towns in the Eighteenth Century," *Perspectives in American History, 8* (1974), Appendix C and from Gary B. Nash, *The Urban Crucible* (Cambridge, Mass. 1979), Appendix, Table 1.

Carters from Correction to Burghers and Freeman List, 1756–1765

Name	Original Occupation	Date of Freemanship	Date of Cartman's License
Rynier Nack	Brewer	1734	1761
James Lowns	Cooper	1744	1756
Rynier Hopper	Laborer	1744	1757
John Emott	Cordwainer	1760	1763
James Carr	Laborer	1747	1758
Isaac Delameter	Laborer	1757	1757
Dirck Ammerman	Laborer	1737	1759
Hendricus Ackerman	Laborer	1758	1758
John Allen	Cordwainer	1740	1756
Thomas Allen	Schoolmaster	1741	1760
Albert Ammerman	Baker	1758	1758
Elias Anderson	Blacksmith	1765	1765
George Anderson	Laborer	1759	1759
Elias Bailey	Laborer	1759	1759
Stephen Baldwin	Cordwainer	1752	1758
Thomas Bedford	Laborer	1758	1758
William Bell	Breechesmaker	1773	1773
Cornelius Bennet	Cordwainer	1761	1765
Paul Blanck	Cordwainer	1761	1765
Isaac Blauveldt	Laborer	1758	1758
John Brasell	Laborer	1758	1759
Alexander Brevoort	Laborer	1759	1759
Aldrick Brower	Laborer	1757	1759
Abraham Brower	Laborer	1747	1756
David Brower	Laborer	1757	1757
Everadus Brower	Feltmaker	1749	1756
Staats Busch	Laborer	1757	1757
Duncan Campbell	Laborer	1761	1761
Vincent Carter	Laborer	1761	1761
John Coolbaugh	Laborer	1758	1761
Woolpert Cooper	Laborer	1761	1761
Alexander Clarke	Weaver	1759	1763
Shedrick Chettleton	Laborer	1759	1760
Benjamin Comfort	Laborer	1758	1758
Samuel Crosby	Laborer	1759	1759
John Davenport	Laborer	1746	1756
John Davis	Laborer	1756	1756
Samuel De Groot	Laborer	1761	1761
Jacob De Morree	Bricklayer	1759	1759
Daniel De Voe	Laborer	1757	1757
Frederick De Voe	Cordwainer	1761	1765
John Dudley	Baker	1761	1764
Marmaduke Earle	Laborer	1757	1757
Peter Ennis	Laborer	1757	1757
Isaac Germand	Innholder	1753	1759
Andrew Gibbs	Carpenter	1744	1756
James Gleen	Carpenter	1758	1765
Peter Hannion	Laborer	1757	1758
Jacob Hansen	Blacksmith	1749	1761
Gerradus Hardenbrook	Bricklayer	1759	1762

James Hillend	Laborer	1758	1758
Francis Hooglandt	Cooper	1758	1758
Matthew Hopper	Blacksmith	1765	1765
George Hutton	Laborer	1761	1761
James Johnston	Wigmaker	1748	1765
John Johnson	Sadler	1759	1761
William Kelly	Mariner	1748	1759
Abraham Knickerbacker	Laborer	1760	1760
John Kip	Cordwainer	1765	1765
Richard Lewis	Laborer	1765	1765
Luke Losier	Laborer	1757	1757
Robert Lyng	Laborer	1761	1761
John McDaniel	Laborer	1758	1758
Abraham Martling, Sr.	Cordwainer	1759	1759
Barent Martling	Laborer	1757	1757
Agnus McDougall	Innholder	1756	1765
James McMullen	Laborer	1757	1757
John McIntosh	Laborer	1757	1757
Cornelius Myer	Laborer	1758	1758
Peter Outerberg	Cordwainer	1765	1765
Joseph Paulding	Baker	1761	1762
Henry Palmer	Blacksmith	1759	1760
John Palmer	Carpenter	1757	1761
Richard Palmer	Laborer	1759	1759
John Porterfield	Laborer	1757	1757
Edward Price	Laborer	1759	1762
Cornelius Quackenbos	Laborer	1744	1756
John Roberts	Gentleman	1753	1762
Arie Ryckman	Laborer	1759	1759
John Saxon	Laborer	1759	1759
Isaac Shute	Laborer	1757	1757
Martin Shire	Cordwainer	1761	1765
Soloman Sherwood	Laborer	1758	1758
Walter Steward	Laborer	1757	1757
Peter Stymets	Laborer	1757	1757
John Stymets	Laborer	1749	1756
Abraham Storm	Laborer	1758	1761
Thomas Swartout	Laborer	1756	1756
Abraham Swartout	Laborer	1758	1758
Henry Tiebout	Bricklayer	1761	1765
Martin Van Bueren	Cordwainer	1764	1764
Abraham Van Buskirk	Laborer	1757	1758
Isaac Van Gelder	Shipwright	1742	1758
Johannes Van Horne	Laborer	1757	1757
Jon Van Pelt	Bricklayer	1757	1757
John Van Tassell	Laborer	1753	1761
Jacob Van Wagenen	Baker	1752	1757
Jacob Van Warte	Laborer	1761	1761
Andrew Walker	Laborer	1758	1758
William Walker	Laborer	1757	1757
Jacob Westervelt	Taylor	1756	1758
Abraham Wheeler	Laborer	1765	1765
Thomas White	Shop Joiner	1765	1765
Hercules Wendover	Cordwainer	1760	1760
Wolfert Webbers	Laborer	1757	1757

Subtotals of Carters from Corrections

62 Laborers
12 Cordwainers
4 Bakers
4 Blacksmiths
3 Carpenters
3 Bricklayers
1 Brewer
1 Cooper
1 Breechesmaker
1 Innholder
1 Feltmaker
1 Weaver
1 Schoolmaster
1 Gentleman
1 Sadler
1 Mariner
1 Wigmaker
1 Shipwright
1 Shop Joiner

101 Total

Grand Total of Carters

50 from "Burghers and Freemen"
101 from Corrections
235 from "Cruger License Book

386 Total

Sources: "Burghers and Freemen," *Collections of N-YHS for 1882,* especially pp. 170–210; "License Book of Cartmen, Tavernkeepers and Porters of Mayor John Cruger, 1756–65," N-YHS Manuscript Collection.

NOTES

Preface

1. Robert J. Steinfeld, *The Invention of Free Labor: The Employment Relation in English and American Law and Culture, 1350-1870*, Chapel Hill, 1991, 8-9, 22; Christopher Tomlins, *Freedom Bound: Law, Labor, and Civic Identity in Colonizing English America, 1580-1865*, New York, 2010, 231-233.

2. Edwin G. Burrows and Mike Wallace: *Gotham: A History of New York City to 1998*, New York, 1999; Kenneth Jackson, ed. *The Encyclopedia of New York City*, 2nd ed., New Haven, 2010.

Introduction

1. For this incident, see "Complaint of James Townsend, Merchant," July 19, 1799, New York City Miscellaneous Papers, box 14, no. 104, New-York Historical Society (hereinafter N-YHS) Manuscript Collection.

2. For his freemanship, see *Minutes of the Common Council of the City of New York, 1784–1831*, 22 vols., New York, 1930, Vol. 1, p. 140.

3. See Jacob Price, "Ideology and an Economic Interpretation of the Revolution," in Alfred Young, ed., *The American Revolution*, DeKalb, Ill., 1975, pp. 159–187; George Rude, *Ideology and Popular Protest*, New York, 1980, pp. 7–40; Eric Hobsbawm, "Labor History and Ideology," in idem, *Workers: Worlds of Labor*, New York, 1984, pp. 1–15.

4. See Chilton Williamson, *American Suffrage from Property to Freedom*, Princeton, N.J., 1960, p. 115; Robert Seyboldt, *The Colonial Citizen of New York: A Comparative Study of Certain Aspects of Citizenship Practices in Fourteenth-Century England and Colonial New York City*, Madison, Wis., 1918.

5. For corporate paternalism, see Ibid.; Arthur Everett Peterson and George William Edwards, *New York as an Eighteenth Century Municipality*, 2 vols., New York, 1917; Dirk Hoerder, *Crowd Action in Revolutionary Massachusetts, 1765–1780*, New York, 1977, pp. 21–22 and Shaw Livermore, *Early American Land Companies*, Cambridge, Mass., 1936, pp. 215–243; Carl Bridenbaugh, *Vexed and Troubled Englishmen, 1590–1642*, New York, 1976, pp. 7, 120–150, 253–254.

6. For the nature of the New York merchant community see Cathy Matson, *Merchants and Empire: Trading in Colonial New York*, Baltimore, 1998, 3-4.

7. John Bernard, *Retrospections of America, 1797–1811*, New York, 1886, pp. 52–56.

8. J. G. A. Pocock, "The Classical Theory of Deference," *American Historical Review* 81, no. 1 (1976), pp. 516–523, and Gary B. Nash, *The Urban Crucible: Social Change, Political Consciousness and the Origins of the American Revolution*, Cambridge, Mass., 1979, pp. 4–5. For critique of the concept of deference, see John B. Kirby,

"Early American Politics—The Search for Ideology: An Historiographic Analysis and Critique of the Concept of Deference," *Journal of Politics*, Vol. 32 (1970), pp. 808–838, and John K. Alexander, "Deference in Colonial Pennsylvania and That Man from New Jersey," *Pennsylvania Magazine of History and Biography* 102, No. 3 (July 1978) pp. 422–436. For a good examination of a colonial governor using extensive patronage to conciliate New Yorkers of all ranks, see Mary Lou Lustig, *Robert Hunter 1666–1734: New York's Augustan Governor*, Syracuse, N.Y., 1983. For an example of un-deferential behavior by Boston carters, see Carl Bridenbaugh, *Cities in the Wilderness; The First Century of Urban Life in America, 1625–1742*, New York, 1938, p. 256.

9. Harold J. O'Neill, "The Rise and Development of Anti-British Feeling in Lower New York Colony from 1713–1776" New York University doctoral dissertation, 1961; John Reid, *In Defiance of the Law: The Standing-Army Controversy, the Two Constitutions and the coming of the American Revolution,* Chapel Hill, N.C., 1981; for discrimination against blacks see Thomas G. Davis, "Slavery in Colonial New York" Columbia University Doctoral Dissertation, 1974, pp. 50, 83–85.

10. For "cultures," see Clifford Geertz, *The Interpretation of Culture,* New York, 1973; Robert P. Baker, "Labor History, Social Science, and the Concept of the Working Class," *Labor History,* Vol. 14 (Winter 1973), pp. 98–105; Herbert Gutman, "Work, Culture and Society in Industrializing Society," *American Historical Review,* Vol. 78, pp. 531–588; Charles Stevenson, "A Gathering of Strangers: Mobility, Social Structure, and Political Participation in the Formation of Nineteenth Century American Workingclass Culture," in Milton Cantor, *American Workingclass Culture,* Westport, Conn., 1977, pp. 31–60.

11. See "A Singular Law Case," in David T. Valentine, *Manual of the Corporation of the City of New York for 1866,* New York, 1866, pp. 746–755.

12. For related works, see Howard B. Rock, *Artisans of the New Republic: The Tradesmen of New York City in the Age of Jefferson,* New York, 1979 and R. Sean Wilentz, *Chants Democratic: New York City and the Rise of the American Working Class, 1788–1850,* New York, 1984. For a review of recent literature, see R. Sean Wilentz, "Artisan Origins of the American Working Class," *International Labor and Working Class History,* Vol. 19 (Spring 1981), pp. 1–22, and David Montgomery, "To Study the People: The American Working Class," *Labor History,* Vol. 21 (Fall 1980), pp. 485–512; See also Hobsbawm, "Labor History and Ideology," pp. 4, 12–13. For call for further study of traditional, conservative laborers see David Montgomery, "The Working Classes of the Pre-Industrial American City, 1780–1830," *Labor History,* Vol. 9, no. 1 (Winter 1968), pp. 3–23, esp. pp. 20–21.

13. See Nash, *The Urban Crucible,* p. 16, and Wilentz, *Chants Democratic,* pp. 26–27. The carters constituted nearly 15 percent of the freemen of New York from 1689–1815. See Appendixes 2 and 3.

14. Isaac S. Lyon, *The Recollections of an Old Cartman,* Newark, N.J., 1872, re-printed New York, 1984. For cartmen diseases, see *Montclair New Jersey Times,* March 3–5, 1888.

Chapter 1

1. For price codes of carters, see Henry A. Riley, ed., *London and London Life in the 13th, 14th and 15th Centuries, Being a Series of Extracts from the Early Archives of London,* London, 1867, pp. 253–255, and for other trades pp. 90, 105, 108, 119, 121–122, 138–140, 162, 180, 314; Eric Bennett, *The Worshipful Company of Carmen,* London, 1952, pp. 3–8; see also E. P. Thompson, "The Moral Economy of the English Crowd in the Eighteenth Century," *Past and Present,* No. 50 (February 1971), pp. 76–136 and E. P. Thompson, "Eighteenth Century English society; Class Struggle without Class?," *Social History,* Vol. 3 (May 1978), pp. 133–167. For organization of Parisian carters, see Jeffrey Kaplow, *The Names of Kings: The Parisian Laboring Poor in the Eighteenth Century,* New York, 1972, pp. 41–44.

2. For definitions of "Forestalling" and "engrossing," see *Oxford English Dictionary* (hereinafter *O.E.D.*), *Standard Edition,* 30 vols. London, 1894, Vol. 3, part 2, p. 184; Vol. 4, part 1, p. 443. See also Thompson, "The Moral Economy of the English Crowd." For documents illustrating English attitudes toward forestalling and engrossing, see R. H. Tawney and Eileen Power, *Tudor Economics Documents,* 3 vols., London, 1924, Vol. 1, pp. 144–146, 267–271, 284, 286, 309, 331; Vol. 2, pp. 60, 112; Vol. 3, pp. 47–50, 61, 266, 319, 321.

3. For definition of "carterly," see *O. E. D.,* Vol. 2, part 1, p. 139.

4. Bennett, *Worshipful Company,* pp. 8–15.

5. J. Strype, *Stowe's London,* London, 1720, p. 83.

6. Jon C. Teaford, *The Revolution in Municipal Government in America, 1650–1825,* Chicago, 1975, pp. 9, 22–23, 51–61; Charles Pendrill, *London Life in the Fourteenth Century,* Port Washington, L.I., 1975, reprint of 1925 edn., pp. 68–170; Gwyn A. Williams, *Medieval London: From Commune to Capital,* London, 1963, pp. 43–50. Williams asserts that the freemanship was the basis for public life (p. 43). See also Tawney and Power, *Tudor Economic Documents,* Vol. 1, pp. 121–124, 133, 134, 136–137; Robert Brenner, "Agrarian Class Structure and Economic Development," *Past and Present,* No. 70 (February 1976), p. 55.

7. Bennett, *Worshipful Company,* pp. 3–50; Riley, *London and London Life,* p. 160. The important case in the issue of impressment of carts occurred in 1391 when a carter working on the construction of the new London guildhall was declared exempt from impressment by the King. This was a major victory for the municipality.

8. For "masterless men," see Christopher Hill, *The World Upside Down,* London, 1972, Chapter 3.

9. Bennett, *Worshipful Company,* pp. 30–36.

10. Walter Stern, *The Porters of London,* London, 1960, pp. 210–212. The initial organization of cartmen was based on precedents set in the portering trade, the largest and simplest form of transportation in which goods were carried on a man's back. Because of the narrow streets and abundance of impoverished workers, portering was the dominant form of land transportation in sixteen-century London. Stern estimates that by 1500 this most primitive form of transport employed over 15,000

men in London. The porters carried large parcels on their backs by resting them on padded knots of rope placed on their shoulders. Using frequently spaced designated rest stops along city streets, porters carried goods from the docks to merchants and shopkeepers. When porters used baskets to carry goods they were known as "creelers."

The porters were first organized in the twelfth century and were divided among four fellowships. Each had a specific territory and task orientation and an independent constitution with officers, bylaws and provisions for cooperative mutual protection of members. Unlike the skilled trades, however, porters did not have ultimate self-control. That power lay with city government. The city government was sufficiently concerned about the misconduct of the porters that, as with the carters, the need for discipline became the main reason for establishment of their fellowships. Disobedience, particularly in the allocation of work, brawling, pilfering goods, bribery and rate-gouging were all porters' practices which the city government hoped to stamp out by organizing the fellowship. In order to join the fellowship porters had to become freemen of the city, to make a bond of five pounds and to swear an oath of allegiance. Members of the Fellowship of Billingsgate Porters, the largest such fraternity, took an additional oath refusing to work with anyone who was not a brother. The city government also fixed the rates of porters.

11. Bennett, *Worshipful Company*, pp. 12, 13, 15, 16, 20. For cartmen freemanships see "Carmen's Company Register of Freedom Admissions," 1650–1797, 2 vols. Manuscript L37–4915, Guildhall Library, London.

12. The best overall history of American freemanship and its various clauses is still Robert Seyboldt, *The Colonial Citizen of New York: A Comparative Study of Certain Aspects of Citizenship Practices in Fourteenth-Century England and Colonial New York City,* Madison, Wis., 1918. Seyboldt compared English and American forms of the freemanship and oaths to great effect. The similarities are startling. For review of English freemanship law, see Charles Pendrill, *London Life in the Fourteenth Century,* pp. 68–93. The standard study of the freemanship is Beverly McAnear, "The Role of the Freeman in Colonial New York," *New York History,* Vol. 21 (October 1940), pp. 418–430. McAnear's thesis that the freemanship lost any economic value by 1750 and held political value only at times of contested elections will be under revision throughout this study. See also Richard B. Morris, *Government and Labor in Early America,* New York, 1946, pp. 148–149. For revision of McAnear, see Graham Hodges, "Legal Bonds of Attachment; The Freemanship Law of New York City, 1660–1800," in Conrad Wright and William Pencak, eds., *Authority and Resistance in Early New York,* New York, 1988, 225-246. for positive English attitudes toward trade monopoly, see Tawney and Power, *Tudor Economic Documents,* Vol. 2, pp. 251, 270, 272; Vol. 3, p. 299.

13. See Sidney and Beatrice Webb, *The Manor and the Borough,* 4 vols., London, 1908, Vol. 2, pp. 396–407; Vol. 3, pp. 483, 639.

14. Bennett, *Worshipful Company,* pp. 90–140. For the early history of the woodmongers, see H. B. Dale, *The Society of Woodmongers,* n.d. (c. 1918).

15. Bennett, *Worshipful Company*, pp. 18–19 and George Unwin, *Guilds and Companies of London*, London, 1908, pp. 345–352. See also "An Abstract of the Orders to be Observed by the Carmen of the City of London . . ." published by the Governors' of Christ's Hospital (1670), British Museum Catalog, Vol. 141, p. 701, and "Reasons Offered by the Governors of Christ's Hospital Against the Woodmongers' Bill," London, 1685, British Museum Catalog, Vol. 142, p. 860. And, see Stephen Spratt, "The Carmen's Remonstrance or a Reply to the False and Scurrilous Papers of the Woodmongers," London, 1649.

16. Unwin, *Guilds and Companies*, pp. 22–40, 353–354 and Bennett, *Worshipful Company*, pp. 22–40. A fellowship was much like a guild but lacked true self-governance and appeared to be unique to workers within the various transportation trades.

17. Ibid. and Unwin, *Guilds and Companies*, p. 354.

For evidence of transition through the generations, see "Carmen's Company List of Proprietors and Operators of Carrooms," 68 vols. Manuscript L37–4927, Guildhall Library, London; "Carmen's Company, Documents relating to the sale and transfer of carrooms, draft petitions; case papers, miscellaneous accounts and correspondence," 1665–1840, Manuscript L37–4950, Guildhall Library, London. Widows could also inherit carrooms and transfer them to new husbands.

18. Bennett, *Worshipful Company*, pp. 125–140.

19. Ibid., pp. 13–15.

20. Ibid., p. 18.

21. Ibid., pp. 21–37 and Margaret Baker, *Folklore and Customs of Rural England*, London, 1974, p. 43.

22. Thomas Vincent, *God's Terrible Voice in the City*, London, 1667; *The Diaries of Samuel Pepys*, 12 vols., Berkeley, Calif., 1970–83, Vol. 2, p. 272; the Woodmongers' Hall on Carter Lane was destroyed in the fire. See John Bedford, *London's Burning*, London, 1966, p. 95.

23. John Taylor, the Water-Poet, *The World Runnes on Wheeles, or Oddes Betwixt Carts and Coaches*, London, 1623. See also Anonymous, "The Coaches Overthrow a Joviall Exaltation of Owners, Tradesmen, and Others for the Suppression of Troublesome Hackney Coaches," London, 1636, and Henry Peacham, "Cart Accusing Hackney Coach and Sedan," London, 1636.

24. See complete listing of cartmen's regulations in "The New and Complete Guide to the City of London," London, 1763, 15th edn., pp. 89–100, and "Guide to Stage Coaches, Coach Rates, and Lawes of Carriers, Innkeepers and Carmen," London, 1777.

25. John Jervis (pseud. for William Kitchener), *An Old Coachman & The Traveler's Oracle*, London, 1827, pp. 187, 192.

26. See, "The New and Complete Guide."

27. For cartmen in their frocks, see Thomas Rowlandson, "Characteristic Sketches of the Lower Orders," London, 1817, and Charles Dibdin, *The High Mettled*

Racer, with illustrations by George Cruikshank, London, 1831. Henry Hanson, *The Canal Boatman,* Manchester, 1975, pp. 8, 9, 10–13, 15, 89, 166, notes that canal workers, many of them former carters, derived their uniform from the trade.

28. David McBath Moir, *The Life of Mansie Wauch, Tailor,* London, 1838, pp. 27, 123129. See also Peter Burke, *Popular Culture in Early Modern Europe,* New York, 1978; Gamini Salgado, *The Elizabethan Underworld,* London, 1977; Gillian Bebbington, *London Street Names,* London, 1972, p. 74; P. H. Ditchfield, *Old English Customs,* London, 1896, p. 105; and George Sturt, *The Wheelwright's Shop,* London, 1887. For other comments on the conservative nature of cartmen, see J. I. Lupton, *Modern Practical Farriery,* London, n.d. (c. 1830), pp. 58–59; John Jacob, *Observation on the Structure and Draught of Wheel Carriage,* London, 1773, pp. 70–74; Joseph Marshall, *Rural Economy of Norfolk,* London, 1795. Marshall also discussed cart-racing. See also Sir Walter Gilboy, *Early Carriages and Roads,* London, 1903. Gilboy also notes that coaches are unfair to carts, reviving John Taylor's argument three centuries later. For picture of carters' May-Day procession and contest for longest service, see George R. Sims, *Living London,* 3 vols., London, 1906, vol. 2, pp. 161–162. For importance of such rituals, see Eric Hobsbawm, "The Transformation of Labour Rituals," in his *Workers: Worlds of Work,* New York, 1984, pp. 66–83.

29. Material drawn from Keith Thomas, *Man and Natural World: A History of the Modern Sensibility,* New York, 1983, 19, 96-97, 100, 113-114.

30. William Hone, *The Table Book,* 2 vols., London, 1827, Vol. 1, pp. 374–376.

31. Henry Mayhew, *London Labor and London Poor,* 4 vols., London 1861–62, Vol. 2, pp. 181–338; Robert Malcolmson, *Popular Recreation in English Society, 1700–1850,* Cambridge, 1973; Bennett, *Worshipful Company,* p. 19; and E. P. Thompson, "Patrician Society," pp. 382–406. For carters' ability to maintain standard wages around London, see Eric Hobsbawm, "The Nineteenth Century London Labor Market," in his *Workers,* 134–135. For carmen's attempts to enforce standard wages, see Carmen's Company, "Copy of Proceedings for general purposes, Guildhall, concerning a petition by certain members of the company for revisions of the bye-laws, October 3, 1831," Mss. L 37–4922, Guildhall Library, London.

32. Bennett, *Worshipful Company,* p. 18. For description of this incident see "Carmen's Court Minutes," January 13, 1772, Misc. Mss. L37–4907, Guildhall Library, London.

33. See discussion of this in P. E. Razzell and R. W. Wainwright, eds., *The Victorian Workingclass,* London, 1973, pp. 153–156. For purchase of carrooms by other tradesmen, see "Documents Relating to the Sale of Carrooms." As a sign of the debased value of a carroom, many licenses were given away.

34. Gareth Stedman-Jones, *Outcast London,* London, 1976, pp. 35, 48, 68–71, 147.

Chapter 2

1. See Oscar and Mary Handlin, *Commonwealth: A Study of the Role of the Government in the American Economy: Massachusetts, 1774–1861,* New York, 1946, p. 68; Rich-

ard B. Morris, *Government and Labor in Early America*, New York, 1946, p. 57; E. A. J. Johnson, *American Economic Thought in the Eighteenth Century*, London, 1932; Jon C. Teaford, *The Municipal Revolution in America, 1650–1825*, Chicago, 1975, pp. 3–30; and David Grayson Allen, *In English Ways: The Movement of Society and the Transference of English Local Law and Custom to Massachusetts Bay in the Seventeenth Century*, Chapel Hill, N.C., 1981, pp. 3–14.

2. Teaford, *Municipal Revolution*, p. 10.

3. For initial regulations, see "Lawes Established by James, Duke of York for the Government of New York in the Year 1667," in *Collections of the N-YHS*, Vol. 1, 1809, pp. 307–346.

4. For ease of transition, see William Smith, *History of the Province of New York from its Discovery to the Appointment of Governor Colden in 1762*, 2 vols., New York, 1829, Vol. 1, pp. 20–30; Michael Kammen, *Colonial New York: A History*, New York, 1976, pp. 73–100; Robert Cowan Ritchie, *The Duke's Province: A Study of New York Politics and Society, 1664–1691*, Durham, N.C., 1977, p. 22. For ethnic tensions, see Thomas Archeacon, *New York City, 1664–1710*, Ithaca, N.Y., 1976 and Joyce Diane Goodfriend, *Before the Melting Pot! Society and Culture in Colonial New York City, 1664-1730*, Princeton, 1994. See also Sun Bok Kim, *Landlord and Tenant in Colonial New York: Manorial Society, 1664–1771*, Chapel Hill, N.C., 1977, pp. 8–9, and Albert C. McKinley, "The Transition from Dutch to English Rule in New York City," *American Historical Review*, Vol. 6 (1900), pp. 693–725. Beverly McAnear in "Politics in Provincial New York, 1689–1761," Stanford University Doctoral Dissertation, 1935, p. 2, notes extensive use of patronage by English authorities to pacify Dutch workers.

5. Arthur Everett Patersen and George William Edwards, *New York as an Eighteenth Century Municipality*, 2 vols. New York, 1917, Vol. 1, pp. 4–8. In order to calm ethnic tensions, the new English government respected the vested rights of Dutch tradesmen and extended patronage to them. The Dongan Charter of 1683 required that freemanships be awarded only to residents, a clause which reaffirmed Dutch practices. See James Kettner, *Development of American Citizenship, 1608–1870*, Chapel Hill, N.C., 1978, p. 88, and *Minutes of Common Council of the City of New York, 1675–1776*, 7 vols., New York, 1917, Vol. 1, pp. 371–372.

6. "Burghers and Freemen," *Collections of the N-YHS*, New York, 1885, pp. 1–4.

7. Ibid., pp. 3–4.

8. Ibid., p. 4.

9. Ibid., pp. 19–26.

10. Simon Middleton, *From Privileges to Rights: Work and Politics in Colonial New York City*, Philadelphia, 2006, 67-69; Edwin G. Burrows and Mike Wallace, *Gotham: A History of New York City to 1898*, New York, 1999, 47, 58.

11. Middleton's account of the impact of Dutch and, subsequently, English law on artisans in mid-seventeenth century New Amsterdam and New York relies, oddly, on the experiences of the cartmen and bakers, another group the govern-

ment supervised closely. See *From Privileges to Rights*, 63-69. For comment on variation in early American law, see Christopher Tomlins, *Freedom Bound: Law, Labor, and Civic Identity in Colonizing English America, 1580-1865*, Cambridge, 2010, 232.

12. Bertold Fernow, ed., *The Records of New Amsterdam* (hereinafter *RNA*), 7 vols., New York, 1896, Vol. 6, pp. 73, 74, 76. For porters, see Walter M. Stern, *Porters of London*, London, 1960, p. 6 and Chapter 1 of this study.

13. Daniel Denton, *A Brief Description of New York: Formerly Called New Netherlands*, London, 1670, p. 20. The English continued Dutch "burgher rights" after conquest of New Amsterdam. See Kettner, *Development of American Citizenship*, pp. 87–89; Carl N. Bridenbaugh, *Cities in the Wilderness: The First Century of Urban Life in America, 1625–1742*, New York, 1938, pp. 44–45; Ritchie, *The Duke's Province*, p. 26, notes how deeply the streets of the city were rutted by carts by 1670s.

14. *RNA*, Vol. 6, pp. 105, 175.

15. Ibid., Vol. 6, p. 175.

16 Ibid., Vol. 6, p. 27.

17. Ibid., Vol. 6, pp. 273, 275. See also Bridenbaugh, *Cities in the Wilderness*, pp. 21–22, 232–234.

18. *Second Annual Report of the State Historian of the State of New York*, Albany, 1897, pp. 243–252. Carman David DuFour was charged as an accomplice but later released.

19. *RNA*, Vol. 6, p. 360; Vol. 7, p. 51.

20. Ibid.

21. *Minutes of the Common Council*, Vol. 1, p. 135-137.

22. Ibid., Vol. 1, pp. 136–137; for Dutch treatment of slaves, see Morton Wageman, "Corporate Slavery in New Netherlands," *Journal of Negro History*, Vol. 65 no. 1 (Winter 1980), pp. 34–42.

23. See numerous examples of this in the "Financial Records of Trinity Church, 16971727," Trinity Church Archives, and "Account of Disbursements in the City of New York for Year 1692," New York Municipal Archives. For analysis of race and slavery in New York, see Graham Russell Hodges, *Root and Branch: African Americans in New York and East Jersey, 1613-1863,* Chapel Hill, 1999. Chapter 2. and Gary B. Nash, *The Urban Crucible: Social Change, Political Consciousness and the Origins of the American Revolution,* Cambridge, Mass., 1979, p. 14. George Frederickson, in his analysis of racial attitudes, notes that exclusion of blacks from occupations was a binding force providing a sense of community with the white population . . . which became a way of life and not simply a cover for economic exploitation. See his *White Supremacy,* New York, 1981, p. 70.

24. Hodges, *Root and Branch,* 43; David Roediger, *The Wages of Whiteness: Race and the Making of the American Working Class,* New York, 1991.

25. *Minutes of the Common Council,* Vol. 1, pp. 64–65.

26. Ibid., Vol. 1, pp. 133–138. See also "Petition of Owners and Masters of Sloops and Boats Supplying the City with Firewood to the Mayor and Common Council,

etc. Setting Forth Complaint Against the Cartmen of the City," March 29, 1684, City Clerk's Office, New York City Municipal Archives; for Bolting Act, see Dorothy C. Barck, "The Bolting Monopoly of New York City, 1680–1694," Cornell University M.A. Dissertation, 1922 and C. W. Spencer "Sectional Aspects of New York Politics," *Political Science Quarterly,* Vol. 30 (1915), pp. 397–425. For firewood regulation, see *Colonial Laws of New York from 1664 to the Revolution,* Albany, 1894, pp. 164–165.

27. *Minutes of the Common Council,* Vol. 1, p. 148. See also "Proclamation Regarding Carmen," March 29, 1684, New York Municipal Archives (hereinafter NYMA).

28. For an opposing view, see Richard B. Morris, *Government and Labor in Early America,* New York, 1946, p. 158, and Idem, "Criminal Conspiracy and Early Labor Combinations in New York," *Political Science Quarterly,* Vol. 52 (March 1937), pp. 51–86.

29. *Minutes of the Common Council,* Vol. 1, p. 148.

30. Ibid., Vol. 1, pp. 56, 57, 59.

31. For reference to Smith Street Lane as "Carmen's Street," see David T. Valentine, *History of the City of New-York,* New York, 1853, p. 327 and John J. Post, *Old Streets, Wharves, Piers of New York City,* New York, 1882, pp. 9, 65. A nearby street was named the Glassmaker's Street and is identified only as a "cart-way." See James Paulding, *Men and Affairs of New Amsterdam,* New York, 1843, p. 12.

32. For Van Der Beake, see *Minutes of the Common Council,* Vol. 1, p. 85; Vol. 2, pp. 13, 98, 109, 202. For Teunis Quick, see Ibid, Vol. 1, p. 218; Vol. 2, pp. 117, 147; Vol. 3, p. 343.

33. Ibid., Vol. 1, pp. 65, 73, 206, 216; Vol. 2, pp. 174, 178; Valentine, *History of New York,* p. 327.

34. See Ritchie, *Duke's Province;* David Lovejoy, *The Glorious Revolution in America,* New York, 1975; Jerome Reich, *Leisler's Rebellion,* Chicago, 1953; Nash, *The Urban Crucible,* pp. 45–90; Patricia Bonomi, *A Factious People: Politics and Society in Colonial New York,* New York, 1971, and McAnear, "Politics in Provincial New York," pp. 89–165.

35. "Depositions Respecting the Riot in New York," in E. B. O'Callaghan, ed., *New York Colonial Manuscripts,* 23 vols., Albany, N.Y., 1907–1910, Vol. 3, p. 741.

36. *Minutes of the Common Council,* Vol. 2, pp. 174–178.

37. Ibid., Vol. 2, pp. 245–248, and "Lawes Concerning Carts and Cartmen," published by the City of New York, 1693, Copy in Library Company, Philadelphia.

38. "Burghers and Freemen," *Collections of the N-YHS,* 1885, pp. 59–60; McAnear, "Politics in Provincial New York," pp. 144–145, 163–165, and Nash, *The Urban Crucible,* p. 40.

39. "Burghers and Freemen," *Minutes of the Common Council,* Vol. 1, 174–176; see also "Petition Demanding Expulsion of Strangers," June 12, 1690, NYMA. For a complete enumeration of these and subsequent freemen, see Appendices 1 and 2. See also Nicholas Varga, "Election Procedures and Practices in Colonial New York," *New York History,* Vol. 41, No. 3 (July 1960), pp. 249–277.

40. Nash, *The Urban Crucible*, pp. 88–93; Reich, *Leisler's Rebellion*, pp. 35–37; and Bonomi, *A Factious People*, pp. 75–78. For use of the word "parties" in the seventeenth and eighteenth centuries, see Alison Gilbert Olsen, *Anglo-American Politics, 1660–1775: The Relationship Between Parties in England and Colonial America*, Oxford, 1973, pp. x-xi and McAnear, "Politics in Provincial New York," pp. 1, 172–173.

41. See list in "Burghers and Freemen," *Collections of the N-YHS*, pp. 58–71, and Appendix 1.

42. "John Coursen vs. Hendrick Dominick," New York Mayor's Court Misc. Papers, 1670–1800, New York Public Library (hereinafter NYPL.) For Coursen's career, see *Minutes of Common Council*, Vol. 1, pp. 35, 45, 73. See also Griffith Jones vs. Ana Bolton, November 1711, in Richard B. Morris, *Select Cases of the Mayor's Court of New York City, 1674–1784*, Washington, D. C., 1935, pp. 123, 124. For agreement on laborer's success in courts, see Morris, *Government and Labor*, pp. 216, 221.

43. "Financial Records of Trinity Church," 1697, Trinity Church Archives. The City of New York hired carters to deliver cords of wood to the poor beginning in 1690. See "Minutes of the Church Wardens," 1690–1750, Box 50, New York City Miscellaneous Papers, N-YHS. See also "Disbursements of City of New York," 1692, NYMA, pp. 199–200. For controversy over Trinity Church, see McAnear, "Politics in Provincial New York," pp. 199–200.

Chapter 3

1. Arthur Peterson and George Edwards, *New York as an Eighteenth Century Municipality*, 2 vols., New York, 1917, vol. 1, p. 93; Richard B. Morris, *Government and Labor in Early America*, New York, 1946, p. 20; J. F. Crowley, *This Sheba Self: The Conceptualization of Economic Life in Early America*, Baltimore, 1974, p. 87; Beverly McAnear, "Politics in Provincial New York, 1689–1761," Stanford University Doctoral Dissertation, 1935, pp. 22–23; and Carl Bridenbaugh, *Cities in Revolt: Urban Life in America, 1743–1776*, New York, 1955, p. 271.

2. Peterson and Edwards, *New York as an Eighteenth Century Municipality*, p. 45. McAnear, "Politics in Provincial New York," pp. 273, 312–325, and Carl Bridenbaugh, *Cities in the Wilderness: The First Century of Urban Life in America, 1625–1742*, New York, 1938, p. 197.

3. See lists of various carters in, "Burghers and Freemen," *Collections of N-YHS for 1885*, and Appendix 1.

4. Robert Seyboldt, *The Colonial Citizen of New York: A Comparative Study of Certain Aspects of Citizenship Practices in Fourteenth-Century England and Colonial New York City*, Madison, Wis., 1918 and Chilton Williamson, *American Suffrage from Property to Democracy, 1760–1860*, Princeton, N.J., 1960, pp. 15–17. The Philadelphia City Government awarded nearly 350 freemanships in this period. See *Philadelphia Minutes of the Common Council, 1700–1750*, Philadelphia, 1906.

5. See McAnear, "Politics in Provincial New York" pp. 534–535. For contemporary use of this view, see Gary B. Nash, *The Urban Crucible: Social Change, Political*

Consciousness and the Origins of the American Revolution, Cambridge, Mass., 1979, pp. 29, 31, 35, and Hendrick Hartog, *Public Property and Private Power: The Corporation of the City of New York in American Law, 1730–1870*, Chapel Hill, N.C., 1983, pp. 15–16, 36–40, 101–102, 118–119, 135–136.

6. See Appendix 1 and Jon C. Teaford, *The Municipal Revolution in America, 1650–1825*, Chicago, 1975, pp. 247–350.

7. McAnear, "Politics in Provincial New York," p. 434.

8. Serena Zabin, *Dangerous Economies: Status and Commerce in Imperial New York*, Philadelphia, 2009, chapter 3.

9. "Laws, Ordinances and Regulations of the City of New York," 1729, Copy in the NYPL; see also *Minutes of the Common Council of the City of New York, 1675–1776*, 7 vols., New York, 1917, Vol. 3, p. 149.

10. Ibid.; see also special concern over firewood expressed in *Minutes of the Common Council*, Vol. 1, pp. 41, 76–77, 138, 145–146; Vol. 4, pp. 107–108; Vol. 6, pp. 312, 230–231; Vol. 7, pp. 46, 50, 147–148; and Bridenbaugh, *Cities in Revolt*, pp. 15, 233–234.

11. "Laws, Ordinances and Regulations."

12. For location of various markets, see Thomas F. DeVoe, *The Market Book*, New York, 1862 and Peterson and Edwards, *New York as an Eighteenth Century Municipality*, pp. 70–77.

13. "Records of Payment for Trinity Church," 1701–1723, Folio 434, Folder 2, Trinity Church Archives.

14. Ibid. and *Minutes of the Common Council*, Vol. 3, p. 255, for one of the many examples of the assize on bread.

15. For explanations of methods of wood selling and cartage, see "John Wallace vs. John Shult, "September 29, 1739, New York City Mayor's Court Misc. Papers, NYPL. See also Isaac S. Lyon, *Recollections of an Old Cartman*, Newark, N.J., 1872, reprinted New York, 1984, Chapter 16, for full discussion of credit for firewood cartage and its problems.

16. *Minutes of the Common Council*, Vol. 4, p. 309.

17. For cartmen placing their sons, see citations under the names in "Burghers and Freemen," and sons' licenses in John Cruger, "License Book of Cartmen, Tavernkeepers and Porters of Mayor John Cruger, 1756–1765," manuscript in N-YHS.

18. See *New York Genealogical and Biographical Record* (hereinafter *NYGB*), Vol. 69 (1938), pp. 172–183.

19. Ibid. and see listing of sons in "Cruger License Book."

20. John Albert Bogert, *The Bogert Family*, Scranton, Pa., 1948, p. 37.

21. *Descendants of David Ackerman*, Ridgewood, N.J., 1962, pp. 25, 51.

22. Ibid.; for Dirck Brinckerhoff, see "Cruger License Book"; and James Birney, *A Friesland Family: A Banta Genealogy*, New York, n.d., p. 26.

23. For Vlierboom, see Howard S. Durie, *The Kakiat Patent in Bergen County, New Jersey*, Pearl River, N.Y., 1970, p. 147.

24. For Jacobus DeLaMontagne and his family, see *Minutes of the Common Council,* Vol. 3, pp. 246, 256, 255, 270;Vol. 4, pp. 460, 411.

25. Ibid.,Vol. 4, p. 128. Before taking post as Supervisor of Watch, Crannell, Sr., had been variously a marshall, collector, storekeeper of powder room, librarian of council and apparently also hired carters to cart books of council and for work on powder room. See citation under his name in Ibid.,Vol. 8, pp. 226–227. For Robert Crannell, Jr., see Vol. 3, p. 264. At his father's death Crannell, Jr., was asked to take stock of powder room, was appointed Supervisor of Watch, Cryer and Bell Ringer of Mayor's Court and given a post as a city marshall, all in one council meeting. See also Vol. 4, p. 499 for Bartholomew Crannell and Vol. 7, p. 68 for Robert Crannell, III.

26. *Collections of the N-YHS,* "Abstracts of Wills, on file in the Surrogate's Office, City of New York," 17 vols., New York, 1892–1908,Vol. 4, p. 23.

27. "Burghers and Freemen."

28. E. B. O'Callaghan, ed., *Documentary History of New York,* 1849–1853, 4 vols.; "Census of City of New York, 1702."Vol. 1, pp. 611–624, See also Bruce Martin Wilkenfeld, "New York City Neighborhoods, 1730," *New York History,* Vol. 57, (April 1976), pp. 165–182.

Chapter 4

1. Gary B. Nash, *The Urban Crucible: Social Change, Political Consciousness and the Origins of the American Revolution,* Cambridge, Mass., 1979, p. 57; Cathy Matson, *Merchants & Empire: Trading in Colonial New York,* Baltimore, 1998, 227-230. Jacob Price, "Economic Function and Growth of American Port Towns in the Eighteenth Century," *Perspectives in American History,* 8, (1974), pp. 158–159, 173. New York's advantage in the French-Indian wars even extended to carting. *The New York Gazette and Weekly Post Boy,* August 7, 1749, noted that Albany carters were impressed into service by the British army leaving the city bereft of their service. No such action was taken against New York carters.

2. Governor Clark quoted in Nash, *Urban Crucible,* p. 224. For Watts, see "Letter Book of John Watts," *Collections of the N-YHS for 1928,* New York, 1928, pp. 232–233.

3. Nash, *The Urban Crucible,* pp. 251–255; for maintenance of regulations in the quartercentury before the Revolution, see Virginia Harrington, *The New York Merchant on the Eve of the Revolution,* New York, 1935, pp. 244–288.

4. For lengthy charter tenures, see Bruce Martin Wilkenfeld, "The Common Council of New York City, 1689–1800," *New-York Historical Society Quarterly* (hereinafter *N-YHSQ*) (1979), pp. 249–273. For impressment and other problems, see Jesse Lemisch, "Jack Tar in the Streets: Merchant Seamen in the Politics of Revolutionary America," *William and Mary Quarterly,* 3rd series, 25, No. 4 (July 1968), pp. 371–408, esp. p. 383.

5. "Lawes Governing Carts and Cartmen in the City of New York," James Parker, Printer, 1749, Copy in NYPL.

6. For biographical material on Cruger, see John Stevens, *The Chamber of Commerce of Colonial New York: Biographical and Historical Sketches, 1768–1784*, New York, 1867, pp. 5–18. For agreement on rise of mayor's power, see McAnear, "Politics in Provincial New York," p. 21.

7. Milton M. Klein, ed., *The Independent Reflector*, Cambridge, Mass., 1964, p. 152 and McAnear, "Politics in Provincial New York," pp. 674–677.

8. Carl Bridenbaugh, *Cities in Revolt: Urban Life in America, 1743–1776*, New York, 1955, p. 84.

9. Beverly McAnear, "Politics in Provincial New York, 1689–1761," Stanford University Doctoral Dissertation, 1935, pp. 312–325, 896.

10. "License Book of Cartmen, Tavernkeepers and Porters of Mayor John Cruger, 1756-1765," manuscript in N-YHS. Cruger licensed six new cartmen when he became mayor in later 1756. He then granted licenses to 40 more in 1757, 48 in 1758, 56 in 1759, 49 in 1769, 50 in 1761, 36 in 1762, 25 in 1763, 20 in 1764 and then 46 in 1765. See Appendix 3.

11. "Burghers and Freemen"; "Cruger License Book." For verification of Cruger's freemen, compare his license list with freemen listed in "*A Copy of the Poll List, 1768, 1769,*" New York, 1880. The addition of laborers to the number of cartmen also means that the statistics in Nash and Price are too low. Both list only those cartmen identified as such in "Burghers and Freemen"; for a complete list of freemen from the 1750s, see Appendix 3.

12. "Lawes Governing Carts," 1749, NYPL.

13. Nash, *Urban Crucible*, pp. 14–16 and Appendix 5; Price, "Economic Function and Growth," pp. 130–131. Although neither Nash nor Price provides figures for New York City artisans, their charts of personal wealth in Boston and Philadelphia give the carters status well above seamen, laborers, shoemakers and tailors. By Nash's charts cartmen are placed around the level of shipbuilding artisans.

14. Eric Foner, *Tom Paine and the Revolutionary America*, New York, 1976, p. 46.

15. For Blanck, see *Collections of the N-YHS*; "Abstracts of Wills on File in the Surrogate's Office, New York City," 17 vols., New York: 1892–1908, Vol. 4; pp. 301–302 and "Account Book of Evert Blancker," N-YHS. For Thomas Montanje, see "Abstracts of Wills," Vol. 5, pp. 89–91.

16. James Birney, *A Friesland Family: A Banta Genealogy*, New York, n.d., p. 34.

17. Ibid., p. 57

18. "Abstracts of Wills," Vol. 5, pp. 54–55.

19. Ibid., p. 234.

20. "License Book of Mayor John Cruger"; *A Copy of the Poll List, 1768.*

21. *A Copy of the Poll List, 1769.*

22. Compare "License Book of Mayor John Cruger" with the "License Book of Richard Varick, Mayor, 1789–1801," N-YHS and *Longworth's Directory of the City of New York for 1796*, N-YHS.

23. "Abstract of Wills," Vol. 5, pp. 391, 402, and "Account Book of Bancker Family," N-YHS.

24. See "Trinity Church Book of Indentures, 1750–1775," Trinity Church Archives. As not all indentures list occupation, comparison with the "License Book of Mayor John Cruger" is necessary for confirmation of some cartmen. Trinity Church divided up its property north of Partition Street into some 400 lots measuring 20 feet by 100 and for leases of two pounds per annum. The church corporation rented this area, known locally as the Church's Farm, to members of the church. Leases were for periods of 33, 66 and even 99 years, much like agricultural freeholds used in English farmlands.

25. For cartmen signs, see Esther Singleton, *Social Life in New York in the Era of the Georges,* New York, 1902, p. 230. For Abraham Montanje's tavern, see I.N.P. Stokes, *Iconography of Manhattan Island,* 7 vols., New York, 1915–1928, Vol. 4, p. 797. For general use of taverns by politicians to court votes, see McAnear, "Politics of Provincial New York," pp. 959–965. For elements of "working-class culture," see Bruce Laurie, "Nothing on Compulsion, the Lifestyles of Philadelphia Artisans, 1820–1850," in Milton Cantor, ed., *Workingclass Culture,* Westport, Conn., 1976, pp. 91–120.

26. For appearance of leopard at Montanje's, see *New York Mercury,* August 7, 1769. See Rita Gottesman, *Arts and Crafts in New York, 1726–1776,* New York, 1938 for other amusements.

27. Carl Abbott, "The Neighborhoods of New York, 1760–1776," *New York History,* Vol. 15, no. 1 (January 1974), pp. 35–53.

28. "Trinity Church Book of Indentures"; Steven Wheeler, "The Physical and Social Structure of the King's Farm, 1750–1770," New York University M.A. Dissertation, 1982.

29. For discussion of Cartmen's Ward, see Chapter 7 and Betsy Blackmar, "Re-Walking the Walking City: Housing and Property Relations in New York City, 1780–1840," *Radical History Review,* No. 71 (1979), pp. 131–148.

30. *A Copy of the Poll Lists, 1768, 1769,* and "License Book of Mayor John Cruger."

Chapter 5

1. For descriptions of New York City after the close of the French-Indian War, see Gary B. Nash, *The Urban Crucible: Social Change, Political Consciousness and the Origins of the American Revolution,* Cambridge, Mass., 1979, p. 259; Bayard Still, *Mirror for Gotham,* New York, 1956, pp. 30–35; and Virginia Harrington, *The New York Merchant on the Eve of the Revolution,* New York, 1935, pp. 283–288.

2. For best descriptions of this evolution, see Patricia Bonomi, *A Factious People Politics and Society in Colonial New York,* New York, 1971, pp. 230–267; Robert J. Christen, "King Sears, Politician and Patriot in a Decade of Revolution," Columbia University Doctoral Dissertation, 1968; L. Jesse Lemisch, "New York's Petitions and Resolves of December 1765: Liberals vs. Radicals," *N-YHSQ* 49, No. 4 (October 1965), pp. 313–326; Roger J. Champagne, *Alexander MacDougall and the Ameri-*

can Revolution in New York, Schenectady, N.Y., 1975, pp. 11–52; Alfred F. Young, *The Democratic-Republicans of New York: The Origins, 1763–1797,* Chapel Hill, N.C., 1967, p. 3–83; and Edward Countryman, *A People in Revolt: The American Revolution and Political Society in New York, 1760–1790,* Baltimore, 1981, pp. 32–71.

3. "License Book of Mayor John Cruger, 1756–1765," Manuscript in N-YHS.

4. *Minutes of the Common Council of the City of New York, 1675–1776,* 7 vols., New York, 1917, Vol. 6, p. 323.

5. Ibid., Vol. 7, pp. 323, 330, 437, 314.

6. "Accounts of H. M. Office of Ordinances, 1757–1761," N-YHS.

7. "Evert and Gerard Bancker's Account Book, 1760–1761," manuscript in N-YHS: for New Jersey woodcutters, see Adrian C. Leiby, *The Revolutionary War in Hackensack Valley,* New Brunswick, N.J., 1980, 2nd edn., pp. 262, 263.

8. "Laws of the City of New York Governing Carts and Cartmen," 1762, Broadside Collection, NYPL.

9. See *Official Directory of the City of New York, 1980,* published by the City, pp. 2–4, for lists of all city mayors. For stability in politics, see Bruce M. Wilkenfeld, "The Social and Economic Structure of the City of New York, 1695–1796," Columbia University Doctoral Dissertation, 1973, pp. 149–152.

10. For discussions of these elections, see Bonomi, *A Factious People,* pp. 230–257; Young, *Democratic-Republicans;* Leopold Launitz-Schurer, *Loyal Whigs and Revolutionaries: The Making of the Revolution in New York, 1765–1776,* New York, 1980, pp. 80–82; and Champagne, *Alexander MacDougall.*

11. "Waste (Account) Book of John and Henry Cruger, 1762–1768," Manuscript in N-YHS; "Commissaries and Paymasters of Province of New York, 1760–1770"; *Cruger Papers,* N-YHS. For full compilation of cartmen votes, see Graham Hodges, "The Cartmen of New York City, 1667–1801," New York University Doctoral Dissertation, 1982, p. 85.

12. Lemisch, "New York's Petitions and Resolves"; Christen, "King Sears," p. 29; Martha J. Lamb, *History of City of New York,* 3 vols., New York, 1877, Vol. 3, pp. 725–728. For impressment raids, see Jesse Lemisch, "Jack Tar in the Streets: Merchant Seamen in the Politics of Revolutionary America," *William and Mary Quarterly,* 3rd series, 25, No. 4 (July 1968), pp. 388, 393; Richard B. Morris, *Government and Labor in Early America,* New York, 1946, pp. 272–278, 280. See also Dora Mae Clark, "The Impressment of Seamen in the American Colonies," in *Essays in Colonial History Presented to Charles McLean Andrews by His Students,* New Haven, Conn., 1931, p. 216.

13. Lemisch, "New York's Petitions and Resolves"; Pauline Maier, *From Resistance to Revolution; Colonial Radicals and the Development of American Opposition to Britain, 1765–1776,* New York, 1972, pp. 68–79; Countryman, *A People in Revolt,* pp. 38–39. For innovative looks at the riots, see Peter Shaw, *American Patriots and the Rituals of Revolution,* Cambridge, Mass., 1981, and Paul A. Gilje, *The Road to Mobocracy: Popular Disorder in New York City, 1763-1834,* Chapel Hill, 1987, 46-52.

14. Lemisch, "New York's Petitions and Resolves." Non-importation was also a

popular measure because it placated the rising anger of the common people against the luxurious living of the wealthy. See Countryman, *A People in Revolt,* pp. 60–62.

15. Launitz-Schurer, *Loyal Whigs,* p. 78; Esther Singleton, *Social Life in New York in the Era of the Georges,* New York, 1902, pp. 160–161; Carl Abbott, "The Neighborhoods of New York, 1760–1776," *New York History,* Vol. 55 (Fall 1968), p. 49; "Indentures of Trinity Church, 1750–1776," Manuscripts, Box 29, N-YHS; "Papers Relating to the Montanje Family of New York, collected by James Riker," MSS Documents, Genealogical Division, NYPL. William Smith mentions in William H. W. Sabine, ed., *Historical Memoirs from 16 March to July 9, 1776,* New York, 1956, p. 103 that Montanje's was "the House where all the Riotous Liberty Boys met in 1765 and 66."

16. Gilje, *The Road to Mobocracy,* 53-54; Peter Thompson, *Rum, Punch, and Revolution: Taverngoing and Public Life in Eighteenth-Century Philadelphia,* Philadelphia, 1999, 141-145. Benjamin L. Carp, *Rebels Rising Cities and the American Revolution,* New York, 2007, chapter 2.

17. Bonomi, *A Factious People,* pp. 280–282 and Young, *Democratic-Republicans,* pp. 10–11.

18. Bonomi, *A Factious People,* pp. 239–44.

19. "The Voter's New Catechism," New York, Published by John Holt, March 3, 1768, Broadside Collection, NYPL.

20. "A Card" broadside handed out in streets in February 1768 in Collection of Political Cards Circulated in 1768 and 1769, NYPL, Evans 10849. For replies, see "The Querist," Broadside Collection, 1768, NYPL. Across the river in New Jersey anti-lawyer riots occurred in Monmouth County at the same time. Monmouth County was a source of firewood for New York City and also a resort of the common people of New York. See Edwin Salter, *This Old Monmouth of Ours,* Freehold, N.J., 1847, pp. 96–100; Larry R. Gerlach, *Prologue to Independence: New Jersey in the Coming of the American Revolution,* New Brunswick, N.J., 1976, pp. 185–192.

21. For a full compilation of cartmen voting, see Hodges, "Cartmen of New York," p. 92. Results were derived from *A Copy of the Poll List for Elections to the Assembly in the Colony of New York, 1768,* New York, 1880.

22. Bonomi, *A Factious People,* pp. 248–252. For Cruger as President of the Chamber of Commerce, see J. C. Stevens, *Colonial Records of the New York Chamber of Commerce, 1768–1784,* New York, 1867. The Chamber took great pains during this time to continue price fixing. See negotiations with repackers of beef, fisheries, and sellers of flour and nails on pp. 49, 63, 176–177, and Harrington, *The New York Merchant,* pp. 286–287.

23. "Whereas on the late Examination Before the House of Assembly, it Appeared that Mr. Jauncey . . ." January 16, 1769, Broadside Collection, NYPL.

24. "A Contrast, Read, My Fellow Citizens, and Judge for Yourselves," Broadside, n.d. 1769, Broadside Collection, NYPL.

25. Bonomi, *A Factious People,* p. 253; Champagne, *Alexander MacDougall,* pp. 16–17.

26. For a full compilation, see Hodges, "Cartmen of New York," p. 95. Results derived from *A Copy of the Poll List for Elections to the Assembly in the Colony of New York, 1769,* New York, 1880.

27. For DeLancey bullying, see Launitz-Schurer, *Loyal Whigs,* p. 70. For cartmen on Trinity Church Farm, see "Licence Book of Mayor John Cruger, 1756–1765," Manuscript in N-YHS; "Records of Marriages in Trinity Church," Vol. 1, 1746–1818, Trinity Church Archives.

28. See "Accounts Payable for Year, 1770–1774," Trinity Church Archives, Folio 434, File 4.

29. For best discussion of this riot, see Lee R. Boyer, "Lobster Backs, Liberty Boys and Laborers in the Streets: New York Golden Hill Riots and Nassau Street Riots," *N-YHSQ,* Vol. 57 (October 1973), pp. 281–308; Abbott, "Neighborhoods of New York," p. 49, John Phillip Reid, "In a Defensive Rage," *New York University Law Review,* Vol. 49 (December 1974), pp. 1043–1097; George Markham, "An Analysis of the Treatment of George III in New York City Newspapers," New York University Doctoral Dissertation, 1963; Lamb, *History of City of New York,* Vol. 3, pp. 746, 759; Countryman, *A People in Revolt,* pp. 63–66.

30. Boyer, "Lobster Backs, Liberty Boys, and Laborers," p. 304.

31. For the council decision, see *Minutes of the Common Council,* Vol. 7, p. 230. In general the council was much more conservative than the populace during the prerevolutionary period. See George Edwards, "New York City Politics Before the American Revolution," *Political Science Quarterly* 36, No. 4 (1921), pp. 586–602.

32. "Petition of the Cartmen of New York to the Common Council," August 13, 1771, NYMA, Box 6412. See also Arthur Peterson and Edwards, *New York as an Eighteenth Century Municipality,* New York, 1917, pp. 74–78; Thomas F. DeVoe, *The Market Book,* New York, 1862, pp. 275–277, 310–312; and I.N.P. Stokes, *Iconography of Manhattan Island,* 7 vols., New York, 1915–1928, Vol. 4, p. 818.

33. "Petition of the Butchers," March 31, 1771, NYMA.

34. *Minutes of the Common Council,* Vol. 7, pp. 300–304.

35. "Petition of the Cartmen to the Common Council," August 26, 1771, NYMA, Box 6412.

36. DeVoe, *Market Book,* pp. 310–312; Peterson and Edwards, *New York as an Eighteenth Century Municipality,* pp. 78–80. For importance of custom, see Eric Foner, *Tom Paine and Revolutionary America,* New York, 1976, p. 159.

37. Whitehead Hicks, Mayor, "To the Inhabitants . . . Concerning the Exstreme Danger of Carrying Gunpowder," January 18, 1773, Broadside Collection, NYPL. "Lawes and Ordinances of the City of New York," 1772, NYPL.

38. For Kelly, see New York *Gazetteer,* November 17, 1773. For Hake see New York City Mayor's Court Misc. Papers, NYPL. For Van Brockle and Page, see *Gazetteer,* June 20 and 27, 1774.

39. For Liberty Boy suppers at Montanje's, see *New York. Mercury,* October 16, 1769; May 23, 1772; May 9, 1773; March 8, 1774; March 13, 1775. After the war the

tavern was taken over by a Mr. and Mrs. Amory and became once again a prominent meeting place for cartmen and mechanics. See Chapter 7. For importance of Committees of Mechanics, see Staughton Lynd, "The Revolution and the Common Man: Farm Tenants and Artisans in New York Politics, 1777–1788," Columbia University Doctoral Dissertation, 1962; idem, "The Mechanics in New York Politics, 1774–1788," *Labor History* Vol. 5, no. 3 (Fall 1964), pp. 224–245; and Jesse Lemisch, "Jack Tar vs. John Bull: The Role of the Seamen in Precipitating the Revolution," Yale University Doctoral Dissertation, 1962.

40. List of Loyalists compared with Cruger License Book. For Loyalists, see "Orderly Book of Three Battalions of Loyalists Commanded by Brig. General Oliver DeLancey, 1776–1778," to which is appended a list of New York Loyalists in the City of New York, compiled by William Kelby: *Collections of N-YHS for 1916,* pp. 115–130. For Patriots, see comparison of Cruger License Book with "Alphabetical Roster of New York State Troops, in Bertold Fernow, ed., *Documents Relating to the Colonial History of New York State,* 15 vols., Albany, N.Y., 1887, Vol. 15, pp. 311–524. See also, Wallace Brown, *The King's Friends; the Composition and Motive of the American Loyalist Demands,* Providence, R.I., 1965, p. 87.

41. See relationships in James Birney, *A Friesland Family: A Banta Genealogy,* New York, n.d., and for others, see Chapter 3, pp. 50–51, 56–60.

42. See battalion members of Marinus Willett's regiment and compare with Cruger License Book. For Lamb, see accounts in "Alexander Lamb Papers," N-YHS. Willett's regiment included cartmen John W. Ackerman, James Allen, Dirck Ammerman, Abraham Arnold, Mathew Bell, James Bishop, Henry Bogardus, John Burk, Archibald Campbell, Duncan Campbell and Peter Adam. See Willett's N.Y. regiment, National Archives, Section 881, Reels 773–774. Lamb's company included cartmen John Berwick, John Betters, Marmaduke Berwick, Daniel Brower, Anthony Clark, George Dalzell, Francis DeVoe, Henry Houck, John Martin, Caspar Slymett and Richard Walsh. See Muster List, National Archives, Section 881, Reel 777.

43. Cruger License Book.

44. See "Orderly Book of Three Battalions" for examples and Oscar T. Barck, *New York City During the War of Independence,* New York, 1931, pp. 98–120. See also Morris, *Government and Labor,* pp. 92–136.

45. Stevens, *Colonial Records of the New York Chamber of Commerce,* pp. 210, 214. See also Ann Beganson, *Prices and Inflation During the American Revolution* Philadelphia, 1951, esp. pp. 36, 48–49, 56, 257, 313.

46. Thomas F. Jones, *History of New York in the Revolutionary War,* 2 vols., New York, 1879, pp. 68–70.

47. "Various Accounts of John Smythe, Treasurer of the British Administration of New York City, 1778–1780," N-YHS. Smythe's accounts include license fees from tavernkeepers and from the Brooklyn Ferry.

48. Benjamin Quarles, *The Negro in American Revolution,* Durham, N.C., 1961, pp.

134–135; Thomas Wertenbacker, *Father Knickerbocker Rebels: New York City during the Revolution,* New York, 1957, pp. 161–162; Morris, *Government and Labor,* p. 306.

49. Jones, *History of New York,* p. 81.

50. "Orderly Book of Three Battalions of Loyalists," pp. 1–16.

51. Harry B. Yoshpe, *Disposition of Loyalists Estates in the Southern District of the State of New York,* New York, 1939, pp. 200, 204.

Chapter 6

1. For descriptions of New York City after the war, see Sidney Pomerantz, *New York: An American City, 1783–1801,* New York, 1939, pp. 3–40, and Edward G. Burrows and Mike Wallace, *Gotham: History of New York City to 1898,* New York, 1999, chapter 17.

2. Pomerantz, *An American City,* pp. 20–30, and Oscar and Mary Handlin, *Commonwealth: A Study of the Role of Government in the American Economy: Massachusetts, 1774–1861,* New York, 1946, p. 68.

3. Pomerantz, *An American City,* pp. 20–40.

4. "Marinus Willett to John Jay, December 11, 1977," Jay Papers, Columbia University; Staughton Lynd, "The Revolution and the Common Man;" Columbia University Doctoral Dissertation, 1962, p. 197.

5. *Independent New York Gazette,* November 28 and December 6, 1783.

6. See "Juvenis," December 23, 1783; "Cincinatus," December 23, 1783; "A Friend to Mechanics," December 23, 1783; "A Battered Soldier," December 27, 1783. Broadside Collection, N-YHS.

7. Staughton Lynd, "The Mechanics in New York Politics, 1774–1788," *Labor History,* Vol. 5 no. 3 (Fall 1964), p. 236. For the election, see *Independent Journal,* December 22, 1783, and *New York Packett,* January 1, 1784.

8. "Broadside Petition to Governor Clinton," September 1, 1783, N-YHS. "Petition of Refugee Mechanics, Grocers, Retailers and Innholders," in *Independent Journal,* January 24, 1784.

9. *New York Packet,* March 18, 1784; *Minutes of the Common Council of the City of New York, 1784–1831,* 22 vols. New York, 1930, Vol. 1, pp. 102–103; English, "New York City," p. 98; Pomerantz, *An American City,* pp. 65–66; Robert Seyboldt, *The Colonial Citizen of New York,* Madison, Wis., 1917, pp. 33–34.

10. *Minutes of the Common Council,* Vol. 1, p. 103. See also pp. 132, 160, 206, 216, 242, 334, 391, 400, 402, 403, 410, 460.

11. *Independent Gazette,* June 18, 1784; English, "New York City," p. 92. Simmons himself received a license. Thereafter, his inn was the site of frequent council meetings. At these meetings, Simmons served food and drink, charged to the city, and watched as the aldermen awarded each other contracts to work with the cartmen. For granting the freemanship of cartmen in this two-month period, see *Minutes of the Common Council,* Vol. 1, pp. 240–248. For Duane Agreement, see "Note" in *Duane Papers,* Reel 4, N-YHS.

12. For Duane, see E. P. Alexander, *A Revolutionary Conservative: James Duane of New York,* New York, 1938, and *Dictionary of American Biography,* 22 vols., New York, 1928, Vol. 5, pp. 465–466.

13. See Bertold Fernow, ed., *Documents Relating to the Colonial History of New York State,* 15 vols., Albany, N.Y., 1887, Vol. 15, pp. 311–524, compared with freemanship carters in "Burghers and Freemen" for 1784–1785; for New Jerseyans coming to New York, compare freemanship carters with William S. Stryker, *Official Register of the Officers and Men of New Jersey in the Revolutionary War,* Baltimore, 1967.

14. See the petitions of Isaac Woolcock, Bernardus VanderWater, Isaac Donaldson, Daniel Demorary, Samuel Arnot, John Hendrick and others, Box 6412, City Clerk's Office, NYMA.

15. For Ackerman, see *Minutes of the Common Council,* Vol. 1, pp. 24, 438, 597, 749; for others, see individual names in *Collections of N-YHS* "Abstracts of Wills on File in the Surrogate's Office, City of New York," 17 vols., New York, 1892–1908, and "Petitions of Dirck Brinckerhoff, Jr., and Henry Lines," Box 6412, NYMA.

16. Banta is listed in "Orderly Book of Three Battalions of Loyalists Commanded by Brig. General Oliver DeLancey 1776–1778," as working for loyalist troops. Nonetheless, he received a freemanship and license, *Minutes of the Common Council,* Vol. 1, p. 20.

17. See Moses Ely, Pension Application, National Archives, Revolutionary War Pension Application, W921.

18. See Enoch Hoyt, Pension Application, National Archives, W21404.

19. See Abraham D. Brower, Pension Application, National Archives, A17352; for blockhouse, see Adrian C. Leiby, *The Revolutionary War in the Hackensack Valley* 2nd Ed., New Brunswick, N.J., 1980, pp. 164–167.

20. See John Casparus and Benjamin Westervelt, Pension Applications, National Archives, A1775, W9981, R6130.

21. See John, Peter and Abraham Riker, Pension Applications, National Archives, R8538, S11294, R8822.

22. See Abraham Martling, Jr., Pension Application, National Archives, W18473. Martling was recommended for a pension in 1832 by Gulian Ver Planck. For his father and uncle, see the Cruger License Book; for other cartmen veterans, see Pension Applications, National Archives: Samuel Hubbs, S13497; Isaac Blauveldt, W18204; Peter Sypher, W24699; Henry Crum, S12623; Morris Earl, W849; John Ten Broek, S42469; John Terhune, S14668; and James Throckmorton, S763, among many others.

23. "Petition of Daniel Demorary for a Cartman's License," Box 6412, NYMA; James Bierney, *A Friesland Family: A Banta Genealogy,* New York, n.d.

24. See note 15.

25. For warrants presented by cartmen, see *Minutes of the Common Council,* Vol. 1, pp. 6, 8, 46, 54, 60, 62, 127, 133, 142, 162, 167, 194–195, 297, 332, 498, 500. See also English, "New York City," pp. 260–262, 218–225, 77–80.

26. For Day's appointments as grain measurer, see *Minutes of the Common Council,* Vol. 3, 670; Vol. 6, 592; Vol. 14, 169; for coal inspector, Vol. 4, 147; for charcoal measurer, Vol. 11, 757, and Vol. 16, p. 301. For freemanship, Vol. 1, p. 20.

27. "Richard Varick's License Book, 1789–1796," N-YHS and *Minutes of the Common Council,* Vol. 3, pp. 669, 345.

28. *Minutes of the Common Council,* Vol. 1, p. 21; Vol. 3, p. 670 for appointment as lime measurer; Vol. 4, p. 162 for wood inspector; and Vol. 5, p. 636 as watchman. For his other careers, see Vol. 8, p. 434; Vol. 10, p. 631; Vol. 19, p. 350; and as brassfounder, Vol. 14, p. 47. For George Brown, see Vol. 1, p. 438; Vo1. 18, p. 263. For Alexander Buchanan, Vol. 6, p. 309. For John Harriot, Vol. 4, p. 77; Vol. 7, p. 631; Vol. 10, p. 126. For Francis Passman, Vol. 10, p. 559; Vol. 12, p. 338.

29. See "Pay Vouchers on Watch," 1784–1796, New York City Misc. Papers, N-YHS.

30. For admonitions to inspectors, see "Lawes and Ordinances of the City of New York Concerning Carts and Cartmen," printed by the City, 1793, 1795, 1799, NYPL; for problems with watchmen, see James F. Richardson, *The New York City Police,* New York, 1970, pp. 8–21.

31. *Minutes of the Common Council,* Vol. 1, pp. 19, 326, 405, 480, 599, 675, 750; Vol. 2, 40, 106, 185, 285.

32. Other cartmen included John Ackerman, Henry Bridsall, William Campbell, William Cummings, David C. Demarest, George Duryea, Samuel Hutchings, John Leonard, James J. Martin, William Post, John Reins, Casparus Romaine, James Smith, Gideon Sprague, John Van Orden and Charles Fisher. See *Minutes of the Common Council* citations for each.

33. For discussion of value of patronage, see Edmund C. Willis, "Social Origins and Political Leadership in New York City from the Revolution to 1815," University of California-Berkeley Doctoral Dissertation, 1967, p. 59.

34. See "Tenant Rolls for Trinity Church, 1780–1796," Trinity Church Archives. The twelve are Abraham Martling, Sr. and Jr., Alexander Lamb, Jr., John Hendricks, Marmaduke Earle, Samuel Brower, Christopher Stymets, John McKim, John Steele, John Blanck, David and Hugh Ross.

35. See rent rates in "Trinity Church Farm Tenant Rolls, 1780–1794," Trinity Church Archives. See also, Betsy Blackmar, "Re-Walking the Walking City: Housing and Property Relations in New York City, 1780–1840," *Radical History Review,* No. 21 (1979), pp. 131–148.

36. Frank Monaghan and Marvin Lowenthal, *This Was New York: The Nation's Capital in 1789,* Garden City, N.Y., 1943, p. 37. "Burghers and Freemen," pp. 240–260; "Richard Varick's License Book"; *Longworth City Directory for 1789,* New York, 1789; "Trinity Church Farm Rent Rolls, 1780–1794"; "Census of Electors in the State of New York, 1790," in *Daily Advertiser,* January 15, 1791.

37. *Minutes of the Common Council,* Vol. 1, p. 117.

38. For the politics of race and freedom in this era, see Graham Russell Hodges,

Root and Branch: African Americans in New York and East Jersey, 1613-1863, Chapel Hill, 1999 and Shane White, *Somewhat More Independent: The End of Slavery in New York City, 1770-1810,* Athens, 1991, 157-163.

39. Pomerantz, *An American City,* pp. 93–98; *Independent Journal,* December 22, 1784.

40. Lynd, "The Mechanics in New York Politics," pp. 169–170.

41. "Petition of Subscribers Cartmen of New York City," March 3, 1784, NYMA; Monaghan and Lowenthal, *This Was New York,* p. 77.

42. Lynd, "The Mechanics in New York Politics," p. 172.

43. *New York Packett,* April 7, 1785.

44. Ibid., April 14, 1785.

45. Ibid., April 21, 1785.

46. *Minutes of the Common Council,* Vol. 1, p. 4.

47. Ibid., pp. 41, 63.

48. Ibid., Vol. 1, p. 288, 295, and "Petition of the Cartmen of New York City, March 3, 1789," NYMA.

49. For approval, see *Minutes of the Common Council,* Vol. 1, p. 629. For controversy, see Chapter 7.

50. See "Petition of Subscribers Cartmen," n.d. (1785), NYMA.

51. See memo by James Duane in front of Richard Varick's License Book, and *Minutes of the Common Council,* Vol. 1, p. 352.

52. See Richard Laslett, *The World We Have Lost,* New York, 1960, pp. 25–52. See also *Oxford English Dictionary, Standard Edition,* 30 vols., London, 1894, Vol. 2, p. 345.

53. See "Petition of Several Cartmen regarding the Request of Nicholas Naugell," February 27, 1787, NYMA.

54. *Minutes of the Common Council,* Vol. 1, p. 299.

55. See examples in John Kouwenhoven, *Columbia University Historical Portrait of New York,* New York, 1954, p. 109, and Mahlon Day, *New York Street Cries in Rhyme,* New York, 1825. Interestingly, most street vendors were black. See Chapters 9 and 10.

56. *Minutes of the Common Council,* Vol. 1, p. 299.

57. *New York Independent Journal,* September 22, 1785; *Minutes of the Common Council,* Vol. 1, pp. 335, 365.

58. Samuel B. McKee, *Labor in Early New York,* New York, 1935, p. 66. See also Pomerantz, *An American City,* pp. 211–212, and Alfred F. Young, *The Democratic-Republicans of New York: The Origins, 1763–1797,* Chapel Hill, N.C., 1967, p. 583, 3n.

59. Lynd, "The Mechanics in New York Politics," pp. 169–170.

60. For descriptions of the Federal Procession, see *New York Packett,* August 5, 1788; I.N.P. Stokes, *Iconography of Manhattan Island,* 7 vols., New York, 1915–1928, Vol. 5, pp. 129–131; William A. Duer, *Reminiscences of an Old New Yorker,* New York, 1852; "Ode to the Federal Constitution upon Adoption of the New Government Constitution by Mr. L——," 1788, NYPL. There were so many cartmen in the pro-

cession that parade organizers were forced to put some of them in other divisions. See "Broadside of Federal Procession," Library of Congress, Manuscript Collection, and also Martha J. Lamb, *History of the City of New York,* 3 vols., New York, 1877, Vol. 2, pp. 323–327.

61. R. Sean Wilentz, "Artisan Culture in New York," in Daniel Walkowitz and Michael J. Frisch, eds., *Working Class Culture: Essay on Labor, Community and American Society,* Urbana, Ill., 1983, pp. 37–78; Seymour Mandelbaum, *Boss Tweed's New York,* New York, 1966. Sean Wilentz, *Chants Democratic: New York City and the Rise of the American Working Class, 1788–1850,* New York, 1984, p. 87.

Chapter 7

1. For descriptions of New York in the late 1780s, see Sidney Pomerantz, *New York: An American City, 1783–1801,* New York, 1939. For wages and other description, see Frank Monaghan and Marvin Lowenthal, *This Was New York,* p. 77. For 1790s' wages, see United States Department of Labor, Bureau of Labor Statistics, *Bulletin #499,* "History of Wages in the United States from Colonial Times to 1928," p. 21.

2. For licenses, see "License Book of Richard Varick 1789–1796," N-YHS. There is no official record of a decision to stop giving freemanships to cartmen, but succeeding material in this chapter and consultation of list of freemen in "Burghers and Freemen" demonstrates that it did occur.

3. Daniel Phoenix, Treasurer, "Order to Pay," New York City Accounts for 1790, slip 57, NYMA.

4. "Warrant of David Demarest, Cartman," September 24, 1789, Box 2475, NYMA.

5. "Accounts of David Walton and Richard Lewis, Cartmen," January 30, 1789, Box 2745, NYMA.

6. Daniel Phoenix, Treasurer, "Orders to Pay," 1790 and numerous accounts for watch service, Boxes 6455, 6456 and 6457, NYMA.

7. Alfred F. Young, "The Mechanics and the Jeffersonians: New York, 1789–1801," *Labor History,* Vol. 5 no. 3 (Fall 1964), pp. 246–248.

8. Dominic DeLorenzo, "The New York Federalists: Forces of Order," Columbia University Doctoral Dissertation, 1979, pp. 8, 23. Duane was not, however, above bullying at the polls. See Alfred F. Young, *The Democratic-Republicans of New York: The Origins, 1763–1797,* Chapel Hill, N.C., 1967, pp. 95–96.

9. For Duane, see E. P. Alexander, *A Revolutionary Conservative: James Duane of New York,* New York, 1938, and for Varick, see Arthur Rommel, "Richard Varick, Federalist Mayor," Columbia University Doctoral Dissertation, 1938; *Dictionary of American Biography,* 30 vols., New York, 1928, Vol. 29, pp. 226–227; For Varick's life in New Jersey, see Adrian C. Leiby, *The Revolutionary War in Hackensack Valley,* New Brunswick, N.J., 1980, 2nd edn., pp. 238–240.

10. *Minutes of the Common Council of the City of New York, 1784–1831,* 22 vols., New York, 1930, Vol. 1, p. 605.

11. See memo in "License Book of Richard Varick."

12. See lists of freemen in "Burghers and Freemen."

13. Varick License Book.

14. *Daily Advertiser,* January 13, 1791.

15. *Daily Advertiser* and the *Weekly Museum,* September 24, 1791.

16. *Daily Advertiser,* September 25, 1791.

17. *Daily Advertiser,* September 27, 1791; "William Livingston to Richard Varick," September 29, 1790 and "Richard Varick to William Livingston," September 29, 1790, Misc. Papers in Varick Papers, N-YHS.

18. *Daily Advertiser,* September 27, 1791.

19. Ibid. Skaats' son, Rynier, Jr., was a cartman from the close of the Revolution until his death in 1794. See "Burghers and Freemen" and Varick License Book.

20. *Daily Advertiser,* September 27, 1791.

21. Ibid.; Varick's insecurity may also have been related to his participation in the Benedict Arnold affair of the Revolutionary War. Varick had been Arnold's personal secretary and was implicated in his treachery. After a lengthy inquiry, he was acquitted. Afterwards, George Washington took pains to alleviate Varick's anxieties by appointing him to gather his papers as Commander-in-Chief. See Leiby, *The Revoltuionary War in Hackensack Valley,* pp. 282–288; Alfred Bushnell Hart, ed., *The Varick Court of Inquiry to Investigate the Implication of Colonel Varick in the Arnold Treason,* Boston, 1907.

22. *Minutes of the Common Council,* Vol. 1, pp. 511, 624; Pomerantz, *An American City,* pp. 111–112.

23. See Edmund C. Willis, "Social Origins and Political Leadership in New York City from the Revolution to 1815," University of California-Berkeley Doctoral Dissertation, 1967, p. 70.

24. *New York Journal,* April 7, 10, 1792, for Republican opposition to mayoral election reform. See Young, *Democratic-Republicans,* p. 255.

25. *New York Journal,* April 10, 1792.

26. *Daily Advertiser,* April 24, 1792.

27. *New York Daily Advertiser,* June 1, 1792, and Young, *Democratic-Republicans,* p. 302.

28. For Society of Cartmen, see list of officers, in *Longworth's Directory of the City of New York,* New York, 1797.

29. *Minutes of the Common Council,* Vol. 3, p. 735; Vol. 5, p. 67 for Mattias Nack; and Vol. 2, pp. 35, 546 and 621 for Samuel Arnet.

30. See "Varick License Book" and "Cruger License Book."

31. *Daily Advertiser,* June 1, 1792 and August 27, 1792.

32. *Daily Advertiser,* August. 28, 1792.

33. *Daily Advertiser,* August 29, 1792

34. *Daily Advertiser,* August 30, 1792.

35. *Minutes of the Common Council,* Vol. 1, p. 589; Daniel Phoenix, Treasurer, "Order to Pay," 1971 N-YHS; For militia appointment, see *Military Minutes of the Coun-*

cil of Appointment of the State of New York, 1783–1821, 4 vols., Albany, N.Y., 1901, Vol. 1, pp. 293, 297, 451.

36. For licenses of scavengers, see "Varick License Book." Many scavengers have notations next to their names that they were subsequently elevated to cartmen.

37. Young, "Mechanics and Jeffersonians," p. 254n.

38. Ibid., p. 253.

39. For street commissioners, see *Daily Advertiser,* September 23, 1793.

40. See assorted wills in *Collections of N-YHS,* "Abstracts of Wills on File in the Surrogate's Office, New York City," 17 vols., New York, 1892–1908, including Rynier Skaats, Jr., Vol. 12, p. 364; Aaron Banta, Vol. 15, p. 249; John Armstrong, Vol. 15, p. 250; Barney Egbert, Vol. 15, p. 250; William Wedman, Vol. 15, p. 250.

41. "Trinity Church Rent Rolls, 1780–1796," Trinity Church Archives.

42. Rommel, "Varick," p. 201.

43. *New York Journal,* April 24, 1793.

44. Young, "Mechanics and Jeffersonians," pp. 255, 258; *New York Journal,* April 24, 1793.

45. *Daily Advertiser,* April 19, 1794.

46. *Daily Advertiser,* April 15, 1794.

47. *New York Journal,* June 7, 1794.

48. Young, *Democratic-Republicans,* pp. 420–421.

49. *New York Journal,* February 7, 1795.

50. *New York Journal,* April 29, 1795.

51. Young, *Democratic-Republicans,* p. 430.

52. *Daily Advertiser,* April 30, 1795.

53. See "Petition of Alexander Lamb and other Foremen of the Cartmen," April 29, 1795, NYMA.

54. *New York Journal,* May 30, 1795.

Chapter 8

1. For Lamb's father, see the many citations in *Minutes of the Common Council of the City of New York, 1784–1831,* 22 vols., New York, 1930, and Patricia Bonomi, *A Factious People,* New York, 1971, pp. 304–310; for Lamb's birth records, see his listing in "Trinity Church Genealogical Records," Trinity Church Archives. For his activities as a fireman, see *Minutes of the Common Council,* Vol. 7, p. 385, and for his leaseholds see "Indenture Book of Church's Farm, 1750–1775," Trinity Church Archives. For his revolutionary activities, see Papers of Alexander Lamb, N-YHS; Lamb served first as a private under Colonel James Hay, then as a wagonmaster, before earning a promotion to a quartermaster—see Revolutionary War Muster Rolls, National Archives. While with Colonel Hay, Lamb fought alongside future cartmen Harmanus Blauvelt, Daniel Cornelius, Abraham Collard, Daniel Conklin, John Demarest and John DeGraw. For contracts with the city, see *Minutes of the Common Council,* Vol. 1, pp. 488, 597, 618.

2. Alfred F. Young, *The Democratic-Republicans of New York: The Origins, 1763–1797*, Chapel Hill, N.C., 1967, pp. 429–445.

3. Ibid., pp. 445–455.

4. Ibid., pp. 455–457.

5. Ibid., p. 451, and for petitions against the treaty, see *Argus*, December 5, 1795. For stoning of Hamilton, see *New York Gazette*, July 20, 1795, and Paul Gilje, "Mobocracy: Popular Disturbances in Post-Revolutionary New York City, 1783–1829," Brown University Doctoral Dissertation, 1980, p. 58.

6. *Journal of the Assembly of the State of New York*, 19th Session, 1796, pp. 14–15, 51, 64, 65.

7. See statistics on voters in Young, *Democratic-Republicans*, p. 588; for Federalist expectations of deference, see David Hackett Fischer, The Revolution in American Conservatism, New York, 1965, pp. 1–49.

8. For the first comments on the Thetis incident, see *Argus*, December 5, 1795; Young, *Democratic-Republicans*, pp. 478–479.

9. For two ferrymen affair, see *Argus*, December 28–30, 1795. After that, letters appeared almost daily in *Argus*. See especially January 27, 30, February 1–4, 9, 13, 22, and April 5–12, 1796.

10. Poem is listed in Account 7765, New York State Library, Albany.

11. *Argus*, March 20, 1796.

12. *Argus*, for entire month of April, 1796, but especially April 26 and 27. Upon Ketaltas' release from prison he was cheered through the streets by the carters. See *New York Journal*, April 15, 19, 22, 1796, and Paul A. Gilje, *The Road to Mobocracy: Popular Disorder in New York City, 1763-1834*, Chapel Hill, 1987, 104-107. For Lamb's vote, see *Journal of Assembly*, 1796, pp. 70–71.

13. *Argus*, April 26 and 27, 1796.

14. *New York Journal*, June 19, 1796, and Edgar A. Werner, *Civil List and Constitutional History of the Colony and State of New York*, Albany, N.Y., 1894, p. 320.

15. *Minutes of the Common Council*, Vol. 2, p. 320.

16. For resumption of his foreman's post, see list of carters in *Longworth's City Directory of 1798*, New York, 1798, and for his death, see his personal listing in the Trinity Church Genealogical Records, Trinity Church Archives. His father outlived him by 11 years before dying at the age of 88. In his lifetime he had seen the city grow from a few thousand to over 100 thousand people.

17. *New York Journal*, June 4, 1797, and *Argus*, April 24, 1797.

18. *Daily Advertiser*, November 14 and 16, 1797.

19. *Daily Advertiser*, November 20, 1797.

20. Howard B. Rock, *Artisans of the New Republic: The Tradesmen of New York City in the Age of Jefferson*, New York, 1979, p. 55.

21. *New York Journal*, February 28, 1798.

22. *Argus*, April 27, 1799.

23. *Argus*, April 30, 1799.

24. *Argus*, May 2, 1799.

25. *Argus*, April 30, 1799. For discussion of Federalist bullying of laborers and cartmen in Baltimore, see Charles G. Steffen, *The Mechanics of Baltimore: Workers and Politics in the Age of the Revolution,* Urbana, Ill., 1984, p. 96.

26. *Argus*, May 2, 1799.

27. *Argus*, May 2 and 3, 1799.

28. Ibid., May 1, 2, 7 and 8, 1799, and for results see May 7 and Edmund C. Willis, "Social Origins and Political Leadership in New York City from the Revolution to 1815," University of California-Berkeley Doctoral Dissertation, 1967, pp. 70–72.

29. *Argus*, May 8, 1799.

30. James Cheetham, *A Dissertation Concerning Political Equality and the Corporation of the City of New York,* New York, 1800.

31. *American Citizen,* April 29, 1800.

32. See "Varick, the worst card in the Federal Pack . . ." Broadside, 1800, N-YHS.

33. *American Citizen,* April 29, 1800.

34. Broadside of "Laws of the City of New York Governing Carts and Cartmen." Published by order of Robert Benson, Clerk, April 28, 1800, N-YHS.

35. *Argus,* May 5, 1800; Willis, "Social Origins," p. 70.

36. *American Citizen,* April 29, 1800.

37. Ibid., April 25, 1801.

38. *American Citizen,* August 28, 1801. For official passage of mayoralty, see *Minutes of the Common Council,* Vol. 3, p. 57.

39. *American Citizen,* August 28–September 8, 1801.

40. *Republican Watchtower* and *American Citizen,* October 29 and December 8, 1801.

Chapter 9

1. See Howard B. Rock, *Artisans of the New Republic: The Tradesmen of New York City in the Age of Jefferson,* New York, 1979, pp. 184–199. Even the bakers, however, retreated to regulation when faced with the spectre of competition from heavily financed speculators. See pp. 190–191.

2 Seth Rockman, *Scraping By: Wage Labor, Slavery, and Survival in Early Baltimore,* Baltimore, 2008.

3. See "A List of Cartmen and Porters," 1801–1802, NYMA, and *Longworth's Directory for the City of New York,* New York, 1801; for racial comparisons, see *Republican Watchtower,* March 27, 1802.

4. See wills of Timothy Jarvis, Carnelius Ryan, James Caldwell, David Demarest, John Blauveldt, Jacobus Bogert and Garret Westervelt in "Wills of New York City," 1801–1849, typescript, Long Island Historical Society; see also Howard Durer, *Kakiat Patent of Bergen County, New Jersey,* Pearl River, N.Y., 1970, pp. 43 and 56.

5. *Republican Watchtower,* April 16, 1802. No voter tabulations are available for these or subsequent elections in this era; therefore no full accounting of cartmen

participation is possible. The many appeals by the political parties, however, indicate strong involvement by the trade.

6. *American Citizen,* April 27, 1802.

7. *Watchtower,* April 16 and May 5, 1802; *American Citizen,* April 23, 1802; Rock, *Artisans of the New Republic,* pp. 59–60.

8. *Watchtower,* January 1, February 19, May 2, April 25, 1803.

9. See *Watchtower,* January 2, 4, February 13, 1804; "Portrait of Liberty in the City of New York," n.d. (1804), NYPL Broadside Collection.

10. *Watchtower,* April 21, 1804.

11. Ibid. See also "Laws Governing Use of Carts and Cartmen," City of New York, 1804, NYPL. See also "Oaths of Inspectors of the City of New York, 1804–1810, NYMA.

12. *Watchtower,* October 22, 1804.

13. Ibid., November 22, 1804; See list of "Oaths Sworn by Hay and Wood Cartmen in City of New York, 1802–1810," NYMA; for oil paintings, see "An Account of the Grand Procession Given by the Citizens of New York in Honor of the American Constitution on July 23rd, 1788, and As Is To Be Presented by Paintings at the Vauxhall Gardens on the Fourth of July, 1806," New York, 1806, pp. 17–18.

14. See Chapter 6, note 35, for Martling's early career; for Tammany meetings of his tavern, see *Republican Watchtower,* April 2, 1802; Dixon Ryan Fox, *The Decline of Aristocracy in the Politics of New York, 1801–1840,* New York, 1919, p. 71.

15. For party quarrels, see Fox, *The Decline of Aristocracy,* pp. 61–75, and Alvin Kass, *Politics in New York State, 1800–1830,* Syracuse, N.Y., 1965, pp. 112–113. For effects of the Embargo, see John Lambert, *Travels through Canada and the United States, 1806–1808,* London, 1815, pp. 62–63; Rock, *Artisans of the New Republic,* pp. 78–80; *Watchtower,* April 30 and November 13, 1806.

16. *Watchtower,* February 2, 23, March 14, April 3 and 24, 1807; *Evening Post,* April 24, 1807.

17. *Watchtower,* March 14, 1807.

18. *Evening Post,* October 24, 1807.

19. Ibid.

20. Ibid.; for a melodramatic presentation of these incidents, see *Rambler's Magazine and New York Theatrical Register,* Vol. 2 (1809), pp. 155–156; Rock, *Artisans of New Republic,* p. 213.

21. Lancelot Langstaff, *pseud.* (Washington Irving, et al.), *Salamagundi,* New York, 1807, reprinted Boston, 1977, p. 211.

22. *Columbian,* February 12, 1808.

23. *Watchtower,* January 5, 1808.

24. See George Daitsman, "Labor and the `Welfare State' in Early New York," *Labor History,* Vol. 4 (1963), pp. 248–256; *Minutes of the Common Council of the City of New York, 1784–1831,* 22 vols., New York, 1930, Vol. 5, p. 96; see also Raymond A. Mohl, *Poverty in New York, 1783–1825,* New York, 1971, pp. 110–114.

25. "A List of Cartmen, Porters, Butchers and Tavern-keepers for the Year 1808 in the Mayoralty of DeWitt Clinton, Esq.," New York, 1808, Copy in N-YHS.

26. *Public Advertiser*, December 28, 1809; "Citizen" to Common Council, October 19, 1807, NYMA; *Morning Post*, October 1, 1811; "Petition of Cartmen," September 24, 1810, NYMA; Rock, *Artisans of New Republic*, pp. 220–222; *Minutes of the Common Council*, Vol. 6, pp. 351 and 395.

27. *Commercial Advertiser*, April 16 and 22, 1808; *Daily Advertiser*, April 23, 1808; for Republican response, see *Watchtower*, April 22–23, 1808.

28. *Commercial Advertiser*, April 28, 1808.

29. *Watchtower*, April 29, 1808.

30. *Commercial Advertiser*, April 21, 1809; *Watchtower*, April 21, 1809; Fox, *Decline of Aristocracy*, pp. 109–114.

31. Ibid., and Note 13; Graham Russel Hodges, *Root and Branch: African Americans in New York and East Jersey, 1613-1863*, Chapel Hill, 1999, 232-233.

32. See "Petitions from Citizens of Inhabitants of Bullock Street," June 18, 1810, NYMA; *Minutes of the Common Council*, Vol. 5, p. 581; Vol. 6, pp. 22, 166, 178, and 226. The residents of Bullock Street particularly complained that the cartmen hauling night-soil raced street and spilled much ordure on their sidewalks.

33. *Watchtower*, June 10, 1809.

34. *Minutes of the Common Council*, Vol. 6, pp. 226–227.

35. Ibid., Vol. 6, pp. 231, 239, and 251. For additional licensing of minors, see Ibid., Vol. 6, pp. 208, 216, 227, 240, 249, 267, 288, 302, 333, 341, 345, 364, 390, 450, 601, 627, 658; Vol. 7, pp. 60, 144, 154, 520, 604; Vol. 8, pp. 166, 174, 209, 218, 238, 246, 253, 274, 348, 357, 372, 466, 562, 604; Vol. 9, pp. 96, 107, 180, 211, 220, 243, 244, 299, 356, 372, 549; Vol. 12, p. 73; Vol. 13, pp. 209, 333, 356, 540, 541. The practice was not stopped until 1826. See Chapter 10.

36. Gareth Stedman-Jones, *Outcast London*, London, 1975, pp. 52–66, esp. 56–58. A trade became casualized when the number of applicants outstripped the demand, when skills were debased, and when reliable workers were no longer needed by employers.

37. See "List of Cartmen Prepared by Superintendent of Carts," 1811–1812, NYMA.

38. Percentages prepared by analysis of "List of Cartmen," 1811–1812, NYMA.

39. See "Jury Lists for Sixth and Seventh Wards," Klapper Library, Queens College, New York, and from addresses on "List of Cartmen," 1811–1812, NYMA.

40. R. Guernsey, *New York in the War of 1812*, 2 vols., New York, 1889–1895, Vol. 2, p. 321; *Minutes of the Common Council*, Vol. 7, p. 427.

41. See "List of Cartmen Prepared by Superintendent of Carts," 1817, NYMA; Rock, *Artisans of the New Republic*, pp. 224–226.

42. "Report of Committee of Cartmen," April 22, 1816, NYMA.

43. *Minutes of the Common Council*, Vol. 6, p. 144.

44. "Report of the Committee Reviewing the Petition for the Committee of Cartmen, April 8, 1816," NYMA.

45. *New York Advocate*, April 21, 1816; *New York Evening Post*, April 22, 1816.

46. See "Report of the Committee Reviewing the Petition for the Committee of Cartmen"; for Society of Cartmen, see *Digest of Special Statutes Relating to the City of New York, February 1, 1778–January 1, 1921*, Albany, N.Y., 1922, p. 1219.

47. For discussion of cordwainers and other groups see Christopher Tomlins, *Law, Labor, and Ideology in the Early American Republic*, New York, 1993, 138-150.

48. See "John McComb, Sr., Receipt Book, 1817–1821, as Overseer of Roads of New York City," N-YHS; John McComb, Sr., "Receipt Book, 1787–1816," N-YHS.

49. "Petition of the Committee of Cartmen," May 26, 1818, NYMA.

50. "Mayor Cadwallader Colden to Committee of Cartmen," June 1, 1818, NYMA.

51. *Minutes of the Common Council*, Vol. 9, p. 617; Charles Haswell, *Reminiscences of an Octogenarian*, New York, 1870, p. 196; *Evening Post*, May 26, 1818.

52. *Minutes of the Common Council*, Vol. 9, p. 622.

53. *Evening Post*, May 26, 1818.

Chapter 10

1. For number of cartmen in 1830, see Edwin Williams, ed., *New York As It Is in 1830 and Citizen's Advertising Directory*, New York, 1830, p. 160; for election of 1824, see *New York American*, March 5 and 6, 1824, and *New York Patriot*, November 6, 1824.

2. See Douglas Danforth, "The Influence of Socioeconomic Factors upon Political Behavior: A Quantitative Look at New York City Merchants, 1828–1844," New York University Doctoral Dissertation, 1974, pp. 27, 34 and 252–264.

3. *New York Patriot*, November 6, 1823; *New York American*, April 4, 1823. For continued description of neighborhoods as "Cartmen's Wards," see *New York Evening Post*, September 21, 1826, March 23 and August 21, 1829; *New York American*, August 27, 1826; *New York Statesman*, October 27, 1828; *New York Gazette*, April 26, 1829; Gilje, "Mobocracy," pp. 247–248.

4. *New York Evening Post*, April 18, 1818. See also, complaints against William Christian, November 21, 1821 (drunken driving); against Reuben Barton, July 26, 1822 (running over a child); against John Sweeney and Charles Darcey, April 14, 1822 (racing); against James Lerner, July 17, 1821 (reckless driving)—all in Msc. Mayor's Court Records, N-YHS; and "Presentment of Grand Jury Against Horse Racing, April 19, 1813," NYMA.

5. Thomas Earle, *Review of New York or Rambles Through the City*, New York, 1814. See also, Maria Child, *Letters from New York*, 2nd Series, New York, 1843, pp. 283–284.

6. Andrew Bell, *pseud.* (A. Thompson), *Men and Things in America* London, 1838, p. 26; Solon Wood, *Hot Corn*, New York, 1846; Samuel Wood, *The Cries of New York*, New York, 1816; Mahlon Day, *New York Street Cries in Rhyme*, New York, 1825; Charles Haswell, *Reminiscences of an Octogenarian*, New York, 1870, p. 61. For cartmen's races, see *National Advocate*, August 1, 1828; *New York Gazette*, August 1, 1828; Paul A. Gilje, *The Road to Mobocracy: Popular Disorder in New York City, 1763–1834*,

Chapel Hill, 1987, p. 236. Citing these incidents Girje notes that in one an elderly man was nearly killed when he threatened to report the license numbers of cartmen holding the races. In a second incident a violent argument occurred over the outcome of a race and a cartman's ear was bitten off.

7. *Minutes of the Common Council of the City of New York, 1784–1831,* 22 vols., New York, 1930, Vol. 8, pp. 489–492.

8. *Minutes of the Common Council,* Vol. 9, pp. 95 and 106.

9. For John Johnson's career, see Ibid., Vol. 2, pp. 472, 474, 564, 574, 576; Vol. 3, pp. 3, 386; Vol. 5, pp. 586; Vol. 6, p. 592; Vol. 8, pp. 489, 522; Vol. 9 pp. 1, 534, 614; Vol. 13, pp. 411, 732; Vol. 14, pp. 170, 768; "License Book of Richard Varick, 1789–1801"; "License Book of Superintendent of Carts," 1801, 1802, 1807, 1811, 1812, 1817, and 1818, NYMA.

10. For a similar incident, see "Case of Amos Bacon," June 20, 1821, Mayor's Court Records, N-YHS. Two other cartmen accused Bacon of owning several carts employing other carters and monopolizing firewood. Bacon's license was suspended. See *Minutes of the Common Council,* Vol. 14, p. 768.

11. For Hitchcock's career, see *Minutes of the Common Council,* Vol. 1, pp 203, 219; Vol. 4, p. 219; Vol. 5, pp. 462, 507, 530, 595; Vol. 6, pp. 403, 791; Vol. 7, pp. 5, 420; Vol. 11, p. 110. Hitchcock's sons Daniel and Edward worked for him and eventually succeeded him in the business.

12. Ibid., Vol. 11, p. 110, and see "Memorials of Edward and William Hitchcock to the Common Council," Box 3183, NYMA; Howard B. Rock, *Artisans of the New Republic: The Tradesmen of New York City in the Age of Jefferson,* New York, 1979, pp. 227–228.

13. *Minutes of the Common Council,* Vol. 9, p. 652.

14. Ibid., Vol. 10, p. 538.

15. See Ibid., Vol. 15, pp. 429–430; "Lawes and Ordinances of City of New York Concerning Carts and Cartmen," New York, 1826, NYPL.

16. See "List of Cartmen of the City of New York of the Superintendent of Carts," 1824, 1826, 1827 and 1828; 4 vols., NYMA.

17. *Minutes of the Common Council,* Vol. 13, p. 540; for bonds, see "Petition of David Pullis, Minor," March 13, 1826, Public Offices Folder, NYMA. Pullis' bond was paid by his father.

18. Ibid., Vol. 12, p. 319.

19. Ibid. A horse and cart were becoming expensive, costing more than $120; see "Phoebe Hatfield vs. Peter Hatfield," divorce proceedings in New York County Archives, Old Surrogates Court, A1 3822, Liber 370.

20. *Minutes of the Common Council,* Vol. 14, p. 299; by 1826 applicants regularly cited family, lengthy residence in the city, veteran status, and endorsements by leading cartmen. See Public Offices Folders, 1819–1826, NYMA.

21. *Minutes of the Common Council,* Vol. 13, p. 374; Vol. 14, p. 420; and *Minutes of the Board of Assistant Aldermen,* New York, 1831– , Vol. 10, p. 786.

22. *Minutes of the Common Council,* Vol. 14, pp. 351, 446, 783;Vol. 15, pp. 147, 193, 267, 383.

23. "Petition of Erastus Smith, Cartman," November 2, 1818, Box 88, NYMA.

24. "Petition of Gideon Manwaring, Cartman," November 2, 1818, and "Petition of Daniel McLaren, Jr., Grocer," October 2, 1820, NYMA.

25. For firemen, see Kenneth Dunshee, *As You Pass By,* New York, 1951; R. Sean Wilentz, *Chants Democratic: New York City and the Rise of the American Working Class, 17881850,* New York, 1984, pp. 261–263; Rock, *Artisans of the New Republic,* pp. 132–135; Lowell Limpus, *History of the New York Fire Department,* New York, 1940; and Amy Bridges, *A City in the Republic: Antebellum New York and the Origins of Machine Politics,* New York, 1984, pp. 34–76.

26. For Fourth of July appearances see *National Advocate,* July 4, 1823; *New York Post,* July 5, 1823, and *New York Spectator,* July 11, 1823; for reception of Lafayette see *National Advocate* July 7, 1824; *New York Spectator,* July 25, 1824; for celebration of Revolution in France, see *New-York Commercial Advertiser,* July 7, 1831.

27. This section was prepared by analysis of the index for over 400 cartmen listed in the *Minutes of the Common Council.*

28. Ibid.; James Richardson, *New York Police: Colonial Times to 1901,* New York, 1971, p. 13.

29. See *Minutes of the Common Council,* in particular, John Varick,Vol. 9, p. 128; William Waldron,Vol. 9, pp. 106 and 110; Isaac Halsey,Vol. 13, p. 366;Vol. 14, p. 126; Vol. 15, pp. 41 and 688; John Brown, alderman,Vol. 8, p. 501; Gideon Sprague,Vol. 8, pp. 83 and 93 among many others.

30. Moses Myer, *A Full Account of the Celebration of the French Revolution of 1830 in the City of New York,* New York, 1830, pp. 43–44.

31. Ibid., also see Graham Russell Hodges, *Root & Branch: African Americans in New York and East Jersey 1613-1863,* Chapel Hill, 1999, 232-233.

32. *Minutes of the Common Council,* Vol. 15, pp. 295–296.

33. Ibid.,Vol. 12, pp. 222, 294, 722, 725, 809.

34. Ibid.,Vol. 11, pp. 3, 18, 216, 223, 288, 304, 337; see also "Petition of Hay Boatmen in Behalf of Greater Wages for Hay Cartmen," February 14, 1824, NYMA.The boatmen also asked for additional penalties against "monopolizing cartmen."

35. *Minutes of the Common Council,* Vol. 11, p. 726; *Evening Post,* May 18, 1818; Rock, *Artisans of the New Republic,* pp. 228–230; *National Advocate,* August 1, 1828; *New York Gazette,* August 1, 1828; Gilje, *Road to Mobocracy,* p. 236.

36. Haswell, *Reminiscences,* p. 196.

37. See "Memorial of the Executive Committee of Mechanics to the Common Council of the City of New York, March 15, 1830, NYMA. See also Bridges, *City in the Republic,* pp. 50–51, 58–59 and 94–95.

38. Ibid., Walter Hugins, *Jacksonian Democracy and the Working Class,* Palo Alto, Calif., 1960, pp. 68–70, 116, 128 and 164. In his study of the workingman's movement, Walter Hugins pointed to the cartmen as one of the larger supporters of the

party. His analysis, however, was based upon the number of cartmen listed in the city directory, not in the license list kept by the superintendent of carts. As the number of carters licensed by the city went over 2400 by 1830, the 15 carters Hugins found enrolled in the Workingman's party seem insignificant. For agreement on this point, see Wilentz, *Chants Democratic,* pp. 210–214.

39. For merchant's petition and immediate reaction by cartmen, see *Minutes of the Common Council,* Vol. 18, p. 327.

40. "Laws and Ordinances of the City of New York Concerning Carts and Cartmen," New York, 1832, *Minutes of the Common Council,* Vol. 18, p. 345.

41. James Kent, *Charter and Notes,* New York, 1834, pp. 149 and 155.

42. For discussion of Tammany move toward the "Workie" position, see Jerome Mushkat, *Tammany,* Syracuse, N.Y., 1975, pp. 121, 158–159, 160–161, and Bridges, *City in the Republic,* pp. 66–70.

43. Mushkat, *Tammany,* pp. 153–155.

44. *New York Evening Star,* March 7, 1834.

45. Ibid., March 24, 29 and April 2, 1834.

46. Ibid., April 5 and 6, 1834.

47. Ibid., April 7, 1834. For accounts of Milliken's later Whig activities, see Bridges, *City in the Republic,* p. 176n.

48. *Star,* April 16, 1834. For good accounts of the meaning of this election, see Mushkat, *Tammany,* p. 155; Robert July, *The Essential New Yorker: Gulian Cromelin Ver Planck,* Durham, N.C., 1951; Leo Hershkowitz, "New York City Politics, 1834–1840," New York University Doctoral Dissertation, 1960, pp. 31, 34, 49–56, 316 and 499; and F. Byrdsall, *History of the Loco-Foco or Equal Rights Party,* New York, 1842, pp. 15–16.

Chapter 11

1. See print in Margaret Sloane Patterson, "Nicolino Calyo and his paintings of the Great Fire of New York, December 16th and 17th, 1835," *American Art Journal,* Vol. 14 (Spring 1982), pp. 4–22; George G. Foster, *Celio or New York Above and Below,* New York, 1850, p. 11; G. Foster, *An Account of the Conflagration in the First Ward of the City of New York, December 16, 1835,* New York, 1835; Reverend Orville Dewey, *A Sermon on the Occasion of the Late Fire in the City of New York,* New York, 1836. For plague, see William A. Carruthers, *The Kentuckian in New York,* New York, 1834, pp. 22–24.

2. Jerome Mushkat, *Tammany,* Syracuse, N.Y., 1975, p. 121, 179–181; F. Byrdsall, *History of the Loco-Foco or Equal Rights Party,* New York, 1842, pp. 15–16; Leo Hershkowitz, "New York Politics, 1834–1840," New York University Doctoral Dissertation, 1960, p. 460; Walter Hugins, *Jacksonian Democracy and the Working Class,* Palo Alto, Cal., 1960, pp. 38–40, 43–46.

3. Hershkowitz, "New York Politics," p. 460; Mushkat, *Tammany,* pp. 166–185, 210; Seymour Mandelbaum, *Boss Tweed's New York,* New York, 1966, pp. 50–56; Ed-

ward Spann, *The New Metropolis: New York City, 1840–1857,* New York, 1981, pp. 359–381. For Tammany favoritism toward Irish, see R. Sean Wilentz, *Chants Democratic: New York City and the Rise of the American Working Class, 1788–1850,* New York, 1984, pp. 315–316.

4. Mandelbaum, *Boss Tweed's New York,* pp. 41–42. For other comments on popularity of laws against forestalling, see E. S. Abdy, *Journal of a Residence and Tour in the United States,* 3 vols. London, 1835, Vol. 1, pp. 31–34; George G. Foster, *New York Naked,* New York, 185–, pp. 49 and 75; "Joseph," *New York Aristocracy or Gems of Japanica-dom,* New York, 1851; for sense of equality in New York, see Douglas Miller, *Jacksonian Aristocracy: Class and Democracy in New York, 1830–1860,* New York, 1972, pp. 3–25, 28–29.

5. Edgar A. Werner, *The Civil List and Constitutional History of New York,* Albany, N.Y., 1884.

6. Leonard L. Richards, *Gentlemen of Property and Standing: Anti-Abolition Mobs in Jacksonian America,* New York, 1970, pp. 14, 26–30, 43, 48–49, 113–122; John M. Werner, "Race Riots in the United States During the Age of Jackson, 1824–1849," Indiana University Doctoral Dissertation, pp. 149–182; Susan H. Wood, *History of the Broadway Tabernacle Church,* New York, 1901, p. 29. Mobs also attacked extortionate merchants. See Asa Greene, *A Glance at New York Embracing the City Government, Theaters, Hotels, Churches, Mobs, Monopolies, Learned Professors, Newspapers, Rogues, Dandies, Fires, Firemen, Water and Other Liquids,* New York, 1837, pp. 102–103, 108–115; and Amy Bridges, *A City in the Republic: Antebellum New York and the Origins of Machine Politics,* New York, 1984, pp. 10, 79–80.

7. For Lyon's vital statistics, see "Records of Greenwood Cemetery," Boonton, New Jersey, and Isaac S. Lyon, *History of Boonton, New Jersey,* Boonton, N.J., 1872.

8. John H. McCarty, *Reminiscences,* Philadelphia, 1907, p. 12. McCarty was a city marshal who as a little boy earned money painting numbers on the sides of carts.

9. Isaac S. Lyon, *The Recollections of an Old Cartman,* Newark, N.J., 1872, reprinted New York, 1984.

10. Isaac S. Lyon, *Sketches of Parsippany,* Newark, N.J., 1848; Lyon, *History of Boonton* and "Records of Greenwood Cemetery."

11. Lyon, *Recollections,* Chapter 1.

12. Isaac S. Lyon, The Washington Monument: Shall It Be Built?, New York, 1846.

13. Lyon, *Recollections,* p. 43.

14. Ibid., pp. 3 and 56; for English working-class autobiographies and distrust of professionals, see David Vincent, *Bread, Knowledge and Freedom: Study of Nineteenth-Century Working Class Autobiography,* London, 1981, pp. 109–133.

15. Lyon, *Recollections,* p. 15.

16. Ibid., pp. 34–36; Isaac Lyon, *Historical Discourse on Boonton,* Newark, N.J., 1873.

17. Lyon, *Recollections,* p. 12.

18. Ibid., pp. 2–3.

19. Ibid., pp. 15–17.

20. "Form of Cartmen's Oath with Signatures," New York, 1836–1839, NYMA.

21. Ray C. Sawyer, "Abstracts of Wills of New York County," 1801–1849 Typescript, 40 vols., Long Island Historical Society, for wills and relationships of Casparus Romaine, James Brower, James Demarest and Cornelius, William Steven, and Abraham Blauveldt. For William and Charles Vanderhoof, see *Minutes of the Common Council,* Vol. 5, p. 125. For John Ackerman, see Durer, *Kakiat Patent of Bergen County, New Jersey,* Pearl River, N.Y., 1970, p. 57. Ibid., p. 69 for Moses and Mathew Ely. See "Form of Cartman's Oath" for all.

22. *Minutes of the Board of Assistant Alderman,* New York, 1831– , Vol. 10, p. 405, April 11, 1836.

23. Ibid., Vol. 11, p. 315, September 26, 1836.

24. Ibid., Vol. 12, p. 191, July 17, 1837.

25. See "Wages of American Workers from Colonial Times to 1928," *U.S. Department of Labor Publications,* 1929.

26. See *Documents of the Board of Assistant Aldermen,* New York, 1831– , Vol. 2, No. 49, November 23, 1835, pp. 211–212. See also *Minutes of the Board of Assistant Aldermen,* Vol. 10, p. 271, February 29, 1836.

27. Ibid., Vol. 12, pp. 173–175, January 23, 1837.

28. Ibid.; see "Laws of City of New York," 1837, NYMA and "Form of Cartmen's Oath with Signatures" NYMA.

29. *New York Emancipator,* May 5, 1836, New York. For example of a black man working for a white cartman, see Willard B. Gatewood, Jr., ed., *Free Man of Color: The Autobiography of Willis Augustus Hodges,* Knoxville, Tenn. 1982, pp. 44–45.

30. *New York Emancipator,* December 26, 1839, January 23, 1840; *Colored American,* May 9, 1840; *New York Globe,* April 15, 1846; Freeman, "Negro in Antebellum New York," pp. 140, 156 and 293. Freeman noted that carting was the most segregated trade in New York City.

31. *Colored American,* September 16, 1837.

32. *New York Emancipator,* January 5, 1837.

33. Ibid., p. 301; George Edmund Haynes, *The Negro at Work in New York City,* New York, 1912, pp. 71–74. Blacks regularly worked as carters in southern cities. See Ira Berlin, *Slaves without Masters: The Free Negro in the Antebellum South,* New York, 1973, p. 231.

34. Clay McShane and Joel A. Tarr, *The Horse in the City: Living Machines in the Nineteenth Century,* Baltimore, 2007.

35. See "Fifth Census of the United States," 1840, NYPL.

36. Lyon, *Recollections,* pp. 2–3.

37. Ibid.; see also Records of Bureau of Vital Statistics, Morris County, New Jersey, for will of Isaac Lyon, proved August 17, 1881; see also *Second Report [and following] of the Bowery Savings Bank in the City of New York,* 1836–1855, Bowery Bank Archives.

38. Lyon, *Recollections*, p. 5.

39. Dr. Joel Ross, *What I Saw in New York,* Auburn, N.Y., 1851, pp. 157–161; L. Maria Child, *Letters to New York,* New York, 1843, p. 183. See also Henry P. Finn, *Comic Annual of 1831,* Boston, 1831, p. 2, describing how on May Day "mistress and maid . . . pay devotion to the Carman, from the 1st to 4th stories."

40. *New York Patriot,* May 3, 1824.

41. Seba Smith, *May-Day in New York or House-Hunting and Moving,* New York, 1843, p. 23.

42. Ibid., p. 37.

43. Ibid., p. 65.

44. Ibid.

45. *Niles Weekly Register,* May 9, 1835, p. 172.

46. *Minutes of the Board of Assistant Alderman,* Vol. 12, p. 310, February 27, 1837; Hershkowitz, "New York Politics," p. 102.

47. *Documents of the Board of Assistant Aldermen,* Vol. 7, No. 43, pp. 599–609, January 11, 1841; Vol. 8, No. 71, pp. 539–550, February 28, 1842; Vol. 9, Nos. 41–44, pp. 383–425, November 28, 1842.

48. Ibid., Vol. 10, No. 65, pp. 1199–1200, January 2, 1844; Vol. 11, No. 3, p. 44, June 5, 1844.

49. *Minutes of Board of Assistant Alderman,* Vol. 23, pp. 162 and 181, August 1, 1842.

50. Ibid., Vol. 23, p. 256–257, September 5, 1842.

51. *Documents of Board of Assistant Aldermen,* Vol. 9, Document 63, pp. 599–600, January 3, 1843.

52. Ibid., Vol. 9, Document 63, pp. 601, January 3, 1843, Document 86, pp. 977–984, February 16, 1843.

53. See Jon C. Teaford, *The Municipal Revolution in America, 1650–1825,* Chicago, 1975, p. 75; Spann, *New Metropolis,* pp. 45–67; Charles R. Adrian and Ernest S. Griffith, *A History of American City Government, 1775–1870,* New York, 1976, pp. 65–107; and Bridges, *A City in the Republic,* pp. 109–112.

Chapter 12

1. *New York Tribune,* July 9, 11, 14, 17, 20 and 24, 1850.

2. For Irish carters, see Robert Ernst, *Immigrant Life in New York,* New York, 1949, p. 106, and "Superintendent of Carts, Express Wagons, Hacks and Omnibuses License Book, 1853–1856," NYMA.

3. Lyon, *Recollections of an Old Cartman,* chapter 1.

4. Ibid., chapter 2.

5. For use of regulations elsewhere in American law, see Richard Wade, *The Urban Frontier: Pioneer Life in Early Pittsburg, Cincinnati, Lexington, and St. Louis,* Cambridge, Mass., 1959, pp. 76, 80–86 and Harry N. Scheiber, "The Road to Munn: Eminent Domain and the Concept of Public Purposes in the State Courts," in *Perspectives in American History,* vol. 5 (1971), pp. 329–405, esp. pp. 336, 338, 367–368.

For Teamsters Union, see Robert Leiter, *Teamsters Union*, New York, 1955; Herbert Northrup, et al. *The Negro at Work in the Land Transport*, Philadelphia, 1971; Steven Brill, *The Teamsters Union*, New York, 1979; John R. Commons, "Types of Labor Organization—The Teamsters of Chicago," *Quarterly Journal of Economics* 19 (May 1905), pp. 400–433.

6. On transit workers see Joshua Freeman, *In Transit: Transport Workers in New York City, 1933-1966*, New York, 1989; idem, *Working-Class New York: Life and Labor since World War II*, New York, 2000, and Kenneth Jackson, ed., *The Encyclopedia of New York City*, 2nd ed., New Haven, 2010, 1148-1150.

7. See my *Taxi: A Cultural History of the New York City Cabdriver*, New York, 2012.

Index